Edexcel GCSE (9–1)
Music

John Arkell   Jonny Martin

PEARSON

Published by Pearson Education Limited, 80 Strand, London, WC2R 0RL.

www.pearsonschoolsandfecolleges.co.uk

Copies of official specifications for all Edexcel qualifications may be found on the website: www.edexcel.com

Text © Pearson Education.
Typeset by Tek-Art, East Grinstead, West Sussex
Illustrations by Tek-Art, East Grinstead, West Sussex
Original illustrations © Pearson Education
Designed by Colin Tilley Loughrey
Cover photo © abstract/ Shutterstock
Indexed by Sophia Clapham, Index-Now

First published 2016

19 18 17 16
10 9 8 7 6 5 4 3 2 1

British Library Cataloguing in Publication Data
A catalogue record for this book is available from the British Library

ISBN 978 1 292123 14 1

Printed and bound in Slovakia by Neografia

Acknowledgements
For image and text acknowledgements please see page 183.

A note from the publisher
In order to ensure that this resource offers high-quality support for the associated Pearson qualification, it has been through a review process by the awarding body. This process confirms that this resource fully covers the teaching and learning content of the specification or part of a specification at which it is aimed. It also confirms that it demonstrates an appropriate balance between the development of subject skills, knowledge and understanding, in addition to preparation for assessment.

Endorsement does not cover any guidance on assessment activities or processes (e.g. practice questions or advice on how to answer assessment questions), included in the resource nor does it prescribe any particular approach to the teaching or delivery of a related course.

While the publishers have made every attempt to ensure that advice on the qualification and its assessment is accurate, the official specification and associated assessment guidance materials are the only authoritative source of information and should always be referred to for definitive guidance.

Pearson examiners have not contributed to any sections in this resource relevant to examination papers for which they have responsibility.

Examiners will not use endorsed resources as a source of material for any assessment set by Pearson.

Endorsement of a resource does not mean that the resource is required to achieve this Pearson qualification, nor does it mean that it is the only suitable material available to support the qualification, and any resource lists produced by the awarding body shall include this and other appropriate resources.

Contents

Welcome to Edexcel GCSE (9-1) Music

Inspiring the next generation of musicians

The new Edexcel GCSE course is designed to help you develop your musical knowledge, understanding and skills through studying a wide range of music from different cultures.

There are many benefits to taking the Edexcel GCSE Music course:

- It gives equal weighting to performance and composition, providing the opportunity for you to develop and progress equally in both skills.
- It includes four areas of study, each containing two set works, enabling you to learn about musical elements, musical language and musical contexts through specific pieces of music.
- The set works also allow you to learn in-depth appraising skills in preparation for your assessment.
- Suggested wider listening pieces relating to the areas of study will help you to appraise unfamiliar music in the exam as well as appraise and refine your own performances and compositions.
- If you do well in this course you will be in a good position to progress to further study of music at AS or A level. The content of this GCSE is ideal grounding for these qualifications; it has been designed using a similar approach, to make the experience of moving on a smooth one.

How you will be assessed

The GCSE course consists of three separate components:

- Component 1 Performing
- Component 2 Composing
- Component 3 Appraising.

Components 1 and 2 are both assessed by non-examined assessments, each accounting for 30% of the total mark. Component 3 is worth 40% of the mark and is assessed by an externally examined paper. For more information about the Appraising exam, see the 'Preparing for your exam' section on pages 163–170. See pages 20–51 for more information about the requirements for the performing and composing components.

How to use this book

This book contains all the information you need on the eight set works that form the basis of the appraising exam, including biographical information on the composers, notes about context and historical background to the genre, and a detailed analysis of each set work.

It is organised in the same way as the Edexcel GCSE specification. There are three main sections – one for each component – and a fourth section which supports you in preparing for the Appraising exam. Each section gives you all the information you need to know and guides you through the content of the course in a practical and engaging way, making it clear what you will cover and providing useful activities and questions to help you practise what you have learned.

In this student book there are lots of different features. They are there to help you learn about the topics in your course in different ways, understand them from multiple perspectives and get the most from your learning.

- **Learning objectives** – these are listed at the beginning of each topic so you know exactly what you are going to learn and that you understand the related success criteria.

Learning objectives

In the study of this set work you will learn about:
- the life and works of Henry Purcell
- the background to 'Music for a While'
- ground bass form in vocal music of the Baroque era
- how to analyse the song
- the key musical features of the song.

- **Getting started** – an activity or questions to check what you may already know and get you thinking about the topic before you start.

Getting started

- Purcell's song 'Music for a While' tells part of the Oedipus story, an ancient Greek legend. Find a story that interests you from the world of fantasy and myth and try to set some of the words to music. A scene from *Harry Potter* or *The Lord of the Rings* might be a good starting point.
- The song uses music for its calming influence. Discuss how music can generate different emotional responses in the listener. How are moods such as anger, sadness, tranquillity and love captured in music? Find examples to illustrate your points.

- **Glossary** – there are certain terms that you will need to know and be able to explain. Key words that are explained within the main text are in bold to emphasise their importance. Other key words used in the text are highlighted in **pink text** and explained in the nearby glossary boxes. You will find all of these key words put together in an alphabetical glossary at the back of the book.

Glossary

Da capo aria: ABA or ternary form. Often the repeated A section would be ornamented by the singer. Da capo means 'from the beginning again'.

Arpeggiated: the chord is spread, normally from the bottom note to the top.

Introduction

- **Listen** – you'll find a range of listening and appraising tasks based on the set works or other relevant pieces of music to help prepare you for the exam.

Listen

One of the best-known ground bass variations is Pachelbel's Canon.

Listen to this piece and hear how the ground bass is repeated over and over throughout the work.

In 1885, nearly 200 years later than 'Music for a While', the Late Romantic composer Johannes Brahms used a type of ground bass (though not just in the bass) for the last movement of his Symphony No. 4 in E minor. See if you can keep track of it in this much more complex movement.

- **Wider listening** – draws clear links between aspects of the set work and other pieces of music that may not be familiar. This feature will support you in answering any question in the exam on unfamiliar music.

Wider listening

In addition to this set work you should also listen to the following:

Beach Boys: 'God Only Knows' from *Pet Sounds*

Released in 1966, the album *Pet Sounds* was produced and arranged by Brian Wilson. After he had stopped performing live shows with the Beach Boys, he chose to concentrate on his composing instead. This album is a testament to his originality and wide-ranging musical tastes. The album was much better received in Britain than in the USA, but has since become a favourite worldwide.

- **Watch out!** – handy tips to ensure you avoid common pitfalls or misunderstandings about a topic.

Watch out!

If your performances do not last at least 4 minutes in total (when you add them all up), you will get zero marks for the performing component of the GCSE.

- **Activity** – this feature is designed to help you practise what you've learned about a topic or subject immediately.

Activity ?

There are two types of answer in a fugue: **real** and **tonal**. In a **real** answer, the interval between one note and the next is exactly the same as in the subject. Otherwise it is a **tonal** answer.

Look at the **answer** in bars 3–4. In the preceding **subject**, the interval between the first two notes (D to A) is a perfect fifth, but in the answer (A to D) it is a perfect fourth, so this is a **tonal** answer.

1 Can you find other examples of tonal answers in the music?
2 Try to compose a two-bar subject that will work with a *real* answer. Write in C major so that the subject begins on the note C and the answer will begin on G. Make sure that every interval is the same in the subject and the answer. This is tricky!

- **Did you know?** – these interesting facts will amuse and inspire but also provide valuable insight into the background of a set work or genre of music.

Did you know?

Bach's music has influenced music in the 20th century, such as the jazz interpretations of the pianist Jacques Loussier. The 1960s pop band Procol Harum based their classic song 'A Whiter Shade of Pale' on Bach's 'Air on the G string'.

- **Exam-style question** – these questions match the style of questions that you are likely to see in the written exam and will give you useful practice as you go through your course.

Exam-style questions

1 What is the key of this set work? Why is this an unusual key for a rock song? **(1 mark)**

2 Name the studio technique that is used to record the layered guitar parts. **(1 mark)**

- **Exam tip** – hints and tips to aid your learning and help you in the exam.

Exam tip

Firstly, remember to make **three** different points. Secondly, use musical terminology and vocabulary to back up your statements – for example, if you are trying to describe the dramatic use of diminished sevenths. In this question, you should refer to the musical elements of melody, harmony, rhythm, texture, dynamics, tempo and metre. There is a lot to say!

- **Summary** – a handy revision checklist of key points you'll need to remember about each set work.

Summary of the key features

Structure
- Intro – Verse 1 – Break – Verse 2 – Guitar solo – Verse 3 – Coda
- mostly split into 16-bar sections.

Tonality and harmony
- B minor
- jazz harmony
- includes extended, altered and substitution chords.

Instrumentation and sonority
- female vocal
- acoustic bass guitar
- nylon-string acoustic guitar (with second guitar overdubbed for solo).

Rhythm, metre and tempo
- starts in free tempo
- in $\frac{4}{4}$ metre
- based on Bossa Nova rhythm
- very syncopated.

Melody
- vocal melody opens by voicing broken chords
- syllabic throughout
- mostly stepwise movement
- melody notes are often the highest extension of extended chords – for example, the ninth of a ninth chord.

Texture
- monophonic at the very start
- counterpoint between parts
- very sparse in places, creating an intimate feel.

- **Checkpoint** – allows you to check your knowledge and understanding and identify where you need to secure your knowledge a bit more. It also challenges you to take your knowledge further.

Checkpoint

Strengthen

S1 In what ways can this set work be described as a piece of fusion?
S2 How do the players learn songs without traditional staff notation?

Extend

C1 Using the techniques described above, work out all the chords for verse 2. Write out the names of the chords and the notes they contain. Leave out optional notes as the guitar is unlikely to voice them.
C2 Work out an alternative voicing for some of the chords.

Preparing for your Exam

A special exam preparation section with tips and guidance for achieving success in your written exam. You will find example questions and answers, together with notes and explanations about the quality of the answers shown. This will really help you build your understanding of how to write stronger answers.

GCSE Edexcel (9–1) Anthology of Music

References throughout this Student Book are made to a printed Anthology and CD. Working in partnership with Peters Edition and Faber Music, Pearson has published an Anthology of the full printed scores for the set works studied and an Anthology CD containing recordings of all eight pieces. These match the versions that will be used in the written exam and are available for purchase at www.pearsonschoolsandfecolleges.co.uk

Other scores and audio versions are available but may not be an exact match for the Edexcel GCSE (9-1) specification.

Understanding Music

Understanding Music

You don't need to read music to be able to enjoy it or to understand it. Music is something that you hear rather than something you look at, so any written version of music is just a representation of the sound. Many famous musicians say that they cannot read music and some seem to be quite proud of this! On the other hand, being able to read and write musical notation does allow you to communicate music much more easily. If you are a composer, it is much easier to communicate your ideas if you can write them down in some form. If you are a performer, it is easier to learn many different styles of music from written notation than 'by ear'. Being able to read music does not mean that you can sight-read difficult pieces and perform them instantly, but it does mean that you can make sense of the code and can turn the symbols into sounds, much as you would do if you were to read these words aloud.

Reading music is much easier than reading text. If you have never learned how to read musical notation, you will be able to pick it up much more quickly than if you were trying to learn a new alphabet with different symbols (like Greek or Chinese). This chapter will help you to understand what many of the musical symbols mean and how to interpret them on your instrument. If you can already read music fluently, you should still take time to read through this section in case there are gaps in your knowledge.

Reading and writing staff notation

Each instrument (or instrument section such as the first violins) has a single stave. This is the set of five, evenly spaced horizontal lines on which sit the empty or filled dots known as note heads. The vertical arrangement of the note heads tells us how high or low the note is. The horizontal arrangement tells us when the note should be played.

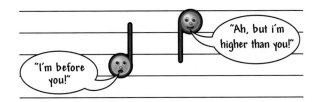

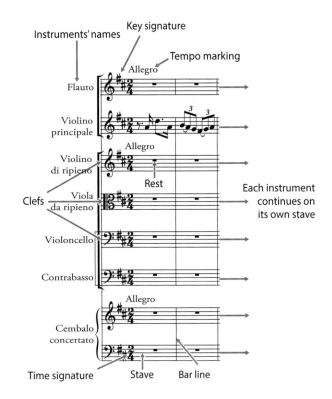

The stems attached to the note heads sometimes have flags or beams attached to them. Along with the note heads, these let us know how long the note should last and will be explained in more detail later. How high or low the note is, when it should be played and how long it lasts are the three most important things to learn and understand when reading music.

Looking at a musical score can be rather daunting, especially if the piece has been written for an orchestra. The trick is to focus on individual parts and to understand them one at a time. Let's look at an example of an orchestral score and pick out the important details. This chapter will explain each of these details and how they fit into the whole.

Duration, rhythm and pulse

Duration

The duration of a note is how long it sounds for. This is determined by the note value. The diagram below shows how the different note values relate to each other. Notice how, as you go down one row, the note value is half of the row above. For example, there are two crotchets for every minim, so a crotchet lasts half as long as a minim, and a minim lasts half as long as a semibreve. Following this logic, there are four semiquavers in a crotchet and eight quavers in a semibreve.

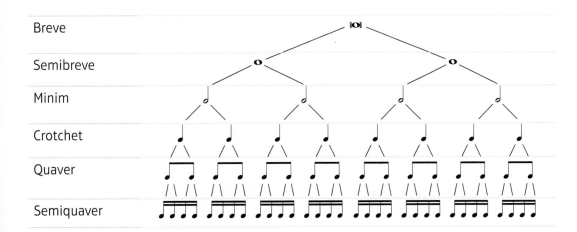

You will be expected to know these terms for your exam.

Understanding Music

Did you know?

The breve is now the longest note in common use, but its name comes from the Latin 'brevis' meaning 'short'. This may be confusing, but it shows how notation develops: there were even longer note values used in Medieval and Renaissance times – called 'longa' (meaning 'long') – though these were used less and less as time went on. In modern times, since the beginning of the 20th century, composers have developed many new ways of notating the musical requirements they have of musicians, with the result that staff notation continues to develop, just like any language.

The note values show how long a note should last, but it is just as important to create space in music by including silences of a particular duration. For this purpose, we have rests. All the standard note values have corresponding symbols to show how long the silence should last.

| breve | semibreve | minim | crotchet | quaver | semiquaver |

Dotted notes

A dot after a note increases its duration by half. For example, if a crotchet lasts for two quavers then a dotted crotchet will last for three quavers.

Rhythm

Combinations of note durations and rests create rhythm. A very simple rhythm might be just four crotchets, one after the other. A slightly more developed rhythm might replace one of the crotchets with a rest. A more complicated one might have a combination of quavers, crotchets and rests. Any combination of durations (with or without rests) will create a rhythm. For a rhythm to make sense it needs to be measured against something – the pulse of the music.

Pulse

The pulse is the steady beat that underpins music. It is well named as it reflects your own pulse, betraying whether you are excited or relaxed, stressed or calm. Just as your pulse will increase in pace when you get more excited or active, so the pulse of music generally increases to reflect excitement or energy or decreases to create a sense of calm or melancholy. The speed of the pulse is called the tempo of the music.

Did you know?

Tempo can be fast or slow, not the rhythm. You can have lots of short notes in a rhythm, but the rhythm is not said to be fast. If lots of semiquavers were played at a very slow tempo, they would not sound fast. The introduction to the Beethoven sonata is a good example.

A metronome

Tempo is traditionally indicated with a descriptive name (normally in Italian) that describes how fast a piece should be; for example, Allegro is 'lively' or 'fast'. In some genres of music it is measured in beats per minute (bpm).

Time signatures

Now that we have a reference point to measure the rhythm against, we need to divide up the music into manageable chunks. We call these chunks **bars**. Each bar will last for a certain number of pulses, or beats. In the example score at the start of this section you can see that the bars are indicated by vertical lines ruled down through the stave, called **bar lines**.

Which note value should we pick to measure the beats? Actually it does not matter and in any case, over the centuries, taste has changed as to what the conventions are. In popular music it is most common to have crotchet beats and to have four of them in every bar. Sometimes quaver beats are more appropriate, and we might have six of these in a bar. Occasionally, minims are used to measure the beats; you will find this a lot in old hymn books, and also in 'Defying Gravity', one of the set works in this book. Even more occasionally, semiquavers are used. To show what note values are used to count the pulse and how many beats there are in a bar, we use **time signatures**. This is where the American terminology for note values comes in handy: if you think of a time signature as a fraction (which it isn't – it doesn't have a line in the middle!), the numerator is the number of beats in the bar and the denominator is the type of beat.

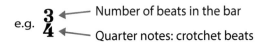

e.g. The time signature is always included at the start of a piece of music, but it can also change in the middle.

> ## Time signature challenge
>
> Count how many times the time signature changes in the first nine bars of 'Defying Gravity'.

Simple and compound time signatures

A **simple time signature** is when the beat naturally divides into two equal halves.

When the bar feels like it needs the beats to be split into groups of three, the time signature is **compound**. In other words, it is like having a group of three 'mini' beats in a 'big' beat. You would feel as if you could count either the bigger beats or the 'mini' beats.

Notice how the crotchets have dots after them, so they can each be split into three quavers. This example would either be counted in two dotted crotchet beats or six quaver beats. This is what gives it the compound feel.

Common and cut common time

There are two other time signatures that you need to be aware of (they both occur in the Beethoven set work):

Common time is represented by the symbol 𝄴 and is essentially the same as $\frac{4}{4}$

Cut common time (also known as **alla breve**) is represented by the 𝄵 symbol and means two minims per bar.

Note values

Ties

The normal note values give a good starting point, though there may be times that you want a note to last just a bit longer than a crotchet but not quite a minim, or just a bit shorter than a quaver but not quite a semiquaver. One option is to use dotted note values, though this still may not quite give the desired duration. Another option is to use **ties**. These are small arcs drawn from one note head to the next, and they mean that you should add up the tied note values and hold the note on instead of sounding it for a second time. Any combination of durations can be tied, and you are not limited to just two notes – three, four or more notes can be tied together.

In this example, the minim is tied to a quaver, so the effect will be to have a single note that lasts for five quavers:

As can be seen from the example above, ties only join notes that are the same pitch.

Triplets

In the main diagram showing how long the note values last, each longer note was subdivided into two shorter ones. There is also a way to notate the music so that a longer note can be divided into three shorter ones called **triplets**. A horizontal square bracket should be drawn to enclose the three notes, or in the case of quavers write a '3' above the beam. This lets the performer know that they should play these three notes in the time it would normally take to play two:

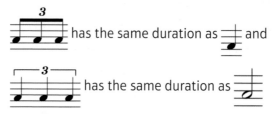

Pitch

In its simplest terms, pitch is how high or low a note sounds. Pitch and combinations of pitches are central to Western music, so this is a longer section split into logical subsections to help you dip in and out of the material as you need to.

Piano keyboard activity ?

The black notes on a piano keyboard are not spaced out randomly – there is a repeated pattern. If you count the keys (white and black notes), you can see that this pattern is repeated every 12 keys: 7 white keys and 5 black keys.

1 Pick out the white note in between the group of two black notes and play it.

2 Find where this note is repeated in the next pattern of 12 keys and play it.

3 Repeat this for the white note in this position all over the keyboard.

The note you played was a 'D'. The distance between two notes is an **interval**. The interval between one D and the next D is an **octave**.

The octave is the most important interval in music. This comes from the physics of sound. For example, the note 'A' just to the left of the lock on an upright piano has a frequency of 220Hz. The next A to the right has a frequency of 440Hz. The next A is at 880Hz, etc. This doubling of the frequency is a physical phenomenon that makes notes an octave apart sound so 'right' if they are played together.

Listen to the effect of combining different notes

- Play two notes together that are an octave apart.
- Play two notes that are next to each other.
- Play three notes together that are all octaves apart (use two hands and stretch!).
- Play two white notes next to each other and the black note in between.

Which combination clashes the most and which sounds most pleasing?

The octave is divided into smaller intervals. As you have seen, on the piano the octave is divided into 12 equally spaced intervals called **semitones**. An interval of two semitones is a **tone**. A guitar fretboard is divided into semitones, too, so if you play a note on the 12th fret and compare it to the open string, you will be demonstrating an octave interval.

A guitar can play notes over three and a half to four octaves. This is the **range** of the instrument. A typical piano keyboard has a range of seven and a bit octaves, spanning most of the range of all the orchestral instruments.

As mentioned previously, pitch is represented by how high or low a note head is on the stave. However, with such a wide range of pitches available, there are ways of trying to make all the notes fit on the five lines of the stave.

Understanding Music

Clefs

One way to do this is the use of clefs. These set a reference point on the stave. The most common clefs you will come across are:

- the treble clef (sometimes called the G clef)
- the bass clef (sometimes called the F clef).

Another clef that you will see in orchestral music is the C clef, which has a different name depending on where it has been placed on the stave:

- the alto clef
- the tenor clef.

| G | F | C | C |
| Treble clef | Bass clef | Alto clef | Tenor clef |

The note on each stave is the alternative name of the clef: the note on the treble clef stave is a G, the note on the bass clef stave is an F, and the note on the final two staves is a C. Notice how these notes correspond to an obvious part of the clef's design – for example, the middle of the C clef. This can be a useful tip for remembering where the notes are for each clef.

There is a special note used as a reference point for all instruments and clefs. This note is **middle C**. On an upright piano it is the C nearest the lock, which funnily enough is in the middle of the piano's range. The figure below shows where middle C is located in each clef.

As you can see, there is a lot of space above middle C in the treble clef and a lot of space below middle C in the bass clef, with the two C clefs being somewhere in the middle. This makes the individual clefs suitable for different instruments with different ranges.

You will need to understand the concept of clefs for your GCSE, but you really only need to be fluent at reading notes from the treble and bass clefs.

Note names

We have been referring to note names such as 'D', 'C' and 'A', but what other note names are there?

Again, this is where the piano keyboard comes in handy to help visualise things. The notes are alphabetical from A to G at which point they go back again to A. This means there are only seven basic note names, corresponding to the white keys on the piano. Graphic representations of keyboards are usually organised so that they start on C, but you can see the same principle in action.

Did you know?

Clefs make music easier to read for instruments with certain pitch ranges:

- Treble clef instruments include: flute, violin, trumpet, soprano voice.
- Bass clef instruments include: bassoon, tuba, cello, bass voice.
- The alto clef is most commonly used for viola music.
- The tenor clef is used for some of the higher notes in parts normally written in the bass clef: trombone, cello, bassoon.

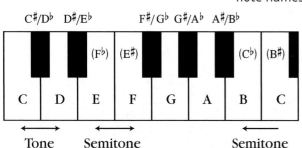

The black keys have a symbol in addition to the letter name – these are sharps (♯) and flats (♭). Notice that if you find any letter name on a white key and move to the black key on the right you will find the same letter name with a sharp. If you move to the left you will find the same letter name with a flat. Another (and more accurate) way to look at this is that when you raise a note by a semitone (that is, you move one note to the right, be it a white note or a black note), you sharpen it, and when you lower a note by a semitone, you flatten it.

This brings up a slightly confusing state of affairs in that some notes have two different names. This is indeed the case, and it depends what other notes they are combined with as to which name you should use. We will look more deeply at this when we study keys and key signatures. When two pitches sound the same but look different on the stave they are called **enharmonic equivalents**.

The musical theory you are learning applies to all instruments, not just the piano. You can see how the same principle of flats and sharps works on a guitar fretboard:

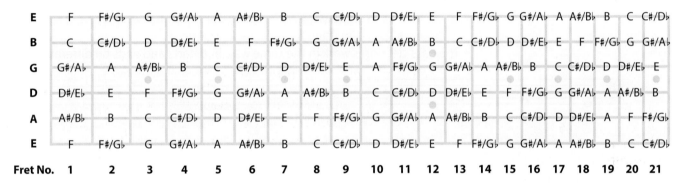

It is not helpful always to have to write out the letter names to refer to pitch, so staff notation uses a system a bit like the rungs of a ladder: the higher up the ladder (or stave), the higher the pitch. When the treble clef is used, the notes look like this:

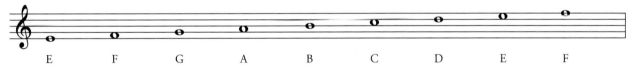

Notice how the notes still go up in alphabetical order, from line to space to line to space, etc. There is no mystery about this – it really is as straightforward as it looks. When you are learning, it takes a while to remember which line or space is which note. You can start by memorising the top, bottom and middle lines and working it out from there until you become more fluent with practice.

If you want a note below an E, the space underneath the stave can be used, but if you want to go even lower, you need to add lines, almost continuing the stave by drawing extra, mini lines:

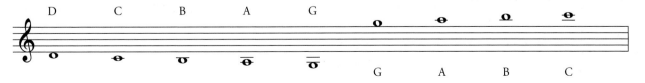

Understanding Music

Octave activity   ?

The piccolo in bars 36–38 of *Star Wars* has an ottava alta symbol. Can you find any other examples in the set works? Can you find a slightly different way of representing the same thing in any of the scores?

These extra lines are called **ledger** lines (or leger lines – either spelling is fine). They can also be used above the stave to extend the pitches upwards.

Notice how middle C in the treble clef is on the first ledger line below the stave.

If you need to go even higher, you can use an **ottava alta** symbol above the stave (a little dotted line with 8va at the beginning) to indicate that the notes should be played an octave higher than written, or an **ottava bassa** symbol below the stave (8vb instead of 8va) for an octave lower.

To represent sharps, a symbol a bit like the 'hash' symbol needs to be before the note head to which it applies. Notice that in text a C sharp would be written as C♯, but in notation the sharp sign is before the note, not after it. The centre of the sharp symbol should be on the same line or space as the note head. The same is true for flats, but in this case the circle part of the 'b' should be on the same line or space as the note head.

The bass clef notes work in the same way, but starts and ends on different notes:

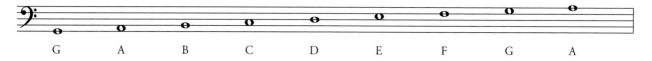

| G | A | B | C | D | E | F | G | A |

Activity   ?

Find where middle C is written in the bass clef.

Ledger lines, octave symbols, and sharps and flats work the same way in the bass clef, too.

We have introduced three intervals already: the octave, the semitone and the tone. Between them they will help us to understand scales and modes. Other types of interval will be explored later in the context of keys and key signatures.

There are 12 different notes to choose from within the octave, but music generally works best when a careful selection of the available notes is made. Scales and modes use some (usually seven) notes from the 12 available and arrange them in ascending order. Each different scale or mode has a unique fingerprint: the pattern of intervals between all of its notes.

Modes and scales

The chromatic scale

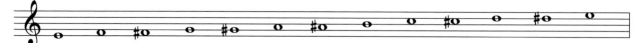

Above is a one-octave chromatic scale starting on E. It doesn't matter which note the scale starts on as it will always use all 12 available notes. The 'black notes' have all been written as sharps to avoid confusion. They could just as easily have been written as the flat version of the letter name above – so F♯ could have been written as G♭. The interval between every adjacent pair of notes is a semitone.

Modes

These are scales that you can form starting on one of the white notes of a piano and playing ascending white notes until you have covered an octave. They were used long before major and minor scales were ever thought of. Even now, modes are used in compositions by many composers, especially those who are influenced by folk music or in jazz. The five examples given are the modes in common use. Notice how the pattern of intervals is slightly different for each mode (T = tone, ST = semitone).

Dorian mode

Phrygian mode

Lydian mode

Mixolydian mode

Aeolian mode

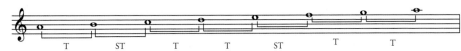

Modes do not have to start on the original starting notes – as long as the interval pattern remains the same they can start on any note. For example, the Dorian mode could start on the note F as long as the interval pattern remained T – ST – T – T – T – ST – T. This would require some flats to be used. Music that is written using modes has a particular sound to it. In fact, each mode has its own unique sound. The folk song 'Scarborough Fair' uses the Dorian mode.

Modal improvisation activity ?

To become used to the sound of modes it is useful to improvise using them. Play the starting note in the lower part of a keyboard and then play up and down the mode. When you become comfortable with this, make up some short melodies using the notes of the mode over the drone.

Major and minor scales

During the 1600s, major and minor scales gradually replaced the use of modes and formed the basis of the key system that we will explore next.

Major scale

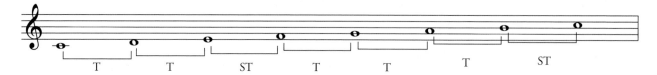

Harmonic minor scale

The harmonic minor scale includes an interval of a minor 3rd which is equal to one tone plus one semitone.

There are also many other scales used around the world, all of which will have a particular sound depending on their unique 'fingerprint', the interval pattern. One that is of interest is a scale that appears in many different cultures across the globe, called the pentatonic scale.

Pentatonic scale

'Penta' means 'five', as in pentagon, a five-sided shape. Pentatonic scales are built up using the first, second, third, fifth and sixth notes of the major scale. They are commonly used in folk tunes and other melodies such as the hymn tune 'Amazing Grace'.

In C major, these notes would be

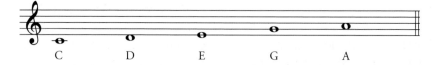

If you used the same notes, but started on A instead of C, you would have the minor pentatonic scale which is the basis of the blues scale.

Harmony and tonality

When two or more different pitches sound at the same time, harmony occurs. The harmony may be pleasant or unpleasant, but the interaction of the pitches is still harmony nonetheless. In Western music, a rather intricate system has developed building harmonies on the major–minor system and three-note chords called **triads** that use notes from these scales. To understand chords we must first have another look at intervals.

Intervals

As previously discussed, the distance between two notes is called an interval. Intervals can be counted in tones and semitones or they can be counted using the degrees of the scale. Starting with the first note of the major scale as number 1, the next note as number 2 and so on, the notes of the scale can be numbered from 1 to 7. Each number or degree of the scale has a technical name as well as its number:

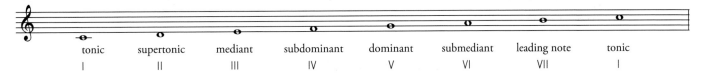

tonic	supertonic	mediant	subdominant	dominant	submediant	leading note	tonic
I	II	III	IV	V	VI	VII	I

Note how the tonic returns to the number 1 again rather than being counted as the 8th degree of the scale. The degrees of the scale have been numbered using roman numerals because this is often how they are referred to when we write about music and when we use them as the basis for chords. So it is good to get used to using the roman numerals when possible.

To work out the interval between two notes, count the lower note as number 1 and then count up each line and space from there until you reach the higher note.

In example 1) the A is the lowest note. Counting this as '1', we get to '4' by the time we reach the D. So the interval between A and D is a fourth. It is probably easier to do this by finding out what the note names are of the two pitches and then, starting with the lowest pitch as '1', just count up the alphabet.

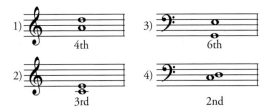

Keys and key signatures

So far we have avoided using sharps and flats as much as possible, but they are nothing to be afraid of. They are often used to make sure that the interval pattern of the scale or mode is maintained while starting on a different note to those you have already encountered. For example, if we build a major scale starting on the tonic note of C then, by keeping to the T – T – ST – T – T – T – ST pattern, only white notes would be used. If we start on G instead, we would need to use an F♯ instead of an F at the end to maintain the pattern. So we say that the key of G major has one sharp, F♯. In staff notation a sharp would need to be added before every single F if we wrote a piece in G major. This would quickly get very tiresome, so a shortcut is to put an F♯ at the start of the stave, just after the clef, to show that every F is to be played as an F♯. This shortcut is called a **key signature**.

People often find key signatures a bit confusing, but if you understand the following principle then it should all fit together: everything revolves around the circle of fifths.

Understanding Music

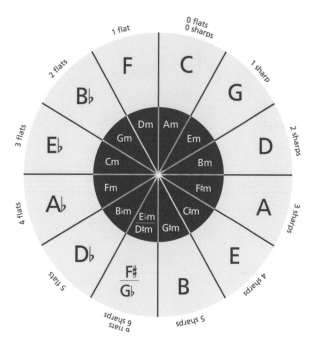

If you want any major key signature, look around the outside of this diagram showing the circle of fifths to find the letter name and you will see how many sharps or flats that key has. For example, A major has 3 sharps and F major has 1 flat.

Moving clockwise around the circle, one sharp is added to the key signature each step and the notes are going up in fifths (C to G is a fifth, G to D is a fifth, and so on). Moving anticlockwise around the circle, one flat is added to the key signature each step and the notes are going down in fifths (C to F is down a fifth, F to B♭ is down a fifth, and so on).

Why does F go down to B♭ instead of B? The fifths used in the circle of fifths are called perfect fifths. If you count the semitone steps, you will find that a perfect fifth has seven semitones. F down to B is only six semitones, so you need to go down an additional semitone to B♭. The same is true when going up from B to F♯: B to F is only six semitones, so an additional semitone brings us to F♯.

The order in which the sharps occur also follows the pattern. The first sharp is F♯, the second is C♯, and so on. The full order in which the sharps occur is FCGDAEB, following the circle clockwise. So, if you know that E major has four sharps, you can calculate that they must be F♯, C♯, G♯ and D♯. Unsurprisingly, the order of flats is the reverse of this: BEADGCF, following the circle anticlockwise.

The minor keys on the inside of the circle share the same key signature as the major keys on the outside. Major and minor keys that share the same key signature are called **relative** major or minor keys. For example, A minor is the relative minor of C major and F major is the relative major of D minor.

This is how key signatures look in staff notation:

Did you know?

- The interval of a perfect fifth has the simplest mathematical relationship of all intervals other than the octave. To go up an octave, double the frequency. To go up a fifth, multiply the frequency by 1.5.
- The fifth degree of the scale is called the **dominant**. Can you see why this is the case?

Key signature activity ?

Copy out the key signatures above but in a different order. Label them by using the circle of fifths. For more of a challenge, see if you can remember the keys without looking at the circle.

Chords and inversions

A chord occurs when two or more notes are played together. Three-note chords are called **triads**. Western harmony has developed using a particular system of triads where the chords are formed by playing a **root note** along with the notes a third and a fifth above it. Each note of the scale can be harmonised in this way:

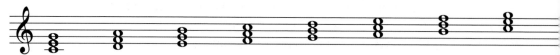

14

Minor scales can also be harmonised with triads:

Notice how the A minor scale has been harmonised using G♯s instead of G♮s. As every key signature is shared by one major and one minor key, you may have been wondering how you could tell which one was being used at any given time. The answer is that in a minor key, the seventh degree is sharpened, but not added to the key signature. In the case of A minor, the seventh degree is G, so this becomes a G♯.

When a triad is built on the degrees of the scale in this way, it is said to be in root position, with the scale degree being the root note. It is possible to play the chords using the same notes but changing the order in which they appear. If the lowest-sounding note is not the root note, the chord has been inverted.

- When the third is in the bass the chord is in first inversion.
- When the fifth is in the bass, the chord is in second inversion.

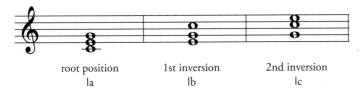

Chord symbols

Chords can be described using roman numerals such as Ib, but they can also be described using letter names – for example, C/E – or a combination of letter names and numbers – for example, C7. This is a convention that is more common in popular music and jazz. The system is generally straightforward although there are some variations in usage between publishers.

In this example from 'Killer Queen', the following can be seen:

- A lower case 'm' shows that the chord is minor (Cm = C minor).
- A '7' means that the chord is a dominant seventh.
- When there are two capital letters, the first letter is the root of the chord and the letter after the forward slash is the bass note. This is another way of writing that a chord is inverted (Gm/D = G minor in second inversion).

Cadences

A cadence is a special chord sequence at the end of a phrase. Cadences are the musical equivalent of punctuation. There are four common types of cadence you need to know, each consisting of two chords:

- The **perfect cadence** (or full close) is chord V to I. This is conclusive, like a full stop, and is often used to end a passage or section of music.
- The **imperfect cadence** (or half close) is chord I to V, or II to V, or IV to V (in fact, anything to V). The imperfect cadence is like a comma. As it ends on the dominant chord, we know that the musical sentence is not complete and that there is more to come.
- The **plagal cadence** (sometimes called the 'amen cadence') is chord IV to I. The plagal cadence is a gentler version of a perfect cadence, chord IV being softer than the strong dominant chord. This cadence has associations with sacred or church music and sounds like an 'amen'. The plagal cadence is still conclusive, however, and is also like a full stop.
- The **interrupted cadence** is chord V to VI. The interrupted cadence literally 'interrupts' a perfect cadence. The listener is expecting chord I after chord V, but is surprised by chord VI. Effectively like a semicolon, the interrupted cadence indicates that the music has more to add before concluding its musical sentence.

The four cadences written out in the key of C major and C minor in four-part harmony set for SATB choir (soprano, alto, tenor and bass) are as follows:

Perfect cadence:

V   I   V   I

Imperfect cadence:

I   V   I   V

Plagal cadence:

IV   I   IV   I

Interrupted cadence:

V   VI   V   VI

The elements of music

To enjoy a piece of music you will listen to it as a whole, but to really understand it you need to break it down into its constituent parts and see how they are combined.

It is possible to think of the musical elements as being a bit like the chemical elements from the periodic table: although each element can exist on its own in some form, it is much more common to find them in combinations forming molecules. More complex materials are built from lots of different chemical elements arranged and combined in different ways. The same is true of music: it is possible to separate out the elements, but they rarely exist on their own.

In this section we will:

- ask the sorts of questions you will need to consider in your exam when describing music
- fill in other aspects of the musical elements that have not been covered already
- consider the musical vocabulary you will need for each element.

Exam tip

In exam questions, you will often be asked to describe the extracts under the headings of the musical elements, so it is important that you learn to hear and describe each element in isolation using the correct musical vocabulary.

Organisation of pitch and tonality

Pitch is organised horizontally in melodies and vertically in chords and harmonies. The chords themselves relate to each other in hierarchies within a key structure, so when we zoom out to look at the overall organisation of pitch, we consider the tonality of the music.

Melody

- Does it move by step or by leap (are the intervals between adjacent notes small or large)?
- In what register of the instrument is the melody played (is it high or low in the instrument's range)?
- Is the melody split into even or uneven phrases?
- How does the melody work with the accompaniment parts?
- Is there any chromatic movement?
- What sort of scales are being used?

Harmony

- Is the harmony consonant or dissonant?
- Are the chords major or minor?
- Are there any added or altered notes in the chords?

Tonality

- What key is the music in?
- How quickly does the key change?
- Is the music major, minor, modal, atonal, bitonal or polytonal?

Structure

A piece of music is organised into smaller chunks or building blocks:

- A song is normally split into verses and choruses.
- A sonata form piece will have an exposition, development and recapitulation.
- A binary or ternary form piece will have an A section and a B section.

Structure

- What is the overall structure of this set work?
- What are the names of the individual sections (for example, exposition, introduction, middle 8)?
- Which section am I listening to now?

Exam tip

You will have studied the structure of each of the set works and will need to be able to tell which section an extract has been taken from, which section comes before it and which section will come next just by listening to the music.

Sonority

This element is the one that describes the sound quality of the instrument. It is more commonly referred to as the **timbre** of the instrument. Think about how it would sound if a trumpet and a xylophone were to play the same melody. Even though they play exactly the same pitches and rhythms, there is still a significant difference in the sound. This is because of the way that the notes are generated by the instrument.

Instruments can be made to sound by:

- striking (for example, percussion instruments, including piano)
- plucking (for example, guitars and harpsichords)
- bowing (for example, violins and cellos)
- blowing through a reed (for example, oboes and clarinets)
- blowing through a mouthpiece (for example, trumpets and tubas).

Each method of producing the sound will produce a different tone quality because the **attack** and **decay** of the notes will differ, the note may or may not be sustained at the same volume, and the combination of harmonics and sound waves that make up the note will differ.

Sonority

- What instrument is playing at this moment in the piece?
- How can I describe the tone quality of this particular instrument?
- Do the performance techniques alter the tone quality in any way (for example, playing closer to the bridge, blowing harder into the trombone, hitting the cymbal in a different place)?

Texture

The number of musical parts, how they move and how they are combined constitute the **texture** of the music.

Texture

- How many parts are playing simultaneously?
- Is the texture sparse or dense?
- Does the texture change and, if so, how frequently?
- Are there specific words I can use to describe the texture (for example, **polyphonic**)?

Rhythm, tempo and metre

Rhythm and tempo have been described in detail earlier in the chapter.

Metre is the time signature of a piece. It is a subtle element in that there are certain beats in the bar that we expect to be slightly stronger than others (accented). For example, the first beat of the bar is almost always accented and the third beat of a four-beat bar is slightly accented, too. Parts of the bar that are not accented are called 'weak' beats. When a weak beat or a note in between beats is purposefully accented, the rhythm is said to be **syncopated**.

Rhythm

- Is the rhythm made up of long or short note values?
- Is the rhythm syncopated?
- Is the rhythm swung?
- Are there any triplets in the rhythm?

Tempo

- How fast is this piece of music?
- Can I use an Italian term to describe the tempo?
- Is the tempo constant or does it speed up / slow down?
- Are there any pauses in the music?

Metre

- What is the time signature of this piece?
- Does the time signature change?
- Is it simple or compound time?

Dynamics

This element refers to the volume of a piece of music. Any music that is played at exactly the same volume throughout will dull our ears and hence sound quite boring. Our ears are used to picking up changes in volume and reacting to it quite sensitively.

Most of the set works have markings included that show the performers how loud or softly the composer intends them to play. Those that don't have many dynamic markings (such as the Bach set work) have other conventions in place that the performers would know about and would interpret accordingly. Some dynamic markings are instantaneous, taking effect immediately, such as **forte** (loud); while some are gradual, such as **crescendo** (get gradually louder).

> **Exam tip**
>
> In a school music room or exam hall the dynamics may be affected by how loud the sound system has been set up, but you can still hear the relative changes from softer to louder, etc. It is a good idea to memorise the dynamic markings in the scores of the set works and become familiar with how these sound when played through another system such as a phone or other digital device.

Dynamics

- How loud is this piece overall?
- Do the dynamics change and, if so, how often?
- Are changes in dynamics sudden or gradual?
- Are all the instruments playing at the same volume?
- Where in the piece do the dynamic changes occur?

Section 1: Performing

- Choose a piece of music you particularly like and search on YouTube for three different versions. Which do you like the most?
- Focus on the performances rather than the music itself. Are there any aspects of the singing or playing that increase or decrease your enjoyment of the music? List these for each version of the piece.

Learning objectives

In this section you will learn about:

- the requirements of the specification
- approaches to performance
- solo performance
- ensemble performance
- preparing for your performance.

The requirements of the specification

Requirement	% of overall GCSE mark	Performance approaches
At least one solo performance lasting at least 1 minute	15%	<ul><li>performing from a score</li><li>improvisation</li><li>performing a live part over a pre-recorded or sequenced backing track</li><li>rapping or beatboxing</li><li>performing a piece from the oral tradition</li><li>performing your own composition</li></ul>
At least one ensemble performance lasting at least 1 minute	15%	The same options as solo performance, but performing as part of an ensemble

You do not need to attempt each possible performance approach – you only need to select one approach for each performance. You can have different approaches for your solo and ensemble performances.

What you need to record

You need to record at least two pieces of music: one solo and one ensemble performance, each of which must be at least 1 minute long.

There is an important additional time requirement: the total duration when you combine your solo and ensemble performances must be at least 4 minutes.

Watch out!

If your performances do not last at least 4 minutes in total (when you add them all up), you may get zero marks for the performing component of the GCSE.

Performing

As long as each individual piece is 1 minute or longer, you can play as many pieces as you need to make up the 4-minute total time requirement. There is no maximum time limit: the specification gives a guideline total duration of no more than 6 minutes.

Each performance must be:

- at least 1 minute long
- recorded live and uninterrupted (you can't edit together different parts of several performances)
- recorded with your teacher present
- announced by you with your name, candidate number, the instrument you are playing and your role in the performance.

Your teacher may let you re-record your performance if you or they feel you could do better. In this case you need to re-record the whole performance, not just the section that went badly.

If you are performing with a backing track, you need to make sure that the part you are playing or singing is not audible on the backing track, too. For example, if you are singing to a backing, you must use a backing track that has no lead vocal. You must not just sing along with the original MP3 or CD.

What you need to submit

You must submit a recording of your performances, but you also need to submit something that will allow a moderator to mark the accuracy of each performance. For most people this will consist of a copy of the score, but different performance approaches may have other requirements. In general, you need to submit something that has enough information about the pitch and rhythm of the music to allow someone to tell if you are playing it correctly or not.

You could submit:

- the musical notation of the part you are playing (you don't need to send the music of the accompaniment)
- a professional recording of the piece you are performing so that a moderator can compare your performance to the one you are imitating
- a lead sheet or chord chart
- a detailed written commentary outlining all the performance information.

As you can see, there are a few other options apart from a score, but these should be treated with great care; it should be left up to your teacher to decide if they are valid or not. If a moderator can't assess the accuracy of your performance from the information you send, then your performance will not be assessed.

Approaches to performance

There is a certain amount of flexibility in the specification to allow performers from a wide range of musical backgrounds to play to their strengths. You should discuss with your teacher what approach will be best suited to your specific skills. You can mix and match approaches for your solo and ensemble performances: you do not have to do the same thing for both. You can even perform your solo on one instrument and your ensemble piece on another. However, there are no additional marks for being versatile, so stick with the approach and instrument that presents your skills in the best light and gives the most musical results.

The following approaches to performance are available for both solo and ensemble performances.

Performing from a score

This is the 'traditional' performance approach and the most widely used. The score can be staff notation or a professional 'reference' recording. If you use guitar tablature, it is important that it contains rhythm information as well as the pitch information. Many books of guitar tab give the staff notation above the guitar tab line, so these are acceptable. Some downloadable sources do not give enough information to be acceptable, so check with your teacher before you start learning the piece.

Popular music singers will often do best to use the original recording as the 'score'. It is likely that any notated music will be a simplified version of the original so, if you are copying a singer, especially one who uses a lot of ornamentation in their singing, it is probably best to submit a reference recording. As mentioned above, you can submit the reference recording instead of the notated score, so you do not need to submit both. If you do submit a notated score and have made some changes then it is important to annotate the score to show where these changes occur. You do not need to transcribe what you sing, but should indicate that you have interpreted a passage with stylistic ornamentation.

If your chosen performance piece has an accompaniment part then you must make sure that you perform with that accompaniment: you are likely to lose marks for 'expression and interpretation' if you do not. It is acceptable to perform to a backing track, but you must ensure that the part you are performing is not audible in the backing track.

Improvisation

It is not necessary to perform exclusively from a score. If your musical style has a significant proportion of improvisation then you can follow this route instead. The requirements are essentially the same as for the traditional performance, but you also need to develop the original stimulus material (the melody, chords or rhythm you are using to inspire your improvisation) and make it sound interesting. If you just repeat four bars over and over with minimal change from one cycle to the next then you are unlikely to do well. If you are confident of being able to develop a melody or chord sequence over the duration of the piece, giving your improvisation a sense of direction while avoiding hesitations, then this may be the approach for you. Note that pieces which contain only a few bars of improvisation count as 'performing from a score' rather than improvisations. An example of this would be a Rock School grade piece in which an eight-bar gap is left for you to fill in a solo.

Performing a live part over a pre-recorded or sequenced backing track

This approach is essentially the same as performing from a score, but just includes a backing track. A sequenced backing is one that you have input into a computer package such as Logic or Cubase. The element of sequencing is not assessed, so whether you have sequenced the backing yourself or bought it from another source is irrelevant. You still need to perform a live track over the top of the backing.

Rapping or beatboxing

It is only recommended that you attempt this approach if you feel particularly confident that it is your best option and that your teacher is confident in being able to assess it. A good way to think about it is to compare yourself to someone who has had a Classical music training and has reached Grade 4 standard. Would you consider yourself to have put as much work into your rapping or beatboxing as that person has into their instrument? If the answer is 'yes', then this is the approach for you.

Performing a piece from the oral tradition

Music from traditions such as Irish folk music, Indian classical music and African drumming will seldom have a notated score as the basis for a performance, but they are still perfectly acceptable styles for your GCSE performance. If a recording or any notation exists for your performance, you should submit it as a guide, but you do not have to worry about accuracy to the same extent. It is important to stick to the spirit of the style and make your performance sound convincing and authentic.

Performing your own composition

It is acceptable to perform your own composition, but the same requirements exist as for 'performing from a score': you need to supply a score with enough detail to allow the moderator to mark the accuracy of pitch and rhythm in your performance.

Activity ?

Record, review, refine

During a practical lesson, use your mobile phone to record a friend performing, and ask them to do the same for you. Afterwards, listen to your own performance (on headphones if possible) and answer the following:

- Did I play too fast or too slow?
- Did I speed up?
- Did I slow down at a tricky section?
- Were there any hesitations?
- Was I in tune throughout?
- Were there any particular passages that went out of tune?
- Did my tone sound different for the high or low notes?
- Did the dynamics change as they were supposed to in the music?

These are things that are sometimes hard to spot while you are actually performing, but are easier to hear when you listen to a recording afterwards. They are also things that can become bad habits, so you need to pick up on them as soon as possible.

Ask your friend to answer the same questions about your performance and do the same for them. Be honest, but supportive, and make suggestions to each other about how you might improve. Put these suggestions into practice and repeat the exercise after two weeks. You will be amazed at how much this will help you to improve.

Solo performance

A solo performance can be in any style and can be on any instrument, including voice. It is considered to be a solo when the part to be assessed has an obvious leading role or is really important for the success of the piece.

Examples of solo performances include:

- a solo piano piece
- the violin part in a violin sonata
- the lead vocal in a song
- the lead guitar in a rock song
- the only live part being performed over a backing track
- a solo drum kit study.

If the piece has an accompaniment then it must be performed with that accompaniment. The accompaniment should not be changed but where possible should be played as it was intended.

Performing

Watch out!

An accompanied solo is not an ensemble performance for the soloist. It can be counted as an ensemble for the accompanist.

Glossary

Undoubled: the part you are performing is not being performed in another instrument or voice at the same time. It is fine if someone is harmonising, but they can't be playing the same notes as you.

Simultaneously sounding: there has to be a significant proportion of the music in which there is more than one part being performed at the same time. You cannot just sing one verse and have someone else sing the next verse, because the parts aren't sounding at the same time.

Independent parts: the instruments or voices are each doing different things. Note that a part that is simply harmonising another (e.g. in thirds) throughout the piece is not considered independent.

Ensemble performance

The ensemble performance can also be in any style and can use any performance approach – it is entirely up to you. There are no extra marks for playing on a different instrument or using a different approach, and there is no penalty for playing the same instrument or using the same approach. Do whatever shows off your musical talents. Don't be modest!

Ensemble performances must consist of two or more people performing **undoubled**, **simultaneously sounding**, **independent parts**.

Backing tracks are still acceptable in ensemble performances, but the backing track does not count as another part – there still needs to be at least one more live performer.

The mark scheme that will be used by the moderator to assess your performance frequently refers to the balance between the different parts in the ensemble. This means that you need to listen to the overall sound of the group, adjusting your volume to support the other parts when you are part of the accompaniment, and coming to the fore when you are supposed to be the lead. It also refers to 'adjusting to other parts': this means that you are able to compensate when other people alter their tempo whether they do it deliberately or not. If you just plough on regardless of what anyone else is doing, you will be heavily penalised.

The solo and ensemble performances are worth the same number of marks for your GCSE. Make sure you put the same effort into your ensemble performance as you do into your solo. In fact, it may require even more effort because you have to learn your own part and then make it fit with other performers.

Preparing for your performance

By far the most important thing to get right if you want your performance to be successful is to choose the best piece for the job.

Picking the best piece

Make sure:

- it is longer than 1 minute
- it is not too long (try not to go over 4 minutes)
- you enjoy playing the piece
- there is something challenging in it
- it is not too challenging – it should not be beyond your ability to conquer every single note in the piece after a few weeks of practising it
- you are convinced that you will be able to play it 100% accurately if you practise enough
- you have the resources the piece needs (backing tracks / accompaniment / appropriate effects pedals / an instrument with the necessary range of notes)
- it contains opportunities for dynamic contrasts and a variety of accents as well as staccato and legato passages
- it suits your style or voice
- you have the ability not just to play the notes but to make it sound like a real piece of music with some emotional content.

Level of difficulty

Note that the difficulty level expected for a GCSE performance is Grade 4 (using any recognised syllabus). If you play a piece that is below Grade 4 standard then it is considered to be 'less difficult', while a piece above Grade 4 standard is considered to be 'more difficult'. If your piece does not appear on a recognised syllabus then your teacher will compare it to other Grade pieces and decide what level it is. Every piece you perform is marked out of 24 and the mark is then adjusted according to how difficult it is. The specification has a 'difficulty levels grid' that shows how these adjustments are made.

For example, if you scored 20 out of 24 marks, your final mark would be:

a Less difficult (Grade 1–3): 20 out of 30

b Standard (Grade 4): 25 out of 30

c More difficult (Grade 5+): 30 out of 30

So, the difficulty level does make a difference, though it is not the be-all and end-all.

It is important to find a piece of music that you enjoy playing but is still challenging

Remember that you have about two years to get this right and to build up to the perfect recording. Start your performing experience by recording a piece that is well within your ability range, even if it is considered less difficult, just to build your confidence. You will have other opportunities to push yourself more, but it is good to get a recording or two secured.

When you prepare for your ensemble performance, make sure that you have practised your own part and mastered it before you get together with the other performers in your ensemble. When you get together you are rehearsing, not learning the parts. It is hard enough to make music sound good when playing together with other people, so don't make it harder for yourself by not putting in the preparation.

Watch out!

Playing a difficult piece badly will result in a worse mark than playing an easier piece well.

Activity ?

Listen to a professional recording of the piece you are going to perform.

Note the aspects of the performance that you particularly like e.g. the tempo, the phrasing of the melody, the changes in tone colour, etc.

Are there any aspects of the performance you are less keen on? List these and write down how you would alter your performance to avoid repeating them.

Performing

Top tips for performance

- Spend time picking the best piece for the job.
- Consult with your instrumental / vocal teacher and your class teacher when choosing your performance piece.
- Remember that the ensemble performance is just as important as the solo performance and probably requires extra effort to get right.
- Never try to record an ensemble performance without rehearsing first.
- It is more important to pick a piece that you can play well than to pick one that is more difficult.
- Longer pieces are not necessarily better.
- Get a recording secured as soon as possible.
- Regularly record yourself; then review the recording and refine your performance.

After recording

When you have recorded your performance, listen to it and ask yourself the following questions:

- Did I perform the piece as well as I could?
- Was my performance accurate to the score **or** did I develop the improvisation enough?
- Was my tone good across the full pitch range?
- Was I always in tune?
- Was the tempo steady when it was supposed to be?
- Did I include dynamic contrasts?
- Can the musical phrases be heard clearly?
- Are there differences between legato and staccato passages and did I use accents appropriately?
- Did I communicate the emotion of the piece well?
- Were there any hesitations in the performance?
- Did it sound as if I was struggling in any passages?

If you can answer 'yes' to the first nine questions in this list and 'no' to the last two, then you have done all you can to record a top-notch performance.

Section 2: Composing

Composing

Getting started

Is there a topic you feel particularly passionate about? Is there a social issue you want to bring to the attention of others but don't know how to go about it? Is there a person you want to share your feelings with, but are afraid to do so? Is there an emotion you feel but can't express in words?
If so, composing gives you the chance to express yourself through music. It is a unique opportunity to throw yourself fully into a creative task and be completely yourself. Take some time to think about what you would like to say through your music.

Learning objectives

In the study of this section you will learn about:

- the requirements of the specification
- approaches to composing
- the set briefs
- how to compose.

The requirements of the specification

Requirement	% of overall GCSE mark	When it can be done
One composition based on a set brief	15%	The brief will be released by Edexcel on 1 September, the start of the academic year. There will be a choice of four briefs, one from each area of study. The work needs to be submitted to Edexcel by 15 May, shortly before your GCSEs.
One free composition	15%	The work may be composed at any stage during the course. It needs to be submitted to Edexcel by 15 May, shortly before your GCSEs.

Watch out!

If your compositions do not last at least 3 minutes in total (when you add them both up), you may get zero marks for the composing component of the GCSE.

What you need to submit

You need to compose two pieces of music. One will be written to a set brief and the other will be a completely free choice. They are both equally weighted, even if one is considerably longer than the other. They both need to fulfil the specification requirements and will be marked using the same mark scheme and criteria. Each piece must last for at least 1 minute.

There is an important additional time requirement: the total duration when you combine your two compositions must be at least 3 minutes.

The specification does clearly state that each piece should be at least 1 minute long, so make sure that you meet this requirement! There is no maximum time limit: the specification gives a *guideline* total duration of no more than 5 minutes, but this is not a strict rule. If your compositions are longer than 5 minutes they will still be marked, but you should not make them longer just for the sake of it – compositions that are longer than they really should be (if they are overly repetitive, for example) will lose marks for coherence.

Each composition must be:

- at least 1 minute long
- recorded either live or using studio techniques as appropriate (including playing back from a sequencer)
- recorded with your teacher present
- announced by you with your name, candidate number and the title of your piece.

You will also need to sign an authentication form stating that your composition is your own, unaided work. This does not mean that you have to compose without being taught how to compose. It means your teacher cannot do any of the actual composition task for you. They can advise you and ask you appropriate questions, but they are not allowed to tell you that you should replace an F♮ with an F♯ or things as specific as that. Your composition will blossom from a series of decisions that you make, not your teacher or anyone else.

Notated scores

You must submit a score of your composition along with the recording. The score and the recording together will be used by your teacher and the moderator (the person who reviews the composition) to assess your work. The score itself is not marked, but it does give the moderator an idea of what your intentions were and can clarify anything that is not clear on the recording. It is just as important to submit a score as it is to submit a recording, and you should not shy away from creating it or do it as a last-minute afterthought.

The word 'score' may be quite frightening and you need to be aware that it means several possible things in the eyes of the awarding organisation (Edexcel). A score can be:

- a full score in staff notation
- a lead sheet or chord chart
- track sheets of a recording
- a (detailed) written account
- a graphic score
- tables or diagrams.

Composing

Although the final deadline for submission of work is 15 May in the year of the exam, your teacher will want your work to be submitted a long time before this. They will want to have a look at it so that they can point out where revisions may be needed and also to leave them enough time to mark a final version.

One final rule to bear in mind is that you must spend at least 5 hours working on your compositions in the presence of your teacher. This is to ensure that your teacher is able to sign the authentication form in good conscience. You are not allowed to do all the work at home and then simply hand it in as a finished article – they must see it progress from fledgling idea to fully realised work of art, confident that this is all your own unaided work.

Approaches to composing

There are probably as many approaches to composing as there are styles of music. Successful composers do not all share a set formula for creating great music and they won't even have one set way to approach composition themselves. A commission with a deadline will have different pressures to a piece of music someone is writing for their own enjoyment. A song written for someone's boyfriend or girlfriend will probably start off differently from an anti-war song. A track written for a 30-second advert will be approached differently from an hour-long symphony. Some people start by writing lyrics; others strum chords on a guitar or noodle on the piano. Some people hum a melody to see where it takes them while others plan the structure of a piece from the outset. There is no right or wrong way to approach composing, and your own approach will change from composition to composition.

'How do I start?'

- Decide that you are going to sit down to compose something.
- Have a recording device handy (such as your phone).
- Keep a notepad (or electronic equivalent) dedicated to scribbling ideas and keep it with you.
- Decide what you want to write about.
- Know who you want to write for.
- Look at artwork, read an article or book, listen to other music – anything that inspires you to start; but set yourself a time limit for gathering inspiration.
- Experiment, improvise.
- Don't make excuses, procrastinate or find anything else to do that feels easier right now. Just make a start!

Starting points

Any artistic endeavour is hard to start. The act of starting will be the most difficult thing that you do in your composition. If you strum a few chords, record them so you have something to listen to and work on. If you just sit staring at the wall, you will have nothing to adapt, change, extend or develop.

The approach you try first will depend on what your task is. If you have some form of stimulus such as a poem then you have a ready-made starting point:

- Read the poem aloud.
- Get a feel for its natural rhythm.
- Analyse its structure.
- Write down the mood it conveys.
- Describe how it makes you feel.
- Do any rhythms leap out at you?
- Does a melody suggest itself to you?

If you are writing for a particular occasion, find other pieces that have been written for the same purpose. How did other composers approach the task? What instruments did they use?

Do you have any limitations in terms of the availability of instruments? If so, then that's a good thing. Boundaries are fertile ground for creativity and innovation. If you don't have any boundaries, set some for yourself.

Sometimes it is good to have a recurring theme. Even something as simple as a number can be a rich source of inspiration. For example, if you choose the number '3', you can have melodies that use lots of thirds, or there may be three main sections, or you could write the piece for three instruments. There may be three main **motifs** that are treated differently in each section and you might make extensive use of triplets. Deciding something like this at the start is a good way to introduce unifying elements to your composition.

Glossary

Motif: a short melodic phrase of just a few notes.

Composing

Another good thing to do at the very start is to consider what your end goal is…

End goal

Considering what we need to achieve as an end result can make it a lot easier to get started.

Activity **?**

Example: Write an eight-bar marching melody

What have you been asked to do? Write out the 'commission'. Now rule out eight bars on a stave or draw eight bar lines on a piece of rough paper. This is drawing out the physical space of the melody, almost like completing the edge of a jigsaw first so that you know what you need to fill.

The thought process:

1   What note values are you going to use? It is supposed to be for a march, so shorter notes will not be appropriate. So, mostly crotchets then. Maybe end with a longer note… a semibreve. Note that thought down in the last bar before you forget.

2   How many crotchets per bar? A quick Google/Wikipedia search reveals that marches normally have four crotchets per bar.

3   Major or minor? It depends on whether you want a funeral march or a victory march. Decide which one it is to be and write in a suitable key signature after the clef. Note down the mood you have decided on.

As you can see from this simple example, just considering the end point immediately gets us started on our composition. Considering the end point at the beginning and revisiting it at different stages of the process ensures that we stay on track in the composing process. It is true that compositions sometimes take on a life of their own, but it is still important to keep the end in sight at all times.

What makes a good composition?

This is a difficult question to answer because everyone may have a different opinion, but it is exactly what the examiners are doing every time they mark a composition. Your answer to the question might be different from the awarding body's answer. Your musical tastes will determine that you like certain styles of music with a particular balance of melody, harmony, rhythm, chord structure, instrumentation, etc. Even if you enjoy a wide variety of musical styles, there will still be music that you write off as being poor, or some that you feel you cannot even listen to. The examiners will have their own tastes, but they need to assess your work according to a defined set of criteria which takes the form of the mark scheme. This will ensure that all their marking is in line with national standards and is as objective as possible (their personal tastes should have no bearing on the mark you receive).

So if you want to do well at this part of the course, you need to consider what the mark scheme says and treat this as the 'ultimate brief' – your composition is primarily written to be assessed by this mark scheme (and hopefully score high marks), not for casual enjoyment or a specific professional commission.

What does the mark scheme require?

There are three criteria, each marked out of 10:

- developing musical ideas
- demonstrating technical control
- composing with musical coherence.

Developing musical ideas

All compositions need a balance between how many ideas they include and how often those ideas are repeated. Some musical styles contain more repetition than others and some styles (such as dance music or ground bass) actually depend on it. However, most music that simply repeats the same thing over and over will become boring, so it is good to alter some aspects of the musical material when particular passages return for a second or third time. For example, the melody or rhythm may be slightly amended, or the instruments playing the material could be different, or the accompaniment parts could be completely fresh even if the melody is unaltered.

It is also important to ensure that there is enough musical material to keep the composition interesting throughout. It is very easy to get stuck in a repetitive rut, even with the most exciting, original idea. The trick is to find the balance between introducing enough musical material and repeating just enough so that the listener recognises and remembers the themes but never gets bored.

The composers of the set works you will be studying during your GCSE course all had different approaches to developing their musical material. Careful study of how they use motifs and themes will help you in your own compositional work. Composers like Beethoven often found lots of different ways to use small musical motifs and were able to create large-scale pieces using only a few notes as the starting point. The first movement of Beethoven's 5th Symphony is a good example of this.

The highest **level descriptors** in the 'Developing musical ideas' criterion of the mark scheme assume that your musical material has been developed and that this has helped to extend the length of the piece, but they also refer to three other areas:

- a sense of the audience
- a sense of occasion
- relevance for the piece's intended purpose.

Glossary

Level descriptors: the parts of a mark scheme that describe what you need to do to achieve that level.

Composing

This means that you will need to be clear about the purpose of your piece. Composing without a sense of why you are doing it will not give you the best results (refer to the previous section on having the end goal in mind). If your composition is suitable for the intended audience and occasion, it will feel appropriate in the intended setting and the people you would expect to have there. For example, a heavy metal song would not feel appropriate in a cathedral service, nor would a choral requiem seem quite right in a nightclub.

Demonstrating technical control

This criterion judges how well you have used the musical elements and the instruments or voices that you have selected for your composition.

The musical elements have not been separated out in this mark scheme, so it is important to ensure that they all work well together. For example, if your melody is fantastic but clashes terribly with the harmony then you will be unable to gain a high mark for this criterion.

Any parts written for instruments or voices must be in a suitable range for those instruments and must show that they are making the most of the instruments in the given context.

The musical element '**texture**' gets its own bullet point in the mark scheme, so it is important to consider how you are combining the different parts in your composition. Introduce variety and space where possible (and where appropriate). Don't have all the parts playing all the time. Think about how you can introduce light and shade into your piece.

As usual, different styles will require different approaches to this criterion, but it is important that you carefully consider the various musical elements as you are composing. Just as you would not repeat the same one-bar melody over and over for an entire piece, you must also change the combinations of instruments at various points and ensure that the **dynamics** are not all at the same level throughout.

Consider the following:

- The **register** your instruments are playing in. For example, if you are using the piano, is all your music in the same two-octave range around the middle of the keyboard? What effect would it have if you used the same motifs higher up the keyboard or played in octaves lower in the range?

- If you are accompanying the melody line with a chordal part in the guitar or piano, how have you 'voiced' the chords? If you are using **block triads** all the time then you are missing an opportunity to make your piece more interesting. Try breaking up the chords, playing **inversions** or playing the chords in a different position on the guitar fretboard. What rhythm would work best for your chords? Do you have to play all the notes all the time?

Glossary

Texture: the character of a piece of music created by the interaction of its various parts.

Dynamics: marks in the score indicating to the performer how loud or soft their part should be played.

Register: refers to how high or low in pitch a piece of music or a musical part sounds.

Block triads: major or minor triads in root position, built up in thirds.

Inversions: major or minor triads with either the third (first inversion) or the fifth (second inversion) in the bass.

- Why have you chosen a particular instrument? Is it really the right sound for the job? Is there another instrument that would work better? Is the part something you would expect to hear on that instrument?

- Can the part be played on the given instrument? An example might be finding that you need chords in a flute part – a bit tricky for just one player to perform! What about those impossible chords in the piano that would need metre-long hands to play? For wind instruments, think about the fast section with no breaks that would leave the player no chance to breathe.

- Why is that instrument playing at this particular point? Does it add to or detract from the music? Does it support the melody or distract from it? On the other hand, do you need to add additional accompaniment parts to give more support to the main part?

- Do your choices sound natural for your chosen style or genre? Do they sound odd? Do the combinations gel together or do they fight against each other? If these instruments were playing live, would one overpower the other?

Composing with musical coherence

Imagine creating a mash-up of all the set works – just taking a theme from here and a chord sequence from there and adding the rhythm part from another piece. Maybe you would go through the themes one by one or give a listener a 20-second 'teaser' of each work before zipping on to the next. Unless you are an incredibly skilled arranger the resulting piece would lack coherence. It would sound like a jumble of several different pieces of work in vastly different styles that just don't belong together in one composition. Almost like taking a few pieces from several jigsaws and trying to fit them together, your task would not be easy and would need some brute force to make things fit in any fashion at all.

When you are composing you have to be careful not to do the same thing with ideas you have composed. Sometimes themes are born to be together and sometimes they should be kept in different compositions.

Every composition should have a sense of direction. It needs to have points where the music is building to a climax, and it also needs points of calm where the listeners can catch their breath. There should be a feeling that the length of the piece is just right – that you have not tried to drag things out longer than the music merits or to cut your composition too short.

This criterion is all about the structure of your composition – how you put together the large-scale building blocks of your piece. For good compositions, most musical styles follow similar principles:

- The different parts of the piece feel as if they belong together.
- One section moves naturally to the next.
- The piece feels like it is the right length.

Composing

- There is a sense of direction – it feels like each part of the structure is where it should be and that the music is 'going somewhere' (building and releasing tension in the right places).
- There is a good balance between repetition and contrast – not too repetitive and not too unpredictable.
- There is a satisfying conclusion to the piece.

Using music technology

Music technology is seen as just another possible resource to be used as appropriate, in the same way as a voice or piano. For some styles it will be absolutely essential to use music technology to create a suitable sound world (for example, dance music or a soundscape for a video game) and for others it may just be used to create the notated score. The specification gives no limitations to what you can use, but the general rule is that you can only gain marks for musical material you have composed. In other words, if you are using **drum loops**, you will not gain credit for the rhythm of the loops unless you created them from scratch. Similarly, if you use vocal samples, you will not gain credit for the melody content of the sample unless you composed and sampled the melody yourself. Be completely clear with your teacher as to what material you have composed yourself and what material comes from pre-recorded loops and samples.

If necessary, you can mix music technology and acoustic instruments. For example, you might use an electric guitar in an otherwise acoustic ensemble or compose some pre-recorded synthesised parts to be played along with live instruments.

You can use music technology to record yourself playing several different parts one at a time, such as if you want to multi-track yourself playing different instruments. Your teacher needs to be present when the parts are recorded.

The set briefs

Each year, the awarding organisation will set four composition tasks from which you must choose only one. The tasks will be released in September at the beginning of the academic year in which you take the exam. There will be one task set for each area of study. The briefs are likely to be rather wide in their scope, so it is possible that you have already composed some work that might fit one of them. However, most students' composition skills are inevitably more developed in the second year of their GCSE studies, so it is probably better to learn from your previous efforts and start afresh, ensuring that your new composition completely meets every aspect of the brief, rather than dropping in an existing piece of work that may not be quite right, no matter how good it is.

The advice given for composing in general holds true for composing to the set brief. The only difference is that in this case you really can't go off on a tangent (which would be fine for your free composition) – you must stick to

> ### Glossary
>
> **Drum loops**: a pre-recorded drum pattern repeated on a loop, over which other music can be laid.

the brief. There are additional sentences in the 'developing musical ideas' criterion of the mark scheme referring to how you have responded to the brief, so make sure you follow it carefully. In fact, embrace the brief – it is giving you a starting point, after all!

Brief 1 – Instrumental Music 1700–1820

- This brief will instruct you to compose for a given number of instruments – for example, a solo instrument with accompaniment, duet, quartet, etc.
- A named composer may be given as a stimulus, such as Bach, Handel or Haydn.
- You may be asked to compose a completely new piece of music or to use a pre-composed melody as a stimulus.
- A specific occasion will be given at which your piece is to be performed – for example, an official ceremony, an audition or a celebration.
- It is unlikely that there will be strict limitations on the specific instruments you are able to compose for – that is, it is unlikely you will be asked specifically to compose a string quartet or a piano sonata.

Watch out!

This brief will always require you to write a piece of **instrumental** music. Do not include vocals in your composition. If you really want to include vocals then choose one of the other briefs.

Brief 2 – Vocal Music

- This brief will ask you to write a piece of music that includes vocals in some way.
- It is most likely to include the option to write a song, but this may not always be the case.
- It will specify whether you can have an instrumental accompaniment or not.
- Lyrics may be provided or you may be asked to either write your own or find them from another source, such as a specific poet.
- A specific occasion will be given at which your piece is to be performed – for example, an official ceremony, an audition or a celebration of some kind.
- You are most likely to be able to write in any style.

Watch out!

This brief will always require you to include vocals in your composition. Failure to do so will be seen as a poor response to the brief.

Brief 3 – Music for Stage and Screen

This brief is the most difficult to predict and could take many possible forms.

You may be asked to write a piece of music for:

- a film sequence such as a trailer, a chase scene or a battle scene
- an instrumental underscore (for a film or show)
- a song for a musical.

You will be given a specific context for your composition, such as a scene in which two characters meet, a science fiction film or a tragedy.

Watch out!

This is the brief in which you will need to pay most attention to creating a specific mood in your composition.

Brief 4 – Fusions

- This brief will ask you to write a composition that fuses two musical styles from different parts of the world.

Composing

Watch out!

If you choose this brief, be careful to actually fuse the two styles together. It is insufficient to present a **ternary form** piece in which the A section is in one of the styles and the B section the other. The composition must mix elements of the two styles together into a single coherent piece of music.

Glossary

Ternary form: a simple musical form in three sections with an ABA structure.

- Both of the styles may be given or you may be able to choose one of them yourself.
- A specific occasion will be given at which your piece is to be performed, such as an official ceremony, an audition or some kind of celebration.
- It is likely that you will have a free choice of instrumental resources, but the fusion styles may give you strong hints as to which would be most suitable.
- You may be given some music as a stimulus – for example, a folk melody – or you may be told to choose a stimulus from a specific source, such as a collection of jazz melodies.

How to compose

The previous sections outline the theory of what makes a good composition and what the awarding organisation is looking for in your work. This section puts the theory into practice by taking one possible approach to composing a piece to a given brief. You may find that you can work in exactly the same way, approaching the task in the same order to achieve good results, or you may need to adapt things significantly to suit your own purposes. As mentioned previously, there is no right or wrong way to compose, but this section does give some guidelines and good working practices. Even if you are composing a piece to a completely different brief with a style that is far removed from this one, you are advised to take note of how the brief has been met and how the composer has repeatedly gone back to the brief to make sure that the composition never strays far from it. The language used reflects the thought process as the composition progresses.

Example brief

Compose a theme and variations for solo instrument and accompaniment. Your theme should be 16 bars long. It is to be performed at the opening ceremony for a new town hall.

Consider the end result first:

We need a piece to be performed at an official occasion, so it should have some sense of a grand theme. Music that has lots of tonic–dominant movement or that has some march or fanfare inspiration would be suitable. The harmony will need to be fairly straightforward – certainly to begin with – and the melody should be simple enough to vary but still be recognisable and have enough character to be interesting.

A 16-bar theme is required. Split this up into two halves of 8 bars each. A melody for an official occasion will need to sound quite regimented, so all the phrases should balance. Four phrases of four bars each should do the job.

Compose a theme

We need an idea to start with. Here is the thought process behind creating a simple melody:

- Pick a key in which to begin. The brief does not specify anything, but D major is as good a place as any to begin. It can be bright and zesty, which suits our brief, and it avoids too many sharps or flats, which might make it harder to figure out the harmonies later.
- Perhaps recent experience of improvising melodies by starting on the tonic has led to some dull efforts, so the third (F♯) might be more promising today.
- A melody wants to get to the tonic quite quickly, so the initial shape of our melody will be downward to the tonic.
- We don't want it all to be stepwise movement, so a leap is in order (to A).
- That leap was nice, so let's have another! The opposite direction this time.
- Back to the tonic by a roundabout route…

We have come up with a little **pentatonic** theme. A nice idea, but it needs to be extended if we are going to have a theme that has enough character to be varied.

- It is a two-bar phrase, so we need another two bars to balance it out and make it into the first four-bar phrase that we originally wanted.
- To ensure that we don't get stuck in a pentatonic rut, let's force ourselves out by starting on a G.
- It should end on a different note.
- If we end on a D again, it will sound like a musical full stop, so let's head for a note that is in the dominant chord – E is a little higher than D and it doesn't belong in the chord of D, so that is a good target.
- We don't want to change everything about the phrase, so starting with the same melodic contour (shape) will work fine.
- A change to the rhythm of the second bar would make things more interesting, too.
- Since we have decided on the **key signature**, we should add that to our notation so we don't have to keep on writing F♯s.

> ### Glossary
> **Pentatonic**: a five-note scale or a melody that uses only five different notes.
>
> **Key signature**: a series of sharp or flat signs placed next to the clef sign on every stave, which tells us the key of the music in the following bars.

Great! We have four bars already, and the last bar is just begging to be continued as the E is like a musical comma (rather than a full stop). We need another four bars, again to balance things out. It would be possible to repeat this theme exactly as it is, but ending on the tonic. Let's keep it simple.

Composing

The last bar needed a little bit of tweaking to make it sound right ending on the D.

What next? Well, we could make the rhythm a little more interesting and a little more fanfare-like if we included a couple of dotted rhythms. The low A's are prime candidates for this and the long D in the second and sixth bars needs something extra…

Remembering the brief, we know that 16 bars are required, and it also needs to sound grand in a way that's fitting for the opening ceremony.

- The last four bars can use the same material again, so we can fill that in straight away and tweak it later if required.
- Bars 9 to 12 need something that is a little more exciting – a higher register is needed.
- Starting on a note in chord IV would give added interest, so we can try a B since that is higher than the rest of the melody so far. Also, the interval of a sixth from the D in bar 8 will sound uplifting.
- Let's keep going up from there! Up to the tonic and then back to earth, and if we end on the dominant (A) then we can have another musical comma, taking a breath before the final four bars.

Great! We have a theme. Just a little tweaking to finish it off. Our original alterations to bar 6 don't sound so good in the context of the full 16 bars. A little experimentation is required to see what we like best in terms of decorating the main theme with dotted notes and passing notes…

Notice how the rhythm of the last bar has changed to make it consistent across all four lines.

Now we need to harmonise the melody. There's no need to write an accompaniment part just yet since we haven't decided what instrument is playing the melody. Just some block triads will do for now.

Write out the triads in the key of D:

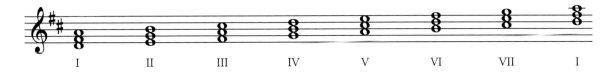

To harmonise a melody, a triad should contain the same notes as the melody notes that fall on the strong beats. There are often several choices of chord to harmonise any given note, but for our brief the primary triads (chords I, IV and V) should be the first choice with other chords used only for added interest.

We also need to decide how often the chord should change; this is known as the **harmonic rhythm**. After some experimentation, it feels right to change the chord every two beats.

Glossary

Harmonic rhythm: the rate at which the chords change.

- For bar 1 we have two very clear choices: I–I or I–V. Write out both choices in pencil underneath the stave and make a decision when the other chords are in place.

Composing

- Bar 2 was always going to be harmonised by chord IV as the melody was designed that way, but chord IV doesn't work throughout the bar, so return to chord I.

- Continuing in this fashion we can harmonise the first line with one chord every two beats:

The whole melody can be harmonised with triads – mostly I, IV and V with the odd chord II (chord II is minor so it is often written in lower case roman numerals: ii). When the chord does not change in the bar it is written once only.

1	2	3	4	5	6	7	8	9	10	11	12	13	14	15	16
I	IV I	IV I	V	I	IV I	IV I	V I	IV I	II I	IV I	V	I	IV I	IV I	V I

Now we have a harmonised theme it is time to revisit the brief and decide what the next step should be…

- Our piece is to be played at an opening ceremony, and we have already decided it should be fanfare-like, so it makes sense for the solo instrument to be a brass instrument.

- The melody is in the range of the trumpet, so this would make a good choice. If we wanted to, we could transpose to another key that is easier for the trumpet (for example, F major), but we originally selected the key of D major because it has a bright sound to it, so we'll stick with that and change if necessary after hearing it played live.

- The harmony works fine, but it is not yet a proper accompaniment. The next stage should be to develop the chords into a piano accompaniment part.

To start with, let's keep things simple and just put the triads into the left and right hands, trying to get rid of some of the leaps from one triad to the next by changing the voicing of the chords.

1 Write out the bass notes of the chords in the left-hand part. We'll start by just having one note in the left hand.

2 The left hand moves a bit better by changing the inversion of the second chord in bars 1, 5 and 13 so that the F♯ is in the bass rather than the D. Re-sounding the D sounds a little clumsy.

3 Even though this is a simple accompaniment part, it is still a bit boring to leave the whole part as just minims. We can add some movement, mirroring the trumpet part from time to time. It's important not to double it too much (such as in bar 3), but a bit of contrary motion (bar 6) and harmonising in thirds (bar 15) will help.

4 The same technique can be used in the bass – bar 11 moves along with the melody line. Too much movement will sound a bit contrived, so we'll leave it there for now.

5 We don't need to use triads in the right hand all the time. Thinning out the part to two notes on some occasions will help vary the texture.

6 Lastly, the harmony really is very simple, so it would be good to add a seventh at an appropriate point. Adding the G at the end of bar 12 flows nicely back to the F♯ in the next bar.

Composing

Glossary

Alberti bass: a figuration commonly used in the Classical period, made up of broken chords used as an accompaniment. Named after a now forgotten composer called Domenico Alberti.

Activity ?

Experiment

Try out different ways of creating an accompaniment part for our theme. Keep the chords the same, but try out other ways of voicing them or different accompaniment styles. Remember that this is the statement of the theme, so you do not want to distract from the solo part.

There are lots of different ways you could elaborate on our simple accompaniment. Some examples include:

* changing the register of the chords
* including more motion in the piano part
* using broken chords instead of the block chords, perhaps in an **Alberti bass** style.

Add variations

Activity ?

Research

Now that we have started the piece, the most difficult part is behind us. The next stage is to decide on what sorts of ways we can vary the theme, so it would be useful to see what other composers have done before us.

There are many examples of theme and variations available. Find one example and make a note of what the composer does in each variation. Use musical vocabulary where possible. Look at the big picture rather than focusing on individual notes.

Your list probably includes some of these:

* The melody moves from the solo instrument to the piano while the solo instrument does something else (normally a fast-moving part to show off the skills of the soloist).
* The accompaniment changes style with almost every variation.
* The time signature changes from 4 in a bar to 3 in a bar (or vice versa).
* The key changes to the tonic minor.
* The composer sometimes imitates other styles – for example, playing the theme in the style of a Hungarian folk song.
* The pitch range of the melody and accompaniment sometimes changes dramatically.
* The texture is sometimes quite busy, with big chords in the accompaniment, and sometimes quite sparse, with minimal accompaniment.

Develop the theme – the minor variation

Let's try a tonic minor (D minor) version of our theme. This is a good opportunity to change the register, too, and maybe some of the melodic contour, so as to make the shift in register sound more natural.

As with any composition work, you can start off with a basic idea, try it out and change anything that doesn't sound as successful as you'd like. Remember – it is your composition! To a great extent you make up the rules. As long as you stick to the brief and have an end goal in mind, it doesn't really matter how you get there. If you stick too rigidly to a given technique, the music often sounds rigid, too, so let your ear be your guide.

Although we have gone straight to the minor variation here, it might not be the best place to put it in the context of the overall piece. Often the minor variation comes a bit later, after two or three other variations.

In this example there are not many changes to the rhythm. You might take the opportunity to change the rhythm along with the register and the key.

What should we do with the accompaniment for this variation? To start with, we need to reharmonise using the triads from the minor key. The easy way to do this is to write out the same chords as before, but with the new key signature, and then add C♯s where the C♮s occur.

It might be nice to be a little more dramatic than in the original theme. To accomplish this, we could:

- use more of the piano
- include octaves in the left hand
- leap from the octaves to a chord
- include more movement in the right hand
- use a higher register in the right hand.

There are a host of other possibilities, but we can try out these suggestions on the first line.

Activity	?

Spot the difference!

What changes have been made to the original theme here?

Can you still recognise the elements of the original theme in the developed melody?

Composing

The motif for the right-hand part hasn't just appeared from nowhere. It is the same as the opening three notes of our original melody, harmonised in parallel sixths. This is an example of trying to use existing material where possible. The accompaniment part is a great place to try to work in old material in different ways. The listener may not notice the reuse of a previous motif, but this will give a sense of unity to the piece that they will appreciate nonetheless. Notice also that dynamics have been included for the first time here. Dynamic contrast adds light and shade and should not be an afterthought, so keep it in mind as you are writing your piece. You don't have to keep one dynamic level through a whole variation – in this case, because we are using a brass instrument, dynamic changes over the duration of even one note can be quite effective.

Activity   ?

Keep experimenting!

Complete the accompaniment part for the minor variation that has been started for you. It might be good to change the right-hand idea a little in the third line to stop it from becoming overbearing.

Try to vary the melody in some of the other ways suggested. Below is an example of what you might do with the trumpet part if you were to move the melody into the piano part. Use this as a starting point to see if you can complete another variation.

How would you change the melody of four beats per bar into one of three beats per bar? In many pieces this will be a successful strategy for another variation, but is it appropriate for our composition?

Glossary

Chromatic: 1 (harmony) from the Greek for 'colour'. The term is used to describe notes that are not diatonic (part of the key of the music). 2 (melody) ascending or descending in semitones.

Diatonic: notes that belong to the key of the piece (literally 'of the key').

Develop the theme – the melody moves to the piano

When the melody moves to the piano, it does not need to be in the same register – it could be played in octaves in the right hand an octave higher than its original pitch or it could make an appearance in the left hand while the right hand plays chords. As mentioned previously, the soloist will probably play a more intricate part which might start like this:

Notice the **chromatic** notes that often occur in the middle of the triplets. These add colour (which is the literal meaning of 'chromatic'), but do not clash horribly because they are not on an accented part of the bar or beat – they fly by quickly but add interest because they do not belong to the key. Try replacing the chromatic notes with the **diatonic** version (the notes that belong to the key, for example, E♮ instead of E♯) and see if you prefer the sound or not.

Where do we stop?

As you can see, this type of composition can go on for some time because there are so many possible ways to vary the original theme. When you look at examples by the great composers, you will find that they often included more than 20 variations of the original theme. You do not need to go this far, but the exercise is a very good one for learning how to develop ideas and hence to do well in the first criterion of the mark scheme.

If you want to submit a piece like this as a GCSE composition, it is important to make it feel balanced and to place the variations in an order that lends a sense of direction to your piece (see criterion 3 of the mark scheme). It would be a good idea to compose more variations than you are actually going to use, maybe six or seven, and then pick the four or five that are most successful and work best together as a whole piece. For our example it would be important to finish on a grand statement with loud dynamics and a dramatic piano part so that it fulfils the brief. This final variation would be in the tonic key and would give a suitable sense of finality to the piece. Knowing that we were going to finish like this, it would be important to include a much quieter variation with a reduced accompaniment part somewhere in the middle of the running order. Why do we do this? Criterion 2 of the mark scheme demands textural contrast, and we are treating the mark scheme as the 'ultimate brief', so we need to make sure we include some textural contrast in our piece!

Composition tasks modelled on the set works

An important component of your course is the analysis of the eight set works in the areas of study. The knowledge acquired through this listening and appraising work – for example, your understanding of musical vocabulary, chord symbols or rhythmic notation – could be extremely relevant to your own compositions. You may find it helpful to use the set works as models for compositions in these particular forms and styles.

Below are suggestions for some compositions you could try.

Bach

Compose a piece for two instruments of your choice. You should be aware of the limitations of the instruments you write for, such as the available pitch range and whether the instruments are limited to single notes. You should also know about any common performing techniques, such as arco (bowed) or pizzicato (plucked).

Your piece must be in a form that includes a theme and at least three episodes. Repetitions of the theme should be separated by an episode. Ritornello and rondo form are good examples of forms you may choose for your composition.

Your composition is to be performed as background music at a formal dinner.

Composing

Beethoven

Compose a ternary form piece for solo piano that includes as many of the following as possible:

- a slow introduction
- tremolo in the left- and/or right-hand parts
- a change of key to the relative major or minor
- another modulation to a more distant key
- use of the full pitch range of the piano
- a range of articulation
- a wide dynamic range
- pedal techniques as a feature of the music
- three main ideas that appear in different guises in the A section and B section
- a dramatic interlude just before the return of the A section.

Your composition is to be used to demonstrate how the modern piano has a wider pitch and dynamic range than the pianos used in Beethoven's era.

Purcell

Compose a piece that has a repeating ground bass of two to four bars' duration. Your piece can be in any musical style but must include at least one instrument and one voice. You might use one of the following as a starting point for your ground bass:

- a blues-inspired riff
- the bass line of a dance track
- one of Purcell's ground basses
- a passacaglia for organ – for example, Bach's Passacaglia (and Fugue) in C minor, BWV 582

Your composition is to be used as an audition piece for performers hoping to get a part in the next school show.

Queen

Compose a song for solo voice with backing vocals and instrumental accompaniment. You should analyse your set works and wider listening pieces to get an idea of structures you might use, but you can also use an original structure or one you have borrowed from a song of your choice. Create textural contrast in your use of the backing vocals.

You should write the song for yourself to sing or for a particular singer you know.

Your song is to be used to showcase the vocal talent of the singer for whom you have written the song, with the backing vocals to be provided by members of the school choir.

Schwartz

Write a short summary (synopsis) of an imaginary musical. Compose a song for one (or more) of the characters in your musical. Your song must either develop an audience's understanding of the character or it must move the plot forward somehow.

You might make your song an alternative to an existing song in a real musical. For example, if your school is putting on a musical this year, you may feel it would have been interesting if the story had taken a different direction. How would you imagine the story developing differently?

The context for this composition is obviously the show of which your song would be a part.

Williams

Compose a 1-minute soundscape for a science-fiction film depicting a post-apocalyptic landscape. In your piece there should be some distinct themes that would be used later in the film in different contexts. You might include musical themes for some of the following:

- the hero
- the love interest
- the main villain
- hope
- despair
- an important object – for example, the ring in the *Lord of the Rings* trilogy.

The context for this piece is the film for which the music is written.

Afro Celts

Compose a piece for percussion ensemble using instruments from two or more of the following musical traditions:

- Indian classical music
- Bhangra
- West African music
- Celtic music
- Western popular music
- Samba.

Your composition is to be performed to local primary schools to inspire younger children to become involved in percussion ensembles.

Spalding

Compose a piece that fuses elements of jazz with any other musical tradition. It must be written for at least two instruments and/or voices. Your piece should use a structure from one musical tradition in the context of another, such as a piece for jazz saxophone in sonata form with tabla and sitar accompaniment.

Your piece is to be performed at the local jazz and blues festival, showcasing the talents of your school's star jazz soloist.

Johann Sebastian Bach: Brandenburg
Concerto No. 5 in D major, 3rd movement

Getting started

- Composing is a job. In the past, many composers worked under a system of patronage. Research what this means, especially for composers like Bach and Beethoven in this area of study.
- What are the pros and cons of such a system? What kind of music would you commission (pay to be composed) if you were given the chance?

Learning objectives

In the study of this set work you will learn about:
- the life and works of Johann Sebastian Bach
- the Baroque era and features of Baroque style
- the background to the six Brandenburg Concertos
- the basso continuo – its role and function
- how to analyse Brandenburg Concerto No. 5 in D major, 3rd movement
- the key musical features.

The life and works of Johann Sebastian Bach (1685–1750)

Portrait of Johann Sebastian Bach

Johann Sebastian Bach was born in Eisenach, Germany, in 1685 and spent his whole life in the country. He came from a family of professional musicians, and his father was a town musician. Bach was the youngest of eight children, but unfortunately both his parents had died by the time he was only 10 years old. He was brought up by an older brother, who was an organist and who helped Bach to develop his skills as organist, violinist and singer.

At the age of 15, Bach became a choirboy at St Michael's School in Lüneburg. A number of church organist and choirmaster appointments followed – for example at St Boniface Church in Arnstadt in 1703 and in Mühlhausen in 1707. In that year he also married his second cousin, Maria Barbara. Bach only stayed at Mühlhausen for one year before taking up a post as organist at the court of the Duke of Weimar.

In 1717, Bach was appointed Kapellmeister (choirmaster) at the court of Prince Leopold in Cöthen. It was during this period that the Brandenburg Concertos were composed. At this time, Bach wrote music at the request of his employers. His work for them consisted of instrumental music, solo keyboard pieces, dance suites for orchestra, and concertos.

His last appointment was as organist and choirmaster at St Thomas Church, Leipzig. Bach was a devout Lutheran – Lutheranism was an early, German form of Protestantism. He wrote music for the Lutheran Church, including over 200 cantatas, as well as choral motets, masses, oratorios and four monumental settings of the Passion (the story of Christ's crucifixion). He also wrote a large repertoire of music for the organ.

Glossary

Ornamentation/ornamented: notes that decorate a melody. They are shown by small notes (grace notes) immediately before the main note or symbols above it. Examples include the mordent, trill, turn.

Diatonic: notes belonging to the key of the piece (literally 'of the key').

Monophonic: refers to a musical texture comprising a single line which can be sung or played by several people.

Homophonic: a texture comprising a melody part and an accompaniment.

Polyphonic: literally, 'many sounds'; more than one melody sounding at the same time or entering at slightly different times so that melodic lines overlap.

Sequence: the repetition of a musical phrase at a higher or lower pitch than the original.

Pedal: a sustained note, usually in the bass part. It may clash with harmonic changes above it. Pedals are usually on the tonic or dominant notes, so would be called a either tonic or a dominant pedal.

Suspension: prolonging a note to create a dissonance with the next chord.

Affection: the prevailing mood in a Baroque movement.

Musical contexts

The Baroque era (c.1600–1750)

This was a creative period in which there was a new exploration of ideas and innovation in the arts, literature and philosophy. Italy was the cultural centre for all things artistic and led the way in exploring new ideas.

Did you know?

The word 'Baroque' comes from the Portuguese for *pearl*. It refers to the ornate and highly decorative architecture, gilded paintings and frescoes (wall paintings) that cover the interior walls and ceilings of German and Italian churches of the period. In music, this decorative element translates into the use of **ornamentation** in melodic lines.

The best-known composers of the Baroque period are Henry Purcell (c.1659–95), Johann Sebastian Bach (1685–1750), George Frideric Handel (1685–1759) and Antonio Vivaldi (1678–1741).

Features of the Baroque style

The following features are typical of music composed during the Baroque:

- the use of **ornamented** melodic lines
- the establishment of the major/minor tonal system
- the use of the **diatonic** chords of I, II, IV, V and VI
- the basso continuo (see below)
- different musical textures such as **monophonic**, **homophonic** and **polyphonic**
- musical devices such as the **sequence**, **pedals** and **suspensions**
- the prevalence of one mood or '**affection**' in a given movement
- contrasting dynamics with just two levels – loud and soft (called **terraced dynamics**)
- use of the Baroque orchestra, based on the new string family (violins, violas and cellos replacing viols) with harpsichord playing supporting harmonies as part of the basso continuo. The use of wind instruments varied from piece to piece depending on availability. The brass instruments were not commonly used within the orchestra yet Bach wrote for whatever skilled players were at his disposal, hence the different combinations of solo instruments in the six Brandenburg Concertos.

Did you know?

The double bass is the only string instrument tuned in ascending fourths, with the rest being tuned in ascending fifths.

Background to the six Brandenburg Concertos

These six famous **concerti grossi** were composed between 1711 and 1720 and were dedicated in 1721 to Christian Ludwig, Margrave (a type of nobleman) of Brandenburg. In 1719 Bach had gone to Berlin to order a new harpsichord and performed to the Margrave. The nobleman was impressed with Bach's music and commanded him to submit some pieces. This is much like the **patronage** that we shall see with Beethoven's composition of the piano sonatas later. It was lucrative for composers like Bach and Beethoven to accept such aristocratic commissions.

The Baroque orchestra comprised a nucleus of stringed instruments: violins, violas, cellos and double basses. The harpsichordist usually directed the ensemble from the keyboard.

In this case, however, Bach was not paid for the set of six Brandenburg Concertos. This was probably because they were delivered two years after the commission and had already been composed during Bach's time in Cöthen; he simply revised these existing works and submitted them!

Bach hoped to secure employment from the Margrave; however, the nobleman did not even bother to acknowledge receipt of the concertos. They were assigned to the library, perhaps because the orchestra of the Margrave only numbered six players of modest ability and was therefore not able to perform these large-scale, almost symphonic, works.

The concerto grosso

The concerto grosso features two groups of instruments played both separately and in combination with each other. The form offers the potential for many types of texture, including **dialoguing** and **antiphonal** effects. The two groups are a smaller group known as the **concertino**, and a larger group made up of a string orchestra, known as the **ripieno**.

Did you know?

Bach's music has influenced music in the 20th century, such as the jazz interpretations of the pianist Jacques Loussier. The 1960s pop band Procol Harum based their classic song 'A Whiter Shade of Pale' on Bach's 'Air on the G string'.

Glossary

Concerto grosso (plural *concerti grossi*): a concerto for more than one soloist. The phrase literally means a large concerto. It is usually written in three movements in the order fast–slow–fast.

Patronage: a system whereby composers earned money from a wealthy individual for writing music. The person who commissioned (asked for) the music was known as a patron.

Dialoguing: instruments literally 'in dialogue', playing one after the other, swapping ideas.

Antiphonal: swapping between different musical groups (e.g. concertino and ripieno).

Concertino: the smaller group of soloists in a concerto grosso – here flute, violin and harpsichord.

Ripieno: the larger group – here a string orchestra.

Glossary

Basso continuo: continuous bass parts are provided for harpsichord and stringed instruments such as bass viol and lute. The players add chords and melody.

Figured bass: a type of musical shorthand for the keyboard player. The figures indicate the chord to be played above the bass note and whether this is in root position or first or second inversion. For a fuller description, see the glossary pages at the back of the book. You will not need to remember this definition for your exam.

The role of the basso continuo in Brandenburg Concerto No. 5, 3rd movement

The **basso continuo** or, more usually, just **continuo**, came into use in the early Baroque period. The term literally translates as *continuous bass* and describes the part played usually by the harpsichord (or organ) and cello (or other bass instrument such as the bassoon or viola da gamba).

The continuo part is an accompaniment and was used extensively in both vocal and instrumental forms of music in the Baroque. It supports and holds together the other parts by providing a bass line and harmonies. The keyboard player would read from a single bass line which had added figures to show which chords to play above the bass notes. This is called **figured bass**. The continuo was still in use at the beginning of the Classical period (c.1750–1820). Haydn and Mozart wrote continuo parts, especially in their earlier work. It became redundant as the classical orchestra evolved and no longer needed support from the continuo instruments. We shall see the continuo used to effectively accompany the Purcell song 'Music for a While' in Area of Study 2.

The continuo role of the harpsichord in Brandenburg Concerto No. 5, 3rd movement

The various functions of the harpsichord continuo in this set work can be summarised as follows:

- The harpsichordist is a soloist in some sections of the movement.
- The harpsichord also forms part of the continuo, providing a background accompaniment.
- The harpsichordist 'realises' the figured bass as chords and melody.
- The harpsichordist may also coordinate and/or direct the ensemble.

Close analysis of Brandenburg Concerto No. 5, 3rd movement

The fifth concerto has always been one of the most popular of the six works. It features the harpsichord prominently, particularly in the first movement. Bach was much admired as a keyboard player and performed this work himself as the solo harpsichordist. The other two solo instruments that feature in this work are violin and flute.

The final movement of a Baroque concerto is fast and lively, and this work is no exception to that rule. It is a **gigue** (a dance-like movement in $\frac{6}{8}$ or compound time) played at an Allegro or fast tempo and in the key of D major, a key suitable for strings.

In the Baroque period the dynamics were left to the performer and there were no dynamic markings in the score. Textual variations were used to vary the dynamics. This being said, as you listen to this movement, you will hear that dynamics are varied according to the number of parts playing. When both the concertino and ripieno groups play together, the music is loud. During the section when only a few parts play, the dynamic level is much lower.

Did you know?

The gigue originated from the British 'jig'. In the mid-17th century it was imported into France and began appearing at the end of a suite of dances. Bach wrote a lot of gigues as last movements to his works.

Structure of the movement

The structure fuses together two forms – the **fugue** and **ternary** form. In a fugue there are three sections: the exposition, middle section and final section. In this movement the first two sections are as we would expect of a fugue.

The third section of a fugue is usually different from the other two sections, but in this set work, it is the same as the first section. The third movement can therefore be regarded as having a three-part (ternary or A B A) form, in which the repeat of the A section at the end is exactly the same as at the beginning. Bars 1–78 are repeated exactly at bars 233–310. This is relatively unusual, as composers tended to alter the repeat of section A for variety. It is possible that Bach felt the opening section was striking enough to merit an exact repetition.

The structure demonstrates both repetition and contrast; the *repetition* of the A section and *contrast* in the new musical material in the B section. The analysis will bear in mind both elements to show how the music is put together.

The complete structure in terms of the three sections is as follows:

Section	Bars
A	Bars 1–78
B	Bars 79–232
A	Bars 233–310

Did you know?

In Baroque times, pitch varied considerably from one town to another. This concerto was probably performed on instruments sounding about a semitone lower than modern instruments, so to us would have seemed nearer the key of D♭ major than to D major.

Commentary on Section A (bars 1–78 and bars 233–310)

The first section starts off in the manner of a **fugal exposition**. The **subject** is played by the solo violin in bars 1–2. The length of the subject is two bars, which means that this will be the space between subject and answer entries.

The characteristics of this sprightly melody are:

- The off-beat semiquaver first note on the **dominant** note A (of D major) is followed by the tonic note D.
- The stepwise (moving in a scale) triplet groupings in bar 2 give the music its gigue-like feel.
- It ends on the tonic.
- The range of each melody is an octave.

Glossary

Fugue: a musical form comprising an exposition, middle section and final section. The music is contrapuntal.

Ternary (or **A B A**) **form**: a simple musical form in three sections with an ABA structure.

Fugal exposition: the initial statements of the subject and answer.

Subject: the short main theme of the fugue.

Dominant: the fifth note of the scale or key – the strongest note after the tonic.

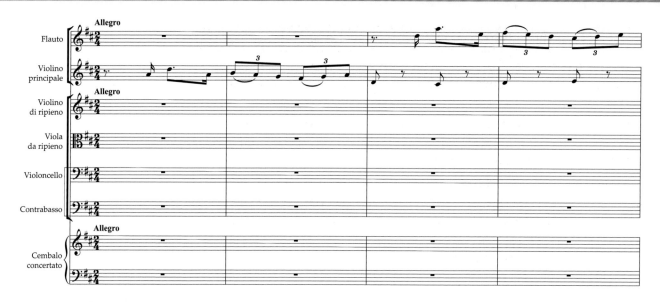

Glossary

Answer: in a fugue, the subject repeated in response to its initial appearance, usually a fourth or fifth lower or higher than the preceding subject. If it is an exact transposition of the subject it is a real answer; if not it is a tonal answer.

Countersubject: the melody played after the subject or answer has been sounded. The melody is literally counter (against) the subject.

Stretto: entries of the subject occur closer together than before, heightening the tension of the music.

In bar 3 we have the **answer** to the fugue subject, played by the flute. The answer starts a fourth higher on the tonic note D and ends on the dominant note A.

Whilst the answer is being played by the flute, the violin has four detached quavers. This is called the **countersubject** (counter means 'against', as in the part going against the subject). This pattern is used throughout the movement. For example, in bars 41–44 the countersubject is played by all parts of the orchestra (except for the right hand of the harpsichord, which has the melody).

At bar 9 the subject is heard in the left hand of the harpsichord, starting on the dominant. The answer is in the right hand, starting on the tonic at bar 11. The order of entries in a fugue is always subject–answer–subject–answer, etc. There are further entries of subject and answer at bars 17, 29, 31, 33, 39, 40, 48, 50, 64, 65, 66 and 75.

Note the trilling on minims by the harpsichord in bars 19 and 21. The sound always dies away rapidly after a harpsichord key is struck, so to make the notes sound for longer it was common practice to trill. See also bars 68 and 70 in this section.

The length of the subject (and the answer too) is two bars, but some of the entries come in after only one bar – that is, before the previous entry has finished. Look for an example at bars 39–41.

This overlapping is called **stretto**, a technique which gives added intensity to the music. Stretto occurs in the cellos, basses and harpsichord. Look at the harpsichord part below, which makes this clear.

(39)

The other part developed in this opening section is the pattern of triplets from the subject. Look at bar 22 in the harpsichord part and bar 52 – the dialogue between the violin and flute and the harpsichord – to see how this is done.

Activity ?

There are two types of answer in a fugue: **real** and **tonal**. In a **real** answer, the interval between one note and the next is exactly the same as in the subject. Otherwise it is a **tonal** answer.

Look at the **answer** in bars 3–4. In the preceding **subject**, the interval between the first two notes (D to A) is a perfect fifth, but in the answer (A to D) it is a perfect fourth, so this is a **tonal** answer.

1   Can you find other examples of tonal answers in the music?

2   Try to compose a two-bar subject that will work with a *real* answer. Write in C major so that the subject begins on the note C and the answer will begin on G. Make sure that every interval is the same in the subject and the answer. This is tricky!

Textures

The whole movement is predominantly **contrapuntal** and fugal.

The texture in the concertino builds up from monophonic, a single melodic line (bars 1–2), to two-part **counterpoint** (bar 3 to the first beat of 9), to three-part counterpoint (bars 9–10) and then four-part counterpoint (bars 10–29). At this point, more ripieno parts join in until all are playing by bar 33. Apart from a few rests, the texture remains quite full until the end of the section at bar 78.

Tonality (keys)

The A section opens and closes in the tonic key of D major. From bar 12 the addition of G♯s starts to modulate the music to the dominant key of A major. A perfect cadence in this key is reached at bars 16–17 (V7–I). The music then modulates to the dominant of the dominant key – E major – through the addition of D♯s from bar 23. This is called the **secondary dominant**. A perfect cadence in that key occurs in bars 24–25. However, within a couple of bars the music has returned to the dominant key of A major with a perfect cadence in bars 28–29. The tonic key of D major is reached at bar 37. There are then a few **passing modulations** (lasting only a bar or so) before a perfect cadence in the tonic key of D major at bars 63–64, and another, final perfect cadence in D again at bars 77–78. The music then moves straight into the relative minor key of B minor for the start of Section B.

Glossary ◥

Contrapuntal: when two melodies are played 'against' each other and interweave – almost the same as 'polyphonic'; written in counterpoint.

Counterpoint: literally means 'tune against tune'. It is the simultaneous combination of two or more melodies with independent rhythms.

Secondary dominant: this refers to a key that is the dominant key of the dominant – for example, in C major, G is the dominant and the dominant of G major is D major, the secondary dominant.

Passing modulations: modulations where the new key only lasts for a few bars (or less) before modulating to another key.

Did you know? ◥

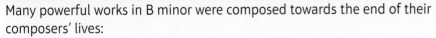

Many powerful works in B minor were composed towards the end of their composers' lives:

- Bach's Mass
- Schubert's Unfinished Symphony No. 8
- Brahms's Clarinet Quintet
- Tchaikovsky's Symphony No. 6, the *Pathétique* (not to be confused with Beethoven's piano sonata of the same name discussed in this book)
- Dvořák's Cello Concerto.

Commentary on Section B (bars 79–232)

The substantial middle or B section starts off with a varied version of the subject played by the solo flute in bars 79–86. The key of the music is B minor, the **relative minor** of the opening key of D major. The dynamics are piano.

(79)

Glossary

Relative minor: the minor key based on the sixth note of the major scale.

Variant: a phrase whose shape resembles the original.

This **variant** of the subject is more lyrical, accompanied by flowing triplet quavers in both solo violin and harpsichord. The repeated tonic Bs provide a tonic pedal. The texture is generally lighter, with fewer instruments playing. As we shall see, this section allows for more of the solo concertino instruments (flute, violin and harpsichord) to engage in dialogue. Look at the section at bars 106–128 (see example below).

The original form of the subject appears in the ripieno violins at bar 87. At bar 89, the variant is heard in the solo violin. Further entries of both forms of melody follow at bar 97 (subject in violins and violas) and bar 99 (variant in the harpsichord right-hand part). The music from bar 97 has moved to F♯ minor, with a perfect cadence at bars 98–99. This key is the dominant of the key of B minor (which itself is the relative minor of the home key of D major). F♯ minor is also chord V of vi. Chord vi in D major is a B minor chord, so the dominant from B minor is F♯ minor. There is also a tonic F♯ pedal at bars 100–106.

(106)

An example of musical dialogue

In bars 106–128, the music mostly features the solo instruments. Bach gives the harpsichord a more soloistic role in this passage, releasing it from the basso continuo function of supporting the harmony with bass line and chords. In this passage the instrument plays in patterns of triplet thirds and features some dialogue with the solo flute and violin also playing in thirds.

There follows further passagework from the harpsichord, with the flute and violin engaged in some two-part counterpoint above (see bars 118–123). This is preceded by a rising sequence in the harpsichord in bars 114–118. Then at bar 123, the solo violin plays the subject in F♯ minor followed one bar later by the answer played by the flute.

The ripieno violins then state the subject at bar 128, followed two bars later by flute and solo violin in **unison**. The texture is now full and features **passagework** in the flute and violin. Notice the rising **scalic** bass and the sequential patterns – for example in bars 137–141. The music is using material derived from bar two of the original subject. The harpsichord has returned to a more sedate chordal style of accompaniment.

For the first time the solo flute and violin are now playing in unison throughout bars 130–148 to reinforce the melody line. The other parts mostly provide accompaniment.

A perfect cadence in A major is reached at bars 147–148. At this point the variant of the subject is heard in both ripieno violins and violas. Throughout bars 148–155 a tonic pedal A is played on the string basses and harpsichord. The two-bar harpsichord link at bars 155–156 takes the music to E minor and we then have a statement of the subject in flute, violin and upper strings followed by another statement at bar 161, this time in B minor. Notice the trilling during this passage on the harpsichord to sustain the sound on the long tied notes.

Another chance for the harpsichordist to take on a solo role occurs from bar 163 to the end of the B section. There is a **canon** between the right and left hands at bars 163–176. It is a canon because the two parts are exactly the same – note for note – but at the interval of an octave. There are short interjections from the solo violin, flute and ripieno violins in bars 177–180. These are based on the opening three notes of the subject. The subject is then heard in these instruments in the tonic key of D major at bar 181.

Another entry based on the shortened variant of the subject occurs at bar 189 in the upper ripieno strings. The subject then undergoes further treatment from bar 193 in solo violin and flute parts in two-part counterpoint. Beneath this, the harpsichord has relentless triplet quaver passagework based on bar two of the subject. This section of music is constantly shifting and passing through minor keys, and there is also a dominant C♯ pedal in the double basses in bars 198–203.

From bar 203, the harpsichord right hand takes on a melody role, making three-part counterpoint with the other two concertino instruments. Fragments of the subject are heard at bars 215–216 in cello and

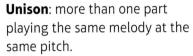

Glossary

Unison: more than one part playing the same melody at the same pitch.

Passagework: a constantly moving passage, often in patterns of quick notes such as semiquavers. It often includes sequences.

Scalic: music that is based on scales ascending and/or descending in pitch.

Canon: parts copy each other in exact intervals, often at the fifth or octave, but at different beats of the bar. The song 'London's Burning' is a good example.

harpsichord left hand. A dominant F♯ pedal of B minor is sustained from bar 217 to bar 222.

Bars 220–224 feature a stretto. In the manuscript example below you can see the order of entries: ripieno violins at bar 220, then one bar later the violas, followed by the cellos, basses and harpsichord left hand together in bar 222, and then in bar 223 the concertino flute and violin.

Exam tips

- When referring to a passage from this movement, make sure you mention the bar number(s) and the instrument(s) playing.
- It might be a good idea to learn by heart bar references for key features such as pedal notes, sequences, stretto, etc., particularly for the essay question.

Exam-style question

1   The middle section starts at bar 79.

(i) What is the key here? **(1 mark)**

(ii) How does this key relate to the opening key of the movement? **(1 mark)**

2   Starting at bar 189, the flute and solo violin play together (in thirds). A bar later the harpsichord plays a similar phrase, imitating them. All three instruments have a minim in the second bar of their phrase, but only the harpsichord has a trill over the minim. Why? **(1 mark)**

Glossary

Cadential: this refers to a progression of chords forming a cadence. Please see the glossary for a fuller definition.

The last eight bars feature rising sequences in the concertino parts, taking the music back to the key of B minor for a full-orchestra **cadential** $\frac{6}{4}$ (Ic–V7–I) in bars 231–232.

Textures

The texture is generally lighter in this section, allowing for the concertino instruments to be heard. The opening bars of the B section feature the solo flute with accompaniment in a homophonic texture, although this is interspersed with some contrapuntal passages, for example, at bars 86–106. Another texture not seen before in this work occurs at bars 106–109. This is called dialoguing (see section on the concerto grosso on page 55), where the harpsichord alternates with the solo flute and violin in a dialogue (see music example on page 60). Further examples of this can be seen in bars 155–162 and bars 187–188.

In bars 128–148 the solo flute and violin play in octaves in a contrapuntal texture. There is also a texture reduced to just the harpsichord in bars 163–178. This is also an example of a canon (see page 61), which in this case occurs at the interval of an octave between right- and left-hand parts; note that, in order to be canonic, each part must be exactly the same, interval for interval. Then towards the end of the B section, at bar 220, the texture increases to full orchestra.

Did you know?

- Three clefs are used in the concerto: treble, alto and bass.
- The alto clef (used mainly for viola parts) was also occasionally used for trombone parts.
- The tenor clef, identical to the alto clef but placed two steps higher in the stave, is also sometimes used in cello, bassoon and trombone parts.
- Historically there were *nine* different clefs…
- … but they all looked identical to one of the three clefs appearing here. It was only their position in the stave that varied.

Tonality (keys)

The B section opens and ends in the relative minor key of B minor (vi), providing tonal contrast to the largely major keys of Section A. Throughout the section the music modulates through a series of mainly minor keys. At bar 97 the key modulates to F# (vi of V) minor, the dominant key of B minor (vi). There is a perfect cadence in this key at bars 98–99. The music modulates to A major in bar 148, and E minor (vi of IV) is reached in bar 156. The music moves back to B minor at bar 161 then to D major at bar 181. A return to F# minor follows from bar 198. The music is quite **chromatic** in this last section and passes through various keys until a dominant pedal on F# in bars 217–222 leads to a perfect cadence in B minor at bar 232 to end the B section. Baroque pieces in a major key only ever modulated to the dominant, the subdominant, or their relative minors, as well as the relative minor of the home key.

Did you know?

The word clef is French for 'key' and clefs literally 'unlock' the pitches, or decode them. They are named after voice parts because that was their first use (trebles being young boys) and that their position changes in order to fit the most notes of that particular vocal range on the five staves, without using ledger lines. Clefs were gradually transferred to instruments of similar range so the right hand of the harpsichord here is roughly the same range as a treble voice, and the left hand the same range as the bass voice.

Glossary

Chromatic: 1 (harmony) from the Greek for 'colour'. The term is used to describe notes that are not diatonic (part of the key of the music). 2 (melody) ascending or descending in semitones.

Glossary

Solo concerto: a concerto for a single instrument accompanied by an orchestra.

Activity ?

Try to identify in the music where each idea in the poem is set to music. How does Vivaldi do this in his music?

Wider listening

To supplement your study of this set work, the following suggested pieces for wider listening provide further examples from the period and will extend the overall breadth and depth of your knowledge.

Listening to these pieces will help you understand how common features from the set works have been used in other contexts, so that the set work is not viewed in isolation.

G.F. Handel: Concerto Grosso Op. 6 No. 5, 2nd movement

Handel's opus 6 concertos were scored for a solo group of two violins and cello, offset by full string sections and *basso continuo*. Handel later added two oboes to the accompanying ensemble for some of these concertos, including this one. The piece includes musical quotations from his *Ode for St Cecilia's Day*, which Handel had recently completed, with the three sections of the Ode's overture appearing as the first, second and final movements of the six-part concerto grosso.

This second movement has similar features to our set work:

- It is in the same major key of D major.
- It is played at a fast and lively tempo.
- It has a fugal texture.
- It uses the concerto grosso ideas of concertino and ripieno groups.
- It features an ever-present basso continuo.

A. Vivaldi: 'Winter' from the *Four Seasons* concertos

Vivaldi's *Four Seasons* was published in 1725, in a set of 12 concertos entitled *Il cimento dell'armonia e dell'inventione* (*The Test of Harmony and Invention*). Each concerto is in the distinct three-movement form of fast–slow–fast.

These four solo concertos are examples of **programme music** (music describing something without using song). Each piece features a poem about the seasons. The lines of poetry (most probably written by Vivaldi himself) are written into the musical score. The essential difference when compared with the Brandenburg Concerto set work is that this is a **solo concerto**, the idea of contrast between the soloist and orchestra being a key element of this type of concerto. Many of the features of Baroque music are still in evidence, however, such as the use of basso continuo and string orchestra. The poem for the three movements of 'Winter' is translated as:

Trembling with cold amidst the freezing snow, while a frightful wind harshly blows, running and stamping one's feet every minute, and feeling one's teeth chatter from the extreme cold; Spending quiet contented days by the fire while the rain outside drenches people by the hundreds; Walking on ice, and moving cautiously, with slow steps, for fear of falling, spinning around, slipping, falling down, again walking on ice and running fast until the ice cracks and splits; Hearing Sirocco, Boreas, and all the winds at war burst forth from the bolted doors – this is winter, but it also brings joy!

Checkpoint

Strengthen

S1 Find *two* examples of different musical textures in the movement. Write a bar number followed by the single word describing the texture: monophonic, homophonic or polyphonic.

S2 In what way is the flute phrase at bar 79 a variant of the opening theme? Name both a similarity of rhythm and a similarity of interval.

S3 Apart from playing the written notes, the harpsichordist was important in other ways. Briefly describe one other role of this instrument.

Challenge

C1 Explain how this piece demonstrates some of the key features of the Baroque style.

C2 In the 20th century Sir Michael Tippett wrote a Concerto for Double String Orchestra. Listen to the opening movement and compare it to this Bach Baroque movement. Can you identify some similarities and differences?

Summary of the key musical features

Key points to remember:

- Bach wrote **six** Brandenburg Concertos dedicated to the Margrave of Brandenburg.

- They are all examples of the **concerto grosso**. This means a 'large concerto' for more than one soloist, written in three movements, usually in the order fast–slow–fast. The work features two groups of instruments played both **separately** and **in combination** with each other.

- The two groups are called concertino and ripieno. The **concertino** is the smaller group of **soloists**, here **flute**, **violin** and **harpsichord**. The ripieno is the larger **orchestra**.

- In all Baroque music there is a **basso continuo**. This is literally a continuous bass played by the harpsichord and low strings.

- The harpsichordist reads a **figured bass**. The bass part is annotated with a **musical shorthand** indicating the **chord** to be played above the notes, which in turn gives a clue about any **melody** that should be **realised** by the player.

- There were **five** main functions of the harpsichordist: soloist, part of the continuo, realising a figured bass part, completing the harmony, and directing the ensemble.

- It was the custom in Baroque music to have **only one mood** expressed in any one movement. This was known as the **affection**. In this set work the mood

is upbeat and uplifting, achieved through the **gigue** dance rhythms (**two beats** of triplet quavers in a bar), the **fast tempo** and the **D major** key, which suits stringed instruments.

- In this movement, Bach explores a number of common musical **textures**. Although it is mainly **fugal** and **contrapuntal**, there are also passages that are **monophonic** and **homophonic**.

- The movement combines **fugue** and **ternary** structure.

- In the opening **fugal exposition**, the **subject** and **answer** enter alternately **every two bars**. The exposition ends when the last entry has been made. The music line played at the same time as the subject is called the **countersubject**.

- Sometimes the entries of subject and answer occur after a shortened duration – **after only one bar** (rather than two bars) in this movement – and seem to tumble over one another. This is called **stretto**. The effect heightens tension and excitement.

- Common Baroque musical devices include **suspensions**, **sequences** and **pedals**.

- As was the custom of the time, **no dynamics** were written into the music. There are instead **terraced dynamics**. This means that the music is soft when just a few instruments play and then loud when all play. There are no crescendos or diminuendos.

Ludwig van Beethoven: Piano Sonata No. 8 in C minor, *Pathétique*, 1st movement

Getting started

- The fortepiano was a new instrument in Beethoven's lifetime. Who invented the first fortepiano and how did this instrument differ from the harpsichord?
- Music of the Romantic era often expressed different emotions and feelings. The title *Pathétique* in this set work refers to suffering. How does music reflect different emotions? Some music lovers say that sad music can make them feel happy, and vice versa. What about you?
- Which other of your set works uses a different keyboard instrument such as a harpsichord, electric piano or synthesiser?

Learning objectives

In the study of this set work you will learn about:

- the life and works of Ludwig van Beethoven
- the development of the piano
- sonata form
- how to analyse the Piano Sonata No. 8 in C minor, *Pathétique*
- the key musical features.

Ludwig van Beethoven

The life and works of Ludwig van Beethoven (1770–1827)

Beethoven was born into a musical family in Bonn in 1770, where his father was a court musician. His father intended to turn Beethoven into a child prodigy and removed his son from school at the age of 11 in order for him to concentrate solely on music. Beethoven first studied Baroque counterpoint with a teacher called Christian Gottlob Neefe, before moving to Vienna in the hope of studying with the two Classical giants, Haydn and Mozart. In the event, Haydn he found too tolerant of his mistakes while he only met Mozart on a single occasion before his death in 1791. Despite these setbacks, during this period Beethoven did begin to make a name for himself as a talented pianist and improviser.

He settled into Vienna and made a living writing music and performing concerts for patrons such as Prince Karl von Lichnowsky, to whom this set work was dedicated. With the dawn of the Romantic era, Beethoven considered himself a pioneer in the new ideas of **Romanticism**. In many ways he was indeed a revolutionary, taking music in new directions and establishing the new, more independent social status that composers who followed him would enjoy.

From 1796, Beethoven started to lose his hearing and eventually he became profoundly deaf. This only makes his later achievements, such as the late string quartets, seem all the more remarkable.

His works can be divided into three periods. The early works were Classical in style and the middle period works Romantic and heroic. In his final period Beethoven wrote string quartets that were unlike anything that had been heard before and are still challenging for many listeners. His output includes nine symphonies, numerous string quartets, the opera *Fidelio*, the *Missa solemnis* (*Solemn Mass*), and 32 piano sonatas as well as many other works. He died at the age of 56 in 1827.

Glossary

Romanticism: an artistic and intellectual movement that began in Europe in the early 1800s and lasted for approximately 100 years. Romanticism is characterised by an emphasis on the individual's expression of emotions and their freedom of imagination, as well as a love of the natural world. Another common theme was the idea of the individual's rebellion against established social rules and conventions, which led to the rise of the virtuoso heroic soloist in Romantic concertos.

Did you know?

At the end of the first performance of Beethoven's last symphony, No. 9, the *Choral*, one of the singers had to turn Beethoven round to face the audience, so that he could see the wild applause that by then he couldn't hear.

Musical contexts

The development of the fortepiano and the 32 piano sonatas

The fortepiano was an early type of piano invented by Bartolomeo Cristofori around 1700 and was the instrument for which Mozart, Haydn and (early on) Beethoven wrote their piano music. Like the piano of today, and unlike the harpsichord, this instrument could vary the volume of each note depending on the player's touch, hence the name 'forte' (loud) 'piano' (soft). Today we call the instrument the pianoforte or, more commonly, just piano.

This ability to vary the dynamics in the music is used to great effect in the *Pathétique* sonata. Particularly effective on these early instruments too were the **sforzando** accents which stood out more strongly than on the modern instrument. Beethoven uses these a lot in the music of the *Pathétique* sonata.

During Beethoven's lifetime the piano started to evolve into the instrument we know today. However, the instrument that Beethoven used to compose his piano sonatas was different from the modern instrument in the following ways:

> **Glossary**
>
> **Sforzando**: an accent showing that a note or chord should be played with greater force than other notes surrounding it. Often shown in the score as *sf* or *sfz*.

Pianos in Beethoven's time	Modern pianos
Delicate structure, housed in a lighter case	More solid, housed in a metal frame
Hammers covered in leather, producing a strident tone	Hammers covered in felt, producing a softer tone
Thin strings, producing a lighter sound	Thicker strings resulting in a more robust sound
Very responsive keys, requiring a lighter touch	Less responsive keys, needing a heavier touch
Keyboard range of about 6 octaves (72 notes)	Keyboard range of about 7⅓ octaves (88 notes)
No sustaining pedal on earlier models	Sustaining pedal invented in 1783 by the Scottish manufacturer Broadwood and used on modern pianos
The bass notes had a buzzing resonance, and the high notes had a light treble sound	The tone quality across the register is more consistent

> **Did you know?**
>
> Inventive musical manufacturers and inventors play a huge role in musical progress.
>
> - Bach was able to extend his harmonic language as a result of scientific innovations in understanding tuning.
> - The recently invented clarinet inspired Mozart and later Brahms to write some of their sunniest music.
> - The weird and haunting sound of the *ondes Martenot*, an early electronic keyboard instrument, inspired the mystic French composer Olivier Messiaen in his powerful *Turangalîla-Symphonie* and has also been used in pop music and in the soundtracks of films such as *Lawrence of Arabia*.
> - The rich orchestral sound of Late Romantic composers such as Mahler and Bruckner would not have been achievable if no one had thought of adding valves to horns and trumpets, allowing them to play chromatically.
> - Instruments such as the Hammond organ, the Fender Rhodes piano and the synthesiser have created whole genres of pop and rock.
> - One prolific and ingenious 19th-century inventor was Adolphe Sax. Where would jazz be without him?

Beethoven composed piano sonatas throughout his life, eventually completing 32, and today these works form the backbone of the piano repertoire. Some of the most breathtaking ones are the *Moonlight*, the *Waldstein*, the *Appassionata* and the *Hammerklavier*.

Beethoven composed his eighth sonata in 1798. It was published in 1799 with a dedication to his friend, Prince Karl von Lichnowsky. The Prince was a great supporter of Beethoven, particularly in his early years in Vienna, and gave the young composer a generous annual allowance (salary) following the dedication. Beethoven is thought to have named the work *Grande sonata pathétique* himself; however, it was actually named by the publisher, to Beethoven's liking. *Pathétique* here does not mean weak or pitiful, but refers to suffering. The subject of suffering was one of the main themes in Romantic music: the notion of the lone artist against the world. Of course, Beethoven himself would have to deal with his own suffering when composing the sonata, as he was already going deaf. For a composer in particular, this must have been hard to come to terms with.

As a former pupil of Haydn and a fan of Mozart, Beethoven would have known the piano sonatas of these two composers. His own works in this form were on a larger scale and full of the intensity and passion that became typical of the Romantic style. Some musicians believe that the work might have been inspired by Mozart's Piano Sonata K. 457, as it is also in C minor and has three similar movements. The themes in the second movements of both works are quite similar, too.

Did you know?

Beethoven spanned two musical periods – the **Classical** and **Romantic eras** – and he is often called a Classic–Romantic. He was known as the composer who made headway into the Romantic style through his use of adventurous harmony and extended structures. He inspired all the Romantic composers who followed him, from Schubert in his own time to Mahler a century later.

Glossary

Classical era: the musical period extending from c.1750 to c.1820.

Romantic era: the musical period extending from c.1810 to c.1900.

Sonata form: a large-scale form invented in the Classical era comprising three sections: *exposition*, *development* and *recapitulation*. Not restricted to sonatas.

Sonata form

The word sonata comes from the Latin word *sonare* meaning *to sound*. The piano sonata was a keyboard work in three movements, in which the first movement (and sometimes the last movement, too) would be in **sonata form**.

The set work uses sonata form as its structure. This form became established in the Classical era and was used by composers such as Haydn and Mozart to structure the first (and sometimes last) movements of their symphonies, concertos, string quartets and sonatas written for solo instruments. The two fundamental ideas expressed in sonata form are:

- repetition
- contrast.

The structure developed from the Baroque binary (two-section) structure (AB, or AABB with repeats) as well as the three-part ternary structure (ABA).

The three sections in sonata-form movements are called:

- exposition
- development
- recapitulation.

This structure gives a balanced arch shape to the movement. The exposition is balanced by the very similar recapitulation (see below).

Contrast is achieved through the two different melodies in the exposition, called the **first** and **second subjects**, which we will study in the analysis. Repetition occurs in the repeat of both first and second subjects in the recapitulation. The central development section provides further contrast and repetition, as these two melodies are explored and developed further in different keys.

Exposition

In this first section the main themes or subjects are stated for the first time. The first theme – the first subject – is always in the home key and is usually the most lively and dramatic, as is the case in this set work. Then comes a short transition or **bridge passage**, the purpose of which is to modulate to the key of the second subject that follows.

The second subject will be a contrast to the first subject in terms of mood. The key will also be different from though still related to that of the first subject – usually the dominant or the relative major or relative minor. In C minor one would therefore expect G minor (the dominant) or Eb major (the relative major), but in this movement Beethoven, with typical originality, chooses something different, as we shall see.

In sonata form, the exposition is traditionally repeated so that the listener becomes familiar with both subjects before the development occurs.

Development

In this central section, composers develop one or both of the subjects from the exposition. This development can be based on a complete melody or a fragment of it. Sometimes the composer will use several fragments and combine them in different ways, thus creating new and sometimes strange variants. The section also features modulations to keys other than the tonic and dominant.

A development section can be adventurous, restless and constantly changing, as the drama unfolds.

Recapitulation

The final section balances with the opening exposition. The composer 'recaps' (states again) the first subject in the home key as before. A transition section follows, as in the exposition, but does not need to modulate this time, as the second subject will now be in the home key. However, in this sonata Beethoven chooses to start the second subject in the subdominant, another original touch.

A sonata form movement often ends with a short rounding-off section called a **coda**.

Glossary

First subject: the first theme or melody.

Second subject: the second theme or melody.

Bridge passage: a linking passage often used to change the key of the music (to modulate) in preparation for the second subject.

Coda: a section sometimes added at the end of a piece or movement.

Close analysis of Piano Sonata, No. 8 in C minor, *Pathétique*

Introduction (bars 1–10) *Grave*

This sonata has a slow introduction of ten bars that is full of intensity and drama. The sonata form structure starts at bar 11 with the exposition. Unusually, Beethoven uses music from the introduction within the main sonata structure, too, as we shall see. These introductory ten bars feature the following musical elements:

- heavy chords (**fp**, *forte* reducing to *piano*) at the beginning of bars 1–3
- use of dotted rhythms
- melody in right-hand part with some dramatic chromatic descending phrases – for example, bar 10
- chordal accompaniment in the left hand. The texture of the whole work is a melody-dominated **homophony**.
- dramatic **diminished seventh** chords – for example, bar 1 (crotchet 3), and bars 2, 3 and 4 (crotchet 1).
- sudden contrasts in dynamics – for example, bars 5–6.

A fortepiano

Glossary

Homophony: a texture comprising a melody part and an accompaniment.

Diminished seventh: a four-note chord made up solely of minor-third intervals.

Area of Study 1: Instrumental Music 1700–1820

Glossary

Codetta: a short coda concluding a section.

Interrupted cadence: most commonly comprises chord V followed by chord VI. So-called because it interrupts an expected perfect cadence V–I.

Pedal: a sustained or repeated note in the bass. It may clash with harmonic changes above it.

Murky bass: the fast octave repetitions in the bass.

Sonata form in the set work

In this movement the sonata form structure is constructed as follows:

- slow introduction (bars 1–10)
- exposition section (bars 11–132) with a **codetta** from bar 121. This section is then repeated
- development section (bars 133–194)
- recapitulation section (bars 195–294)
- coda section (bars 295–310).

Commentary on introduction

The first bar is an intense short melodic statement, repeated a fourth higher at bar 2. The rise in pitch over the first four bars adds to the passionate intensity of the music. Bar 3 repeats the opening melody from bar 1 but in a higher register, developing it over the course of bar 3 and the first part of bar 4, heightening its dramatic potential by speeding up the harmonic rhythm and extending its register up to the top A♭ in bar 4.

The chromatic harmony at the start of bar 4 leads to a climax, with just the note A♭ over a B♭ bass. Despite the missing notes, this feels like B♭7 – the dominant seventh chord in E♭ major. A florid (showy) right-hand phrase then helps us into this new key, the relative major of C minor.

The melody from the opening bar, now in E♭ major, is heard in bar 5 in a quieter, gentler version, until the sudden **ff** left-hand bass chords disrupt it. When the melody reappears in bar 6, we have begun to modulate back to C minor. Look at the chromatically shifting left-hand chords used in bars 6–9, which add to the restless nature of the music in this introduction.

Throughout bars 7 and 8 the melody climbs in pitch and dynamics. It is broken up into smaller units until it reaches a strong dominant seventh chord in C minor at the first quaver beat in bar 9. The cadence that follows tells us that there is more to come as this is an **interrupted cadence** (V–VI). The final bar, bar 10, features a two and a half octave chromatic descent to B♮ below the stave before rising to a solitary accented A♭. Then, after a pause and via the same B♮, we are plunged straight into the sonata form exposition, marked *Allegro di molto e con brio* (very fast and lively).

The exposition section

The exposition section in this sonata has four main characteristics:

- It is fast paced (*Allegro di molto e con brio*).
- It is in $\frac{2}{2}$ (*alla breve*) time.
- It starts in C minor.
- It features two subjects (themes).

Commentary on the exposition section

Exposition first subject in C minor

This is a dramatic rising 'rocket' theme in the right hand covering two octaves. The left hand plays tremolo octaves, which in bars 11–15 (crotchet 2) also form a tonic **pedal** on C. This type of accompaniment is known as a **murky bass**. The theme repeats at the first octave in bar 13 and then ascends to top C. Notice how Beethoven adds excitement by starting *piano* then crescendoing throughout bars 15–18. There is a perfect cadence in C minor (bars 18–19) before the theme is repeated. This time the diminished seventh chord (first heard in bar 18 beat 1) is extended to end on chord V at bar 27, forming an **imperfect cadence**. This cadence is then further developed with exciting accented octave Gs (dominant note) and descending broken chords in the right hand. From bar 35 there is a **transition** section, which is a link section for the music to modulate and prepare for the second subject.

Transition section

This section is based on the first subject theme and uses lots of Romantic chromatic harmony. The tremolo octaves in the left hand rise chromatically and the music modulates to Ab major (bar 39) then Bb major (bar 43). The bass Bb tremolos in bars 43–49 form a dominant pedal; again, notice the dramatic accented chords. This is followed by two suddenly quiet linking bars of unaccompanied right-hand crotchets oscillating around the notes Bb and A♮. The main note is heard as Bb, as it occurs on the beat: this is the dominant note of Eb, preparing for the second subject. We would normally expect this to be in Eb major – the relative major of C minor. However, Beethoven plunges into the unexpected key of Eb minor instead. The minor key fits well with the *pathétique* mood of the music.

Exposition second subject in Eb minor (Section 1, bars 51–88 and Section 2, bars 89–120)

Section 1, bars 51–88

This theme by contrast is much more **lyrical**. It uses grace notes and crossed hands (right hand going over the left into the bass to play the melody) to create a dialogue or antiphonal effect. The left hand plays a simple accompaniment of held semibreves with three two-note chords on crotchets 2 to 4. Notice the dominant pedal (Bb tremolos) throughout bars 51–62.

The theme is repeated in different keys in this section – for example, Db major at bar 67, back to Eb minor at bar 79 and then to F minor at bar 83.

> ### Glossary
>
> **Imperfect cadence**: a cadence ending on chord V and sounding incomplete. Usually preceded by chord I, II or IV.
>
> **Transition**: a section used to take the music from one key to another by modulation. Sometimes also called a bridge section.
>
> **Lyrical**: songlike, flowing.

Area of Study 1: Instrumental Music 1700–1820

Glossary

Articulation: the manner in which a note or sequence of notes is played – for example, staccato, legato, accented.

Staccato: played in a detached fashion.

Legato: played in a smooth fashion (as opposed to staccato).

Mordent: there are two types of mordent: 'upper' and 'lower'. The upper mordent is made up of the main note, the note above the note and the main note again, all played as quickly as possible. The lower mordent again goes from the main note to the note below and back to the main note again.

Alberti bass: a figuration commonly used in the Classical period, made up of broken chords used as an accompaniment. Named after a now forgotten composer called Domenico Alberti.

Look at the contrast in **articulation** in the melody, alternating between **staccato** crotchets and **legato** phrases (for example, from bar 51 onwards). Beethoven also uses **mordents** to decorate the melody (for instance, in bars 57 and 58).

Section 2, bars 89–120

This is in the expected key of E♭ major, the relative major of C minor. Some people have analysed this section as a third subject or as a second part of the second subject, which is another way of seeing the overall form of the piece. The style of the accompaniment at this point has changed to a type of **Alberti bass** figuration. The melody is disguised in the quaver chords, and the left- and right-hand parts start to move chromatically away from each other – the right hand ascending and the left descending in contrary motion.

As the pitch range widens, the music crescendoes from the opening *piano* to *forte* at the climax at bar 98. The pitch then descends abruptly to a low A♭. There follow two bars of stabbing broken chords: IV (A♭) and V7 (B♭7). The repeat starts at bar 101 with a slightly altered end from bar 110 (crotchet 4) to bar 113. Where bar 99 used chord IV, here, at bar 111, it is replaced by an F minor chord in first inversion, that is, IIb.

The next few bars (113 crotchet 2 to 121 crotchet 1) consist of a four-bar phrase, repeated once. The left hand reverts to the simple style encountered at the start of the second subject (bar 51 onwards). The right hand plays a descending scalic melody that crescendoes during bars 117–120, leading to the codetta in bar 121.

Codetta

The codetta sees the return of the tremolo left-hand octaves. These start as a tonic E♭ pedal and then begin to descend to a low F♯–G at the end of the section. The right hand plays a major form of the first subject 'rocket' theme before giving way to simple two-part chords at bar 125. The music contains several accented chords and increases in volume to reach **ff** by bar 132. The section ends at the first-time bar with two chords. The first chord is V7b of chord V (this is called a secondary dominant). The second chord is a dominant seventh chord in C minor – G, B, D, F – preparing for the repeat of the exposition in C minor. At the second time bar, following the repeat, Beethoven twice uses the dominant seventh chord in G minor – D7 – in first inversion – F♯, A, C, D – as the development that follows starts in the key of G minor.

The development section

The development section has the following features:

- Unusually, it starts with the music of the slow introduction.
- It develops music from the first and second subject and transition section and explores distant keys.
- It uses a wide range of dynamics for dramatic effect.
- It ends with a long dominant preparation on G of some 30 bars.

Commentary on the development section

Reprise of four bars of introduction

This *grave* section starts in G minor but ends with a dominant chord in E minor, which is a distant and unrelated key. The music starts loudly and this time decrescendoes to bar 136. The first two bars rise in pitch (just as in the opening bars of the sonata) and in the third bar the E♭ changes **enharmonically** to a D♯ to enable the music to modulate to E minor. The **perfect cadence** links to the start of the fast section that follows.

Development: **Allegro di molto e con brio**

Here at bar 137 in E minor, Beethoven develops music from the transition section of the exposition (bar 35 onwards). The quaver bass of the first two bars is a tonic pedal and resembles the first-subject bass. You can see how this rising figure over two octaves is also similar to the first subject itself (bars 11–14).

Look at the octave melody that follows at bars 139–143 (crotchet 1). Where have you heard this before? It is based on the melody of the introduction, bars 1–2. The rhythms have been made longer or **augmented**. The left hand, too, from bar 139 uses a simple chord accompaniment heard at the start of the second subject at bar 51. Beethoven is joining up ideas from the exposition and developing them together in this section. This music is then repeated in G minor (bars 145–149).

At bar 149, Beethoven uses four bars of B♭ quaver tremolo octaves which then become descending tremolo octaves (as used in the bass of the first subject) in the *right* hand, whilst the *left* hand is assigned the melody part. This melody uses the melody of the transition to develop throughout the section starting in bar 149. The descending right-hand tremolo continues until, at bar 167, the left hand takes over with repeated G quavers covering some 30 bars to the end of the development section. This forms a dominant pedal and is known as **dominant preparation**.

This long section features references to the first subject, for example bars 171–175 and bars 179–187, as well as sections of chromatic broken quaver chords (bars 167–170 and bars 175–179). All this heightens the drama and excitement of the music. Note, too, the crescendo throughout bars 179–187. We now have a two-bar sequence of descending quavers in the right hand in a monophonic texture based on two chords – V7 and IV in C minor – that end in the left hand for the last four quavers G–F–E♭–D. These take us straight down in step to the tonic note of C and the start of the recapitulation section.

Glossary

Enharmonic: two identically sounding pitches with different names – for example, E♭ and D♯.

Perfect cadence: a cadence comprising two chords. A perfect cadence is chord V followed by chord I.

Augmented: doubling (or more) of the original notes' durations.

Dominant preparation: a passage focused on the dominant chord to create expectation for a return to the tonic.

The recapitulation section

The recapitulation section has the following features:

- There is a reprise of first and second subjects.
- The second subject, unusually, is in the subdominant rather than the tonic key.
- It balances the exposition section.
- It ends with a coda that reminds us of the *grave* section.

Commentary on the recapitulation section

Recapitulation first subject in C minor

The first subject is in the tonic key starting at bar 195 (the same as in the exposition bars 11–23) but is then altered at bars 207–221 to form a new version of the transition. If you look at the score you will see descending patterns of minim chords. These chords are accompanied by rising sequences of quaver octave tremolos in the left hand.

Where has this melody pattern come from? If you look at the first subject above it is based on the second half of the theme (bars 199–201). Beethoven was clever at reusing musical material in different ways.

Each one of these patterns modulates as follows:

Key of D♭ major: bar 208 (minim 1) to bar 211 (minim 1), then up a tone to start on B♭

Key of E♭ minor: bar 211 (minim 2) to bar 214 (minim 2), then up a tone to start on C

Key of F minor: bar 215 (minim 1) to bar 219 (minim 1).

Link bars 219–220: these stress the on-beat note C (dominant note of F minor). Refer back to the end of the first subject at bars 49–50 where B♭ is stressed as the dominant note of E♭ minor (the key of the second subject).

Recapitulation second subject in F minor

The second subject is in the unexpected subdominant key of F minor, starting at bar 221. This is short-lived, however, and at bar 233 we have the dominant seventh chord of C minor (G–B–D–F), bringing us back as expected to the home key. The following section, on the other hand, varies a little in detail from the exposition and again shows how composers hardly ever follow textbook descriptions of form!

The second part of the second subject occurs at bar 253 in the expected tonic key of C minor. Whilst keeping to the general structure of the matching section in the exposition, Beethoven again varies the music of this section.

From bar 277 the third part of the second subject and the codetta starting at bar 289 mirror the exposition, though in a different key. This section ends abruptly with a *fortissimo* diminished seventh chord and a pause at bar 294.

Recapitulation: Coda (Grave *and* Allegro di molto e con brio)

In bars 295–298 Beethoven brings back music from the slow introduction for four bars, ending with a dominant seventh chord in C minor. This time it is broken up with rests but still contains the rising figure that is central to the expressive mood of the *Pathétique* and permeates this sonata-form movement. Here it is rather like a last melancholic pang before the final triumph of the rocket theme of the first subject that concludes this movement in heroic fashion. Look at how the dynamics crescendo from *p* in bar 299 to *ff* in the space of seven bars. Notice, too, the dramatic use of further diminished seventh chords at bars 305 and 306 before a **cadential** $^6_4$ progression of chords, Ic–V7–I.

So why do we have a silent bar and pause at the end of the piece? This is to complete a 12-bar phrase, as Beethoven ends with 11 bars of music.

Glossary

Cadential $^6_4$: this refers to a progression of chords forming a cadence. For example, Ic–V7–I is known as a cadential $^6_4$. The $^6_4$ refers to the first chord being in second inversion – that is, a fourth and sixth above the bass (for example, G–C–E).

Activity   ?

Compare these two sections of music of the sonata: exposition bars 88–112 and recapitulation bars 253–276. Can you spot the differences?

Exam-style question   ○

Describe **three** ways in which Beethoven achieves a sense of excitement and drama in this piano sonata movement.   **(3 marks)**

Exam tip   ○

Firstly, remember to make **three** different points. Secondly, use musical terminology and vocabulary to back up your statements – for example, if you are trying to describe the dramatic use of diminished sevenths. In this question, you should refer to the musical elements of melody, harmony, rhythm, texture, dynamics, tempo and metre. There is a lot to say!

Wider listening

The following suggested pieces for wider listening by Mozart and Haydn are also classical piano sonata movements, and make for a useful and interesting comparison to the Beethoven set work.

W.A. Mozart: Piano Sonata in C major K. 545, 1st movement

Mozart composed 24 sonatas for the newly invented piano during the Classical period. This first movement of this piece is well known and sounds very restrained and elegant when compared to the intense drama of the Beethoven set work, composed 11 years later. Like Beethoven's, this first movement is also in sonata form, although Mozart adopts a more straightforward, textbook working of his material. Unconventionally, however, Mozart begins the recapitulation of this sonata in the subdominant key of F major – highly unusual for the time.

The Beethoven movement is far more complex in its key structure and harmony. The keyboard textures are much lighter, too, in the Mozart sonata; and the opening theme in the right hand is accompanied in the left hand by a typical Classical Alberti bass accompaniment. An example of this type of accompaniment can be found in the Beethoven sonata at bars 89–110. Dynamic contrasts too are much more measured, varying soft and loud sections rather than the frequent dramatic crescendos and accented notes of the stormy Beethoven sonata.

Joseph Haydn: Piano Sonata in C major Hob. 50, 3rd movement: (*English Sonata*)

This sonata was written only a few years before Beethoven's *Pathétique*. In all, Haydn wrote 62 piano sonatas, and this work was one of the last three, written in the year 1794. In terms of temperament the sonata has a number of features that link it more closely with the Beethoven work rather than the earlier Mozart sonata. For one thing, the third movement is fast and in the spirit of a scherzo, the lively dance movement that Beethoven would increasingly come to favour. For another, the phrases of the melody are often unbalanced – for example, the main theme has five bars answered by two bars. And there are also sudden moments of silence and then excursions to remote and unrelated keys, just as there are in the Beethoven work.

Listen

1   Choose another piece by Beethoven and give three reasons why the music conveys emotion to you. Try to select a piece with an emotion other than suffering!

2   Compare the very different moods of the Beethoven set work with the Haydn sonata movement described above in wider listening. Make a list of similarities and differences. To get you started, the Beethoven is in C minor and the Haydn in C major.

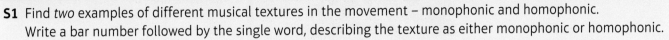

Checkpoint

Strengthen

S1 Find *two* examples of different musical textures in the movement – monophonic and homophonic. Write a bar number followed by the single word, describing the texture as either monophonic or homophonic.

S2 What is unusual about the key of the second subject? Why do you think Beethoven chose this key?

S3 Describe the opening ten-bar introduction highlighting three features of the music.

S4 There are many examples of the dramatic diminished seventh chord in this piece, such as on the third crotchet beat in bar 1. Explain the makeup of the chord – that is, how many notes it has, the size of intervals between notes, and how it resolves onto the following chord.

Challenge

C1 Explain how this piece demonstrates some of the key features of the Romantic style.

C2 Listen to the second, slow movement of this sonata. What mood do you think the music conveys and how does Beethoven achieve this in the music?

C3 The piano underwent changes to its structure, range, etc. during the Romantic period. Why was this necessary?

Summary of the key musical features

Key points to remember:

- Music of the **Romantic era** often expressed powerful emotions. The title *Pathétique* in this set work refers to **suffering**, which the movement expresses through the use of **minor keys**, **dramatic chords**, **accented notes**, **strong melodies**, **Romantic harmony** and chords such as the **diminished seventh**.

- Beethoven was called a **Classic–Romantic composer** as he spanned two stylistic periods in his lifetime, the **Classical** and **Romantic eras**. He was known as the composer who pioneered the Romantic style through his use of **adventurous harmony** and **extended structures**.

- The **piano** started to undergo **development** to strengthen its structure and increase the range of notes (compass) during Beethoven's lifetime to cope with the **increased musical demands** that Romantic composers made in their music.

- Beethoven composed 32 piano sonatas. His eighth sonata was written in 1798. It was published in 1799 with a dedication to his friend, Prince Karl von Lichnowsky. Musicians believe that the work might have been inspired by Mozart's Piano Sonata K. 457 as it is also in C minor and has three similar movements. The themes in the second movements of both works are quite similar, too.

- The first movement of the sonata is in **sonata form** with three sections – **exposition**, **development** and **recapitulation**. Unusually, Beethoven opens the piece with a ten-bar **slow introduction**. He also uses four bars from this introduction at the start of the development section and at the start of the coda.

- The two fundamental ideas expressed in sonata form are **repetition** and **contrast**.

- Features of the introduction include **heavy, accented chords** and right-hand **florid melody** with left-hand **chordal accompaniment**. The texture is **homophonic**, with the use of **dramatic chords** such as the **diminished seventh**.

- The **exposition** includes the following features: (i) **fast tempo**, (ii) in $\frac{2}{2}$ **time** with (iii) two **contrasting themes** in the keys of **C minor (first subject)** and **E♭ minor (second subject)**.

- The **development** includes the following features: (i) It starts with four bars based on the **introduction**. (ii) Beethoven **develops** the first and second subjects, exploring distant keys. (iii) It ends with 30 bars of **dominant preparation**, leading to the recapitulation.

- The **recapitulation** includes the following features: (i) It is a **reprise** of the **first** and **second subjects**. (ii) This would usually be **all** in the **tonic** key of **C minor**, but unusually Beethoven chooses **F minor** as the key to start the **second subject**. (iii) The start of the **coda** features four bars from the **introduction**. (iv) The movement ends with the first subject **'rocket' theme** in the tonic key of C minor.

Area of Study 2: Vocal Music

Henry Purcell: 'Music for a While'

Getting started

- Purcell's song 'Music for a While' tells part of the Oedipus story, an ancient Greek legend. Find a story that interests you from the world of fantasy and myth and try to set some of the words to music. A scene from *Harry Potter* or *The Lord of the Rings* might be a good starting point.

- The song uses music for its calming influence. Discuss how music can generate different emotional responses in the listener. How are moods such as anger, sadness, tranquillity and love captured in music? Find examples to illustrate your points.

Learning objectives

In the study of this set work you will learn about:

- the life and works of Henry Purcell
- the background to 'Music for a While'
- ground bass form in vocal music of the Baroque era
- how to analyse 'Music for a While'
- the key musical features.

The life and works of Henry Purcell (1659–95)

Henry Purcell is one of the greatest composers of the Baroque period and one of the greatest English composers of any time. His father was in charge of the choristers of Westminster Abbey but died when his son was only five. Later, as a teenager, Henry obtained a court position as 'composer in ordinary for the violins'. A little later he became organist at Westminster Abbey and after that, at the Chapel Royal.

Much of Purcell's music, like Bach's, was commissioned by wealthy patrons. The royal family commissioned him to write ceremonial music for royal events. Purcell also wrote **trio sonatas** and **dance suites** in the *stile italiano* as well as songs (in English), including 'Music for a While'. His most famous work is the opera *Dido and Aeneas* (1689), composed for a girls' boarding school in Chelsea. He also worked with the ultra-successful poet John Dryden on *King Arthur* (1691). This 'semi-opera' is a combination of play and opera, not unlike a modern musical. 'Music for a While' is also based on a text by Dryden. Other music for the stage included another successful semi-opera, *The Fairy Queen* (1692). His last work of this kind, *The Indian Queen*, was incomplete when he died in his mid-thirties. He is buried in Westminster Abbey, next to the organ he once played.

Glossary

Trio sonata: a piece for Baroque ensemble comprising two violins, cello and harpsichord (or organ).

Dance suite: in Baroque music the suite comprised a series of dance movements. By the time of Purcell, suites were composed of four main movements called the allemande, courante, sarabande and gigue. These movements are based on dance forms from different countries. Optional extra movements include the air, bourrée, gavotte, minuet and prelude.

Stile italiano: Purcell was influenced by the Italian style, which was characterised by the concertato style (as seen in the Brandenburg Concerto set work), the trio sonata, double-dotted notes, dramatic recitatives and *da capo* arias.

Henry Purcell

Musical contexts

Vocal music

Vocal music is one of the oldest forms of music, since it does not require any instrument except the voice. All musical traditions and cultures have some form of vocal music going back over centuries. For example, in medieval times, wandering singers called troubadours would often entertain at court, singing courtly love songs. In the Renaissance period, vocal music flourished, particularly in the church. Opera, too, started its evolution, with Claudio Monteverdi's *Orfeo* (1607) acknowledged to be the first great masterpiece in this form. In the Baroque era, Bach, Handel, Vivaldi and others wrote songs for solo voice. Large-scale works such as cantatas, oratorios (sacred and secular) and operas all featured the solo voice.

Purcell and the music of the Restoration period (1660–c.1720)

For a century before the Restoration period, the Tudor monarchs had valued music and indeed aspired to be cultivated musicians themselves. In the 17th century, however, King Charles I seemed only interested in music from Italy or France, rather than encouraging British composers. It was Charles II who, returning in 1660 from exile in France, brought with him a new enthusiasm for a more cosmopolitan approach to music.

In an attempt to improve church music, string orchestras were used to accompany verse anthems, and Charles II formed a band of 24 violins for just this purpose. At the same time, Purcell and another composer, John Blow, restored the tradition of opera in England as well as the popular masque – a spoken type of entertainment interspersed with dances, ballet and songs.

One important new development from about 1672 was the establishment of public concerts, whose content the public even had a say in deciding. Purcell devoted many years of his short life to writing music to commissions which might be considered today to be far below what he was capable of. In the society of his time, it was difficult to find opportunities to realise his true potential as a composer. Even a generation later, George Frideric Handel (1685–1759), like Purcell, discovered that London, and indeed England, had no appetite for grand operas, unlike in other parts of Europe. However, Purcell was content with the modest commissions he did receive, and these resulted in some great works, such as *Dido and Aeneas*. Despite the poor resources and lack of support for English composers at the end of 17th century, Purcell showed himself to be a great composer in many diverse genres, including opera, church music, chamber music, keyboard music and music for the theatre.

The Theatre Royal

Purcell's talent and skill as a composer for the stage was therefore somewhat restricted by a lack of public opera in London during his lifetime. Most of his theatre music consists of instrumental music and songs mixed with spoken rather than sung drama, though occasionally there were opportunities for more extended musical scenes.

During Purcell's lifetime, the Theatre Royal in Drury Lane, London was in decline despite the joining together of the King's and Duke's companies in 1682 to form the United Company. The theatre in this decade was a place for political satire and social unrest. But Purcell wanted to avoid any controversy and instead wrote theatre pieces that tried not to offend anyone.

The countertenor

Purcell wrote a significant amount of music for a higher male voice called a countertenor. This is a type of male voice whose range is equivalent to that of the mezzo-soprano, a lower female voice. The term first came into use in England during the mid-17th century and was in wide use by the time Purcell was composing his music. However, the popularity of this type of voice was short-lived. Within a few years of Purcell's death, the young Handel was being influenced by the Italian style of singing in *opera seria* (serious opera) and the countertenor was soon replaced by the castrati of Handel and eventually by the more heroic tenors of the continent.

Purcell's opera *King Arthur* at the Theatre Royal, Drury Lane, London

Background to 'Music for a While' by Henry Purcell

The song 'Music for a While', composed in 1692, is the second of four movements from the incidental music to the play *Oedipus* by John Dryden and Nathaniel Lee. Originally scored for voice and basso continuo, the piece exists in many other arrangements.

The text is divided up in the music as follows:

(Section A)

Music for a while
Shall all your cares beguile.
Wond'ring how your pains were eas'd
And disdaining to be pleas'd
Till Alecto free the dead
From their eternal bands,

Did you know?

Countertenor Alfred Deller's performances in the 1940s led to a rediscovery of the countertenor voice and sparked a renewed interest in Purcell's vocal music. You could investigate Alfred Deller's life to find out more.

A scene from the play *Oedipus*

(Section B)

Till the snakes drop from her head,
And the whip from out her hands.

(Section A1)

Music for a while
Shall all your cares beguile.

Oedipus is one of the most powerful of all Greek legends. Oedipus accidently kills his father and, without realising it, marries his own mother. When he discovers the horror of what has happened, he plucks out his eyes and then commits suicide.

The song comes from Act 1, Scene 3 of the play based on the legend. At this point in the drama, Tiresias, a blind *seer* (someone who can foretell the future), and two priests summon the ghost of King Laius to discover the identity of his murderer. The first three bars of the song are played as the first priest enters. The rising pitch of the ground bass in the first three bars signifies the first priest attempting to raise King Laius from the dead by singing 'Music for a While'. The soloist sings to one of the Furies, Alecto, who is able to '*free the dead from their eternal bands*'. Alecto has snakes for hair and blood dripping from her eyes. Her role in the story is to taunt and persecute Oedipus for killing his father. The effect of the music in the middle section of the song is to calm or '*beguile*' Alecto – that is, to bewitch her – so that the snakes '*drop from her head*' and the whip falls from her hands. So the song itself plays a dramatic role in the play rather than simply commenting on it.

Ground bass form in vocal music of the Baroque era

Ground bass, also known as basso ostinato, was used widely in both instrumental and vocal music in the Baroque era. It is a style in which the music is written above a repeating pattern of bass notes. In instrumental music, this often features a set of variations over this bass 'ground'.

 Listen

One of the best-known ground bass variations is Pachelbel's Canon.

Listen to this piece and hear how the ground bass is repeated over and over throughout the work.

In 1885, nearly 200 years later, than 'Music for a While' the Late Romantic composer Johannes Brahms used a type of ground bass (though not just in the bass) for the last movement of his Symphony No. 4 in E minor. See if you can keep track of it in this much more complex movement.

In vocal music of the Baroque period, the use of a ground bass was also quite common, and Purcell wrote several fine examples in his opera *Dido and Aeneas* (1689). The most touching of these are 'Ah, Belinda' and Dido's lament, 'When I am laid in earth', sung as she says farewell to life.

Features of a ground bass are *usually*:

- a minor key
- a straightforward rhythm made up of quavers, crotchets and minims
- a slow and stately tempo
- ending with a perfect cadence
- a fairly solemn mood
- the use of chromatic notes to give the bass part melodic interest in its own right.

Look at the opening three bars to 'Music for a While'. You will see that all these points all apply. However, in one respect it is unusual. The ground bass was usually one, two, four or eight bars long, but in 'Music for a While' the bass is *three* bars long.

Basso continuo

As we saw in the section on the Bach Brandenburg Concerto movement, the accompaniment is known as the **basso continuo** or simply the continuo. In Purcell's song, the harpsichord, lute and bass viol provide this part to accompany the solo voice. (For more information on the basso continuo, see page 56.)

Glossary

Basso continuo: continuous bass parts are provided for harpsichord and stringed instruments such as bass viol and lute. The players add chords and melody.

Close analysis of 'Music for a While' by Henry Purcell

This piece demonstrates many of the hallmarks of Baroque style. Turn back to the section on Bach's Brandenburg Concerto which explains these features in detail, before looking further at the analysis which follows.

Instrumentation
Solo voice accompanied by harpsichord, lute and bass viol. Our recording sounds a semitone lower than the written pitch of A minor, as it was made using Baroque instruments tuned to Baroque pitch.

Dynamics and tempo markings
As was traditional practice in the Baroque era, these markings are not given in the score. Clearly, however, the tempo is fairly slow and the music must start softly.

Structure of the set work
The piece is structured as a ground bass in ternary (ABA) form, as follows:

introduction (bars 1–3)

section A (bars 4–21)

section B (bars 22–28)

section A1 (bars 29–38).

The structure with a shortened repeat of section A can also be considered to be Rounded Binary Form.

Commentary on Introduction (bars 1–3)

The ground bass is played in the left hand of the harpsichord, doubled by the bass viol. The first chord is A minor, which suggests that this might be the key. Look at the perfect cadence at the next repetition of the ground bass, bar 3 beat 4 to bar 4 beat 1. This confirms the key of A minor.

Glossary

Figured bass: a type of musical shorthand for the keyboard player used in the Baroque era. The figures indicate the chord to be played above the bass note and whether this is in root position, first or second inversion. For a fuller description, see the glossary pages at the back of the book.

Ornament: notes that decorate a melody. They are shown by small notes (grace notes) immediately before the main note or symbols above it. Examples include the mordent, trill, turn.

Mordent: there are two types of mordent: 'upper' and 'lower'. The upper mordent is made up of the main note, the note above the note and the main note again, all played as quickly as possible. The lower mordent again goes from the main note to the note below and back to the main note again.

Appoggiatura: an ornament is often referred to as a 'leaning in' note. The appoggiatura leans on the main note, commonly taking half its value and starting a semitone or tone higher. For example, if the main note is a crotchet and the smaller grace note a quaver, then the player plays two equal quavers.

Characteristics of the ground bass

In this section, the ground bass has these characteristics:

- three bars long
- all equal quavers
- slow tempo.

Each set of four quavers rises in pitch (apart from the last two beats of bar 3), perhaps imitating the rise of King Laius from the dead.

It uses chromatic notes (F♯, C♯), providing tonal ambiguity, unsettling the listener.

The last four quavers (D–F–E–E) are the bass notes of the progression to the perfect cadence (chords IV, IVb, Ic, V).

The right hand is a melodic part. Purcell would originally have provided just a **figured bass**, so each performance would have varied in terms of how the right-hand part was 'realised' by the harpsichordist. This set work is a transcription (written-down copy) of the musicians' performance on the Pearson Anthology CD. Notice the use of **ornaments**, for example, a lower **mordent** (bar 1) and an **appoggiatura** (bar 2) in this interpretation.

Parts of the melody imitate parts of the vocal line. Compare the falling three-note figure at the start of bar 3 (G♯–F♯–E) to the first three notes in bar 7 (-*guile*) and bar 9 (*all*) and so on. The same applies to beat 3 of bar 3 (F–E–D–C–B) and bar 5 beat 4 to bar 6 beat 1 (*for a-while*) and bar 9 beats 3 to 4 (*all your cares*). See if you can find other examples in the score for yourself. The use of dotted rhythms in the right-hand part shows the influence of the *stile italiano* on Purcell.

Commentary on Section A (bars 4–21)

The solo voice enters at bar 4 with the main melody set to the words *music for a while shall all your cares beguile.* The harpsichord adopts a more basic accompanying role and the focus is on the soprano melody.

The key word *music* is sung on the tonic note A then reinforced by repetition a fifth higher on the dominant note E at bar 5. Purcell also draws attention to the word by setting it **syllabically** and with a long note on the first syllable 'mu' (dotted crochet first time and a minim tied to a quaver the second time). This is called **word-painting** and was a favourite Baroque technique. There are many other examples of this practice that we shall identify in the song. Notice too how, in the performance on the Pearson Anthology CD, the second statement of *music* has a crescendo throughout the long note – for expressive purposes. As was the convention of the time, Baroque music did not have any dynamic markings on the score. It was left to performers to interpret the music as they saw fit.

Most of the setting of the first few bars has been syllabic. As the song progresses, there are more examples of the use of a **melisma**, meaning more than one note per syllable.

Glossary

Syllabic word-setting: one note per syllable of a word

Word-painting: depicting a word in music to imitate its meaning

Mu - sic,   mu - sic for_ a_ while   Shall all   your cares be - guile:_   shall all,   all,

Purcell tends to use these to depict the key words of the text, such as the long setting of the word *eternal* at bars 19–21, another example of word-painting.

Notice how the harpsichord also imitates the vocal line at times. Look at the singer's part at bar 5 beat 4, followed by the harpsichord at bar 6 beat 2.

At bar 4 the ground bass and the singer start together. But Purcell chose an *odd* number of bars for the ground bass, whereas the vocal line stretches over mostly *even* numbers of bars. So, from now on, phrases do not align.

At bar 7, the ground bass starts again but the singer is still in mid-phrase. The singer finishes at bar 10 beat 1 as the ground bass starts again – and then the singer starts again on the third beat of that bar – and so on.

This pattern continues in much the same way until the very last chord, when singer and ground bass finally synchronise.

Purcell wanted the song to sound like a continuous stream of music.

The melody of bars 7–10 stresses the word *all* by the use of a short quaver on *shall* followed by a long on-beat crochet on *all*. The repetition of the first *shall all* up a tone matches the ascending bass pattern and adds to the emphasis of *all*. The quaver rest that follows the first three of these phrases also makes the words stand out clearly. Purcell even repeats the word *all* twice on the last quaver of bar 8 and the first beat of bar 9 for further emphasis. This repetition has an almost hypnotic effect in beguiling the Fury into forgetting her mission. Purcell later develops this idea of repetition effectively with the words *eas'd* (starting at bar 13) and *drop* (starting at bar 23).

Notice also how the harpsichord is playing in a narrow register in bars 7–9 to keep clear of the vocal line above it. A perfect cadence in A minor concludes the text at bar 9 beat 4 to bar 10 beat 1.

The new melody set to the word *wond'ring* at bars 10 and 11 is a melisma. This phrase is repeated in an ascending sequence alternating between voice and harpsichord. The first setting starts on D (bar 10 beat $3\frac{1}{2}$), then a note higher in bar 11 in the harpsichord, starting on E and finally on F in the vocal part again (bar 11 beat $3\frac{1}{2}$).

- guile: Won - d'ring,   Won - d'ring how your pains_____ were

Laments

Many vocal pieces using ground bass were laments – songs displaying sorrowful feelings. It was traditional for laments to have:

- falling phrases
- minor keys
- slow tempo.

'Music for a While' has all these features.

Look at the falling phrases just discussed to set the word *wond'ring*, or the setting of *drop* (bars 23–26).

The opening bars in the harpsichord also feature falling phrases (see bar 1). See how many other examples of such phrases you can find in the song.

Glossary

Dissonant intervals: the intervals that are dissonant (clashing) are the minor and major second, the minor and major seventh and the tritone (augmented fourth or diminished fifth).

Purcell often uses **dissonant intervals** between the bass and melody to add feelings of anguish or pain to the music. A good example is the word *pains* at bar 12 beat 3. The soprano sings the note E above a D minor chord. The E is not part of the chord and clashes noticeably with the F in the chord. This E begins a four-note melisma which places further stress on the word *pains*.

The setting of *eas'd* (eased) at bars 13 and 14 has been referred to already. The 'easing' is further emphasised by the descending pitch in three short sequences. There are also dissonances between the melody and bass, especially melody note C above bass note B (bar 13 beat 3) and melody note B above bass note C (bar 14 beat 1). These minor ninth and major seventh dissonances add to the anguish of the music.

The two-bar passage at bars 13–14 starts to modulate to E minor (the dominant key) through the addition of D♯s in the harpsichord part. Notice how the ground bass is altered at bar 14 to allow for this modulation. The melody and basso continuo resolve together on the word *pleas'd* in bar 15 with a perfect cadence in E minor. The progression of chords from beat 2 to beat 3 in bar 15 is Ic–V–I.

Following the cadence, the music moves to G major as the text focuses on the Fury Alecto. The ground bass at bars 16–17 follows the basic pattern of the original, but starts a minor third lower on F♯. The bass is altered in the third bar (bar 18) to modulate to G major – the relative major key of E minor. The whole vocal phrase has the feel of a more optimistic major key. The melody rises in pitch with each short phrase, from G on *Till* (bar 15), to B on *free*, to C on *dead*. Following a long dominant D note on *lec*, the melody descends in step to the tonic note G and a perfect cadence in that key, again through the chords Ic–V–I. The rising ground bass adds to the general optimism at this point.

The original form of the ground bass returns at bar 19 as the singer sings long melismas to word-paint *eternity*. This setting of the word *eternity* is a written out ornament. The first of these centres around the note G and the second starts a major sixth higher. There is some deliberate dissonance between the vocal part and the continuo in bars 19–21 in the form of **suspensions**, which add to the expressive power of the music. The second *eternal* at bars 20–21 is essentially a simple pattern of notes, that is, bar 20 beat 3, the note E, to bar 20 beat 4, note D, then bar 21 beat 2 to note C, then note D on beat 3, and on beat 4 the notes E–D–C. The bass is altered in bar 21 so that we have a modulation, this time to C major, the relative key of A minor. Again a Ic–V–I progression is used from bar 21 beat 4 to bar 22 beat 1. There are some striking **interjections** (swapped phrases) between the voice and harpsichord in these bars. Look at all these features in the bars below:

Glossary

Suspension: prolonging a note to create a dissonance with the next chord.

Area of Study 2: Vocal Music

Glossary

Tierce de Picardie: refers to a sharpened third in the tonic chord in music in a minor key.

Onomatopoeic: the music setting sounds like the word, for example, *drop*.

Commentary on Section B (bars 22–28)

Bar 22 is the start of Section B and we are in the relative major key of C.

This short middle section of only eight bars starts with one bar of harpsichord **link**. This link bar helps to separate Sections A and B, and also gives the singer a chance to take a breath. The bass is similar to the shape of the ground bass, and at the end of bar 22 we have another perfect cadence, this time in C major (the relative major key of A minor). This only lasts for one beat as there is then a perfect cadence back into the key of A minor between the second and third beat of bar 23. Notice the sharpened third at this point on the word *snakes* to create a major rather than minor chord. This is called a **Tierce de Picardie** and highlights the dramatic first use of the word *snakes*. It is another example of word-painting in music.

At this point the original form of the ground bass is heard, this time starting halfway through the bar rather than at the start. The voice comes in slightly before this so that, again, we do not have both parts starting or ending together. This creates a sense of tension and is slightly disturbing.

The music and lyrics in the B section are persuading Alecto to drop the snakes from her head and the whip from her hand. The dropping of both of these is word-painted as the melodic line 'drops' in a sequential pattern of three notes. The rest between each *drop* is equally dramatic, the drama heightened by the fact that Purcell places this short **onomatopoeic** word on the off-beat. Meanwhile the continuo carries on unperturbed in the lower register. Notice how the harpsichord melody features dotted rhythms and lower mordents. Another recurring feature is the descending four-semiquaver patterns (for example, bar 22 beat 2 or bar 25 beat 4). These are derived from the melody of bar 5 on the words *for a while*.

Till the snakes   drop,   drop,   drop,   drop,   drop,   drop,   drop,   drop,   drop

The ground bass finishes at beat 3 of bar 26 and then there are just two and a half bars left of the section. The bass of these bars follows the shape of the original bass with a brief modulation to E minor at bar 28, although by beat 4 of the same bar we have a perfect cadence back to the tonic key of A minor, the home key, for the final shortened version of Section A, which we call A1. There is another Tierce de Picardie at bar 28 with an E major chord: the third (G) has been sharpened to a G♯.

Commentary on Section A1 (bars 29–38)

The shortened repeat uses the first two lines of text, *Music for a while shall all your cares beguile.*

This forms a conclusion to and summary of the whole song. The ten-bar section has three statements of the three-bar ground bass in its original form, followed by a final A minor chord.

From bar 29 to bar 35 beat 1, the music of the vocal and bass line is the same as in bars 4–10, except that in our recording the soprano has ornamented her part in places for variety. It was traditional practice to do this in **da capo arias** where, on the repeat of the A section, the singer would embellish the vocal line. This would vary from singer to singer and would not be written down. However, in the Pearson Anthology, the version sung by Catherine Sampson has been notated for you to see her changes.

These can be seen at the following places:

Bar 31 between *shall* and *all*

Bar 33 on *all*

Bar 35 on *all*

Bar 36 on *all* (beats 1 and 3)

Bar 37 on *be* of *beguile.*

Bars 35 to the end at bar 38 are really just an extension of the previous setting in bars 32–35, rather like a reprise (repeat). The final *shall all your cares beguile* is melodically similar to the previous setting at bar 34. The final chord is a spread **arpeggiated** chord. The harpsichord, as mentioned elsewhere, cannot sustain long chords because each keystroke decays so rapidly, so the slow spreading of the chord helps to sustain it for the length of the semibreve.

Glossary

Da capo aria: ABA or ternary form. Often the repeated A section would be ornamented by the singer. Da capo means 'again from the beginning'.

Arpeggiated: the chord is spread, normally from the bottom note to the top.

Exam-style question

Describe **two** ways in which Purcell gives emphasis to individual words or syllables in this set work. **(2 marks)**

Exam tip

Firstly, remember to make **two** different points. Secondly, use musical terminology and avoid vagueness. In this question, you should refer to **word-painting** through **syllabic** and **melismatic** setting of words. For example, there is a melisma on the word *eternity* to make the word last a long time, albeit not for eternity!

Area of Study 2: Vocal Music

Did you know?

By Mozart's time the Baroque art of high trumpet playing had died out, so in his arrangement of 'The trumpet shall sound' Mozart stole the solo from the trumpet and gave it to the French horn, playing an octave lower than Handel intended. Baroque trumpet playing was not revived until the second half of the 20th century, so for more than 200 years no one knew what it sounded like.

Glossary

Obbligato: an essential melody part that must be played.

Binary form: a structure of two sections, A and B. Each section is repeated. In the A section the music modulates from the tonic to dominant key. In section B, the music starts in the dominant and explores other keys before returning to the tonic at the end of the section.

Cantata: the word derives from the Italian *cantare* and means 'sung'. A cantata is an extended piece in several movements, comprising chorus, recitative, chorale and aria with an orchestral accompaniment.

Wider listening

The three Handel arias and the arias from Bach's *Wedding Cantata* listed below make interesting comparisons to 'Music for a While'. The arias are based on religious texts and come from the oratorio *Messiah*. It is not compulsory to study these but making comparisons between different pieces will help you to appraise unfamiliar music in your exam.

G.F. Handel: 'The trumpet shall sound', 'Rejoice greatly' and 'Every valley' from *Messiah*

'The trumpet shall sound' is a da capo aria for bass soloist with an **obbligato** solo part for trumpet. The string orchestra and continuo provide the accompaniment. The opening A section is uplifting and positive, matching the words *the trumpet shall sound*. However, the B section is much more reflective of the text *for this corruptible must put on incorruption*. As with the Purcell the music is in a minor key, in this case B minor. In the same way as 'Rejoice greatly', the bass soloist would freely ornament the reprise of section A. In Baroque music, only one prevailing 'affection' (mood) is expressed in any one movement. As two-thirds of this da capo aria is in D major, the mood is positive, echoing the words *the dead shall be raised incorruptible*. This contrasts with the mood in Purcell's 'Music for a While'.

'Rejoice greatly' is a soprano aria. The structure is ternary form (ABA). The repeat of the A section is different and the soloist would freely ornament the reprise of the first section when this is repeated. This is similar to the Purcell work where the solo singer ornaments the repeat of the opening section. The aria is scored for strings and continuo. The melody is far more ornate than the Purcell, reflecting the rejoicing nature of the words, but the middle section is quieter and more restrained. Again, like the Purcell, Handel writes descriptively, using rapid runs and sequences to bring the text to life.

'Every valley' is in **binary form** and is scored for tenor voice and strings. The melody is based on two short figures to the words *every valley* and also the *crooked straight*. As in the Purcell song, Handel takes opportunities to word-paint colourful words such as *exaltation*. The continuo, as in the Purcell song, provides the bass line and supporting harmonies.

J.S. Bach: *The Wedding Cantata* BWV202

It is not known for sure for which occasion the *Wedding Cantata* was written. The librettist, the person who wrote the words, is also a mystery. There is some speculation that it might have been for Bach's own wedding in 1721 to Anna Magdalena, who may even have sung it herself at the ceremony. The cantata was composed during Bach's years in Cöthen, where he composed most of his instrumental music.

To judge by the text, the cantata was designed to be performed at springtime, and is one of Bach's most uplifting works. It is written for a solo soprano supported by oboe, strings and continuo, and consists of five arias separated by four short recitatives.

Aria: 'Weichet nur, betrübte Schatten', Give way, sorrowful shadows, is the first aria and depicts in music a portrait of a cold winter scene in gentle string arpeggios with an oboe melody in dialogue with the soprano. The tempo, as in 'Music for a While', is slow (adagio) although it increases to Andante as the text invokes the awakening of spring to the words *Flora's mirth will our breast naught but merry joy now furnish.*

Aria: 'Sehet in Zufriedenheit', Look in satisfaction, is the last movement of the cantata and takes the form of a **gavotte** dance scored for soprano, oboe, violins, viola and continuo. The gavotte is first played on the instruments, then sung, with accompanying figuration passing from instrument to instrument before being finally played by the whole orchestra.

Glossary

Gavotte: a medium-paced French dance in $\frac{4}{4}$ time beginning on the third beat of the bar. It was popular in the 18th century.

Checkpoint

Strengthen

S1 How does Purcell bring this expressive text to life in this song? Can you give one example?

S2 What mood do you think Purcell is trying to achieve in this song? How does Purcell achieve this mood in the music?

S3 In your own words, describe what the words 'syllabic' and 'melismatic' mean.

Challenge

C1 Describe the state of music in England during Purcell's lifetime.

C2 Explain what a ground bass is and how it works in this song.

C3 Name **two** features of the song that show it was written in the Baroque era.

How confident do you feel about your answers to these questions? If you're not sure you answered them well, try the following:

- Re-read the section on the analysis of the song.
- Listen to the set work regularly and practise spotting the features of harmony, melody and so on that you need to learn.
- Try to make connections between what you are learning about the set works and any music you have played or know well. Asking yourself questions about things that are similar or different between two pieces of music can help you to gain a deeper understanding of the set work.

Summary of the key musical features

Key points to remember:

The play *Oedipus*
- The song first accompanies a priest trying to raise the ghost of King Laius.
- Later the song attempts to 'beguile' the Fury Alecto into forgetting her mission.

Style
- lament
- Italian style.

Instrumentation
- solo voice (soprano in the Pearson Anthology CD)
- basso continuo (harpsichord, lute and bass viol in the Pearson Anthology CD).

Structure
- ground bass (basso ostinato); three bars long
- ternary form with third section shortened

- main keys: outer sections in A minor; central section in its relative major, C major
- sequences.

Harmony
- figured bass
- harmonic progressions such as Ic–V–I
- a few modulations away from A minor and C major
- dissonance
- suspensions
- tierce de Picardie.

Word-painting
- dissonance, along with melismatic and syllabic word-setting.

Baroque ornamentation used in the song
- mordents, appoggiaturas, grace notes, arpeggiation.

Queen: 'Killer Queen' from the album *Sheer Heart Attack*

Getting started

Many of Queen's songs were adapted for use in the West End show *We Will Rock You*. This was a **jukebox musical**. Can you name two other bands that have had their music adapted for similar jukebox musicals?

Learning objectives

In the study of this set work you will learn about:
- the background to the song
- Queen's sound
- how to analyse 'Killer Queen'
- music technology as a musical element
- guitar techniques
- the key musical features.

Musical contexts

Purpose and intention

'Killer Queen' is a pop song, intended to be played on the radio and originally sold as a single. It is a particularly well-crafted pop song which draws on several of Queen's trademark musical signatures.

Did you know?

The 'single' was a 7-inch (17.5 cm) diameter vinyl disc which was released at a relatively low cost before a band brought out their full album on an LP (long-playing record). It was intended to whet appetites, so that people had an idea of what the band sounded like before they invested more money in buying the full album. It was also given to DJs to be played as promotional material on the radio. The 'singles chart' was a measure of how popular these releases were amongst the record-buying public, in the same way as the download chart is today.

The birth of Queen

Roger Taylor and Brian May had been in a group called Smile, which broke up in 1970. The following year, along with Freddie Bulsara, a graphic designer, they auditioned a bass player called John Deacon. They were all intelligent, highly educated individuals with potential careers in other fields, but they shared a love of rock music. They knew that they could apply their intelligence to the rock sound and create something unique. Freddie (formerly known as Farrokh) felt that the surname Mercury was much more suitable for a rock singer than his own. He also suggested the band name Queen, which had a certain grandeur as well as connotations of the gay culture with which he was involved. He was to foster a swashbuckling image throughout his career, as well as bringing to the band his intense creativity and sense of theatre. The lyrics of 'Killer Queen' are a good example of this chemistry.

We Will Rock You at the Dominion Theatre, London

Glossary

Jukebox musical: when the score for a musical is made up of existing songs, usually all by the same artist or with a strong thematic link.

Freddie Mercury

Early years

Queen's early years were set against a backdrop of 1970s London, when the city was suffering from economic difficulties and political violence, so their early music offered some welcome escapism. Popular English bands of the time included Yes, Pink Floyd, Black Sabbath and The Who.

The band worked hard to create their own sound, using advanced recording techniques to 'orchestrate' their music. The basic sound was the riff-driven heavy rock of the early 1970s, but to this they added arranging techniques borrowed from big-band jazz. These they applied to distorted electric guitars, treating the guitar tracks almost like the sections of a jazz orchestra.

Mercury's love of theatre and opera also played its part in the band's sound, the culmination of which was 'Bohemian Rhapsody', from their fourth album, *A Night at the Opera*. The album *Sheer Heart Attack*, from which 'Killer Queen' is taken, showcases the contrasting songwriting styles of May and Mercury; the first half of the album is mostly May's work and the second half mostly Mercury's, with a Roger Taylor song sandwiched in between.

Background to 'Killer Queen'

Released in 1974, 'Killer Queen' was the first of Queen's songs to become mainstream, quickly peaking at number 2 in the UK singles charts. It had a much lighter sound than most of their previous work. This may have been because Brian May had a protracted stay in hospital at the time that Mercury was writing the song. May often contributed the harder-edged rock tracks, so when he first heard the new song he was concerned that 'Killer Queen' was too much of a departure from their earlier material. The other members of the band seem to have anticipated his reaction, and had left space for May to add his trademark guitar work. This he did with a quirky, melodic guitar solo (bars 44–61) that is still one of May's favourites.

Mercury usually composed the music first and added the lyrics later, but for 'Killer Queen' he worked the other way around, starting with the lyrics. The pictures evoked through the lyrics are clearly represented by the **vaudeville**-inspired music. His lyrics are both suggestive and vague, leaving listeners to interpret them as they see fit. Speaking to the *New Musical Express* in 1974 Mercury said, 'I'd prefer people to put their own interpretation upon it – to read into it what they like'.

An adaptation of 'Killer Queen' was used as the theme for the evil tyrant character of the same name in Ben Elton's musical *We Will Rock You*. The show is essentially a compilation of many of Queen's most popular songs, with the lyrics often changed slightly or used in new ways to drive the plot. The storyline itself is quite weak, but the strength of the songs ensures that the show remains popular. It also demonstrates the inherently theatrical nature of Queen's songs and the element of **glam** that they consciously introduced into much of their work and public image.

Glossary

Vaudeville: a form of comic musical theatre from the 1880s.

Glam: a genre of rock known for over-the-top, glamorous dress sense including platform shoes, glitter and flamboyant hairstyles.

Queen's sound

Although Queen's music spans many musical genres, there are common threads that run through much of their output:

- adventurous structures
- use of unusual keys (for rock music)
- complex, **multi-tracked** guitar and vocal parts
- **anthemic** melodies ('We Are the Champions', 'Bohemian Rhapsody', etc.)
- melodic, carefully crafted guitar solos
- a sense of theatre blended into a rock song format
- a studio sound that was consciously different and more 'crafted' than their live sound, with the use of music technology playing an important role.

We will look at each of these areas in detail, exploring how this set work bears all the hallmarks of the Queen sound, even though at the time it represented a departure from their established style.

> **Glossary**
>
> **Multi-track**: a recording of a performance (or performances) on separate tracks in which each track can be edited individually to change levels, add effects, etc. In 1975, 24-track tape recorders, such as the one used for 'Killer Queen', would have been available only in the most exclusive studios.
>
> **Anthemic, anthem**: a song with a strong, memorable melody which has rousing or uplifting characteristics.

Close analysis of 'Killer Queen'

Structure

Bar number	Section	Phrase structure
1–2	Introduction	6 finger clicks (starting on the third beat of the first bar)
2–14	Verse 1	4-bar phrase oscillating between C minor and B♭7 chords
		5-bar phrase ending with a rhythmic 'trip'
		3-bar phrase with last bar half-spoken
15–22	Chorus 1	5 bars + echo/answer
		3 bars (dovetails with the next section)
23–26	Instrumental	4 bars, where the first bar dovetails with the end of the chorus
27–38	Verse 2	Same phrase structure as verse 1
39–43	Chorus 2	Shorter than chorus 1, consisting only of the first 5-bar phrase
44–51	Guitar solo part 1	4 bars, borrowing ideas from the second half of the chorus
		3 bars, with syncopated rhythmic motif
52–61	Guitar solo part 2	4-bar phrase – same as verse 1
		5-bar phrase – same as verse 1
		2-bar phrase leading to verse 3
62–69	Verse 3	The phrase structure is broken up into 3 × 1-bar phrases, a 3-bar phrase and a final 1-bar phrase (after a short pause) leading into the chorus
70–78	Chorus 3	5-bar phrase – same as chorus 1
		4-bar phrase – same as chorus 1, but with an additional bar
79–end	Outro	Starts with a one-bar answer to the final vocal phrase and then repeats the syncopated rhythmic motif until it fades out

Area of Study 2: Vocal Music

Glossary

Middle 8: connects two sections of a pop or rock song but is not necessarily eight bars long.

Outro: a concluding section, sometimes like a coda in Classical music.

Capo: a clamp fastened across all the strings to raise their pitch.

Harmonic sequence: when a chord sequence is immediately repeated at a higher or lower pitch.

Extended chord: a chord with at least one added note, such as the ninth.

Scalic: music that is based on scales ascending and/or descending in pitch.

Harmonic rhythm: the rate at which the chords change.

The song appears to be in a simple verse–chorus structure with a brief intro, a guitar solo acting as the bridge or **middle 8**, and an **outro** to reinforce the tonic key. However, the unbalanced phrase structure (for example, the 4-, 5- and 3-bar phrases of verses 1 and 2 and the guitar solo part 2) indicates a need to look deeper into the music, and when we look at the harmony for each of the sections, it is clear that there is more to the structure than first meets the eye.

Tonality and harmony

The chord sequences owe more to songs from musicals than to the blues-based chord sequences of rock music. A standard rock song will often follow an adapted 12-bar-blues sequence for at least one of its sections or, if not, will generally still use chords I, IV and V (and possibly ♭VII) as the basis of the harmony. The middle 8 may briefly venture into something more exciting, but the song will generally stay rooted in the tonic key throughout. Songs from musicals tend to be much more harmonically adventurous, as their composers were often trained in the Western Classical tradition. As you can see from your study of 'Defying Gravity', this can include the use of motifs (including leitmotifs), development of themes and some rather advanced harmony.

It is also interesting to note that 'Killer Queen' is in E♭ major. Rock songs are rarely written in flat keys (unless the guitarist uses a **capo** or detunes the guitar by a semitone). E major and D major, which suit the guitar, are much more common. Queen often explored unusual keys for rock music – for example, 'Bohemian Rhapsody' is in B♭ major.

'Killer Queen' is in E♭ major but modulates frequently and makes use of **harmonic sequences** to create harmonic interest. Tonal ambiguity is purposefully added by playing a C chord first as the listener is not immediately sure what key the piece is in. It includes V–I progressions frequently, using these to move quickly through several different keys in a short space of time. The song contains **extended chords**, while inversions of chords are used to create **scalic** movement in the bass.

Harmonic analysis

Verse 1 (bars 2–14)	
First phrase *She keeps a Moët et Chandon…*	Just two chords are used, each lasting for one bar: Cm | B♭7 | Cm | B♭7 | C minor is chord VI in the key of E♭ major and B♭7 is the dominant seventh, so the key is set fairly clearly, as long as the B♭7 resolves to the tonic…
Second phrase *A built in a remedy…*	Which it does, as the first chord in the second phrase. The **harmonic rhythm** changes to two chords per bar. Notice the change of time signature in the penultimate bar. E♭ Gm/D | E♭7/D♭ A♭ | A♭m E♭/B♭ | $\frac{6}{8}$ A♭/B♭ | $\frac{12}{8}$ B♭7 | This sequence begins with a chromatically descending bass line. Note that some scores mark the chord in the $\frac{6}{8}$ bar as B♭11 rather than A♭/B♭. Both approaches describe the same chord and are equally valid. Mercury was fond of this chord and it is used in many of his other compositions (for instance, 'Somebody to Love').

Third phrase *Caviar and cigarettes…*	The first appearance of a harmonic sequence. Again, the harmonic rhythm is two chords per bar (until the last chord). G7 Cm | Bb Eb | D7 Gm F | Here the chord sequence is a series of three bars of V–I, modulating quickly from C minor to Eb major to G minor with the F chord preparing for a modulation to Bb major in the chorus. The sequence is moving up in thirds each bar rather than a circle of fifths (see Chorus second phrase below).
Chorus (bars 15–22)	
First phrase *She's a killer queen…*	Again, Mercury modulates quickly through several different keys. The chorus starts in Bb major, briefly moving through D minor in the third bar and C major in the fourth bar. The harmonic rhythm is two chords per bar except for the fourth bar, which changes chord every beat. This bar has an ascending bass line and highlights the lyrics *guaranteed to blow your mind*. Bb Dm | Gm Dm | Gm A7 Dm | G7 F7/A G7/B C | Bb |
Second phrase *Ooh, recommended at the price…*	This phrase contains a **circle of fifths** in the first two bars: A Dm | G7 C | Bb | The phrase dovetails with the first bar of the instrumental – it feels as if it needs one extra bar to be complete, but this bar also forms the first bar of the instrumental section, so there is an overlap.
Instrumental (bars 23–26)	

This phrase gives us a little break from fast-moving chords with a piano **vamp** creating variety over an F in the bass. The movement of the piano accompaniment gives the chords F, Bb/F and Eb/F – a variation on a standard rock 'n' roll piano feature.

Verse 2 and Chorus 2 (bars 27–43)

The second verse has the same chord sequence as the first, with the addition of a pedal note on C (the relative minor).

The second chorus has the same chord sequence as the first phrase of the first chorus.

Guitar solo (bars 44–61)	
Part 1	The first four bars sound like a continuation of the chorus, but they are a slight development of the sequence (the first bar repeats and the third bar uses Cm instead of C): A Dm | A Dm | G Cm | G Cm Eb/F | The next three bars make a feature of the Eb/F (or F11) chord, repeating it to draw out the tension before the next section.
Part 2	The second part of the guitar solo (from bar 51) uses the same chord sequence as the verse up until the last two bars, which replace the last three bars of the verse. Last two bars: Eb/Bb Ab/Bb | Bb7 | Note how the last chord is preparing the listener for a return to the tonic key of Eb major, but instead the music modulates to C minor, the relative minor.

Verse 3 (bars 62–69)
The first four bars use the same technique as was seen in the first part of the guitar solo: they take a previously heard chord sequence and extend it by repeating each bar. The sequence is essentially an extended version of the final phrase of verses 1 and 2 followed by an extended preparation for the final chorus. The chorus would have followed on naturally from the fifth bar (as this is the sequence that led previously into the song's chorus), so the extra three bars are unexpected and form another climactic point in the song.
G7 Cm | G7 Cm | Bb Eb | Bb Eb | D7 Gm F | Bb F | Bbm F | $^6_8$ F |

Chorus 3 (bars 70–78)
The third chorus has the same chord sequence as the first chorus with one bar added at the end to sound more final than the 'dovetailing' bar.
This leaves us with a problem: we are still in the key of Bb major and the song is supposed to be in Eb major. It won't sound complete and is certainly out of keeping with other pop songs to finish in a different key.

Outro (bars 79–end)
To solve this problem, Mercury repeats a chord of Eb major over and over to fade. It is not the subtlest modulation in the song, but it does create a satisfying and unusual ending.

Glossary

Circle of fifths: a series of chords in which the root note of each chord is a fifth lower or a fourth higher than that of the previous one.

Vamp: a short repeated accompanying phrase.

 ## Listen

Spotting differences in chord sequences

It can be hard to learn how to listen to music critically instead of just for enjoyment. You need to train your ears to spot subtle changes and to pick up detail that the casual listener will miss.

Now that you have studied how the various sections use the chords differently, see if you can hear the differences listed.

1   Listen for the difference in harmonic rhythm from the first four bars of the verse onwards. What effect does this have? What effect does it have when the chords start changing on every beat (for example, in bar 18)?

2   Listen to the circle of fifths sequence in bars 20–21 (and the corresponding bars in chorus 3). Do you think you would recognise this sequence if you heard it in an unfamiliar piece of music?

3   Do you think the ending is effective when the song returns to Eb major at the end? What words would you use to describe the key change here?

Instrumentation and sonority

Queen make clever use of a limited number of instruments in this song. These are:

- vocals
- piano
- 'jangle' piano

- electric guitar
- bass guitar
- drum kit and percussion.

Note that no **synthesisers** were used in the making of the album *Sheer Heart Attack*. Queen were proud of this, as synthesisers (synths) were very popular in the music of the 1970s and provided all sorts of options for crafting the sound. Queen did things the hard way, creating similar effects with their voices and guitars.

Part of Queen's distinctive sound is the way they build the guitar and vocal textures by recording one layer on top of another – a process called **overdubbing**. In the chorus, there is a four-part choir that has been built up by recording Mercury himself singing each part individually. May and Taylor also recorded some backing vocals at different points in the song.

The backing vocals often move in parallel, but a swooping effect is created by the parts crossing over. For example, in bars 8–11 in the score, the vocals have been written in three parts. If you imagined singing the middle part, your vocal line would cross both the higher part and the lower part over the first two chords. The immaculate tuning and timing combine to create a vocal texture that is clearly inspired by groups such as the Beach Boys. Remember that this was recorded in the days before autotune was invented, so what you hear is what was sung!

Glossary
Synthesiser: an electronic musical instrument that creates sounds by manipulating combinations of waveforms or by modifying existing sounds.
Overdubbing: recording an instrumental or vocal part over previously recorded music.
Gospel music: a musical style with roots in the black oral tradition in which vocal harmonies play a prominent role.
Timbre: the particular tone colour of an instrument or voice.

The vocal writing is a really important part of the Queen sound. Since no synths were used in this album, the vocals have the dual role of 1) creating **gospel**-inspired parallel harmonies that weave in and out of the main vocal and 2) providing harmonic support, almost like synth chords.

To achieve the distinctive piano sound, two pianos were recorded. One is a standard piano (a Bechstein grand) and the other has become known as a 'jangle piano' (as printed on the sleeve of the album *Sheer Heart Attack*). The jangle piano was of unknown brand and had a honky-tonk, out-of-tune sound. The two instruments play the same part, so a hybrid **timbre** has been created.

Did you know?

Multi-tracked, layered electric guitars were another major part of the Queen sound. Brian May was extremely particular as to how he recorded his guitar parts. He played with an old sixpence rather than a plectrum so that he could use the serrated edge to create a rasping sound when he altered the angle of attack on the string. He is famous for having built his own guitar (with the assistance of his father), the Red Special, with mahogany from a 100-year-old fireplace. He was able to customise every aspect of the guitar's sound. Apart from his customary Vox AC30, he also used an amplifier built by John Deacon to record some of his guitar parts, just because of the unique sound it produced.

The harmony guitar parts in bars 70–73 are typical of how May created a sound reminiscent of a saxophone section in a big band. Bars 55–61 of the guitar solo are a more obvious example of how he overdubbed three parts to create a harmonised melodic line.

The bass guitar provides unobtrusive harmonic support by playing melodic bass lines that work within the complexity of the musical texture. The bass guitar has a warm, 'round' sound provided by the Fender Precision bass played through an amplifier customised by John Deacon.

Roger Taylor's drumming gels seamlessly with John Deacon's bass playing to complete the rhythm section. More often than not he keeps time with one hit per beat alternating between the bass and snare drums, but he also adds colour with cymbal and **snare rolls** at the beginning of Verse 2 and some subtle additional touches such as emphasising the important rhythmic motif in bars 47–50 and dropping to just hi-hat cymbal at different points (for example, bars 51–52) to create textural contrast. He also makes a major contribution to the dynamic contrast of the song by altering his use of the hi-hat between the verse and chorus. Tasteful fills and use of the cymbals complete a drumming performance that again is more akin to a jazz band or show band than a rock outfit.

Glossary

Snare roll: a rapid succession of hits on the snare drum.

Exam tips

When you are asked to describe music under a heading such as melody, texture or dynamics, it is important to be able to say three things:

1. the location in the extract you are talking about – for example, at the beginning or in the second chorus
2. what instrument is involved – for example, the lead vocal
3. what happens to that element – for example, the pitch range is much wider or the dynamics are quieter.

Use appropriate musical vocabulary to describe the points you can hear. Practise this by using it when you describe music in everyday speech.

Listen

Instruments

Can you identify the extra percussion used in the song? Other than the finger clicks in the introduction there are only two *additional* percussion instruments. These can be heard at the start of bar 29 and the end of bar 68.

Can you hear the one bar in the song where a second bass guitar has been overdubbed?

It is a descending run somewhere in Verse 2…

Exam-style questions

1. What is the key of this set work? Why is this an unusual key for a rock song? **(1 mark)**
2. Name the studio technique that is used to record the layered guitar parts. **(1 mark)**

Brian May playing the Red Special in a Queen perfomance

Rhythm, metre and tempo

The time signature of the song is $\frac{12}{8}$. It could also be thought of as $\frac{4}{4}$ with **swung** quavers, but for the purpose of studying this set work, it has been written in the Pearson Anthology in **compound metre** to make it easier to read. If it were written in $\frac{4}{4}$ then there would be endless triplet markings over the crotchets and quavers.

This means that when we refer to a beat, we mean each dotted crotchet rather than a single crotchet. The tempo is ♩ = 112, which means that there will be 336 quavers per minute. You can see how it is much easier to count 4 quick dotted crotchet beats per bar than 12 extremely quick quaver beats!

Syncopation is a rhythmic feature used a lot in this set work. The most important rhythmic motif of the piece uses syncopation:

This motif appears to emphasise important parts of the music. Its effectiveness comes from the emphasis on the last quaver of the triplet group, making it feel like the music is pushing ahead slightly. Examples can be found at the end of bar 23 and bar 25 and, more obviously in bars 47–50, where the motif alternates between groups of instruments creating an **antiphonal** texture.

The other rhythmic motif used throughout the piece is first heard in bar 6 in the vocal line, *just like Marie Antoinette*:

just   like___   Ma - rie   An - toi - nette.___   A   built - in___   a - re - me - dy___   for

This is immediately developed in *a built-in a-remedy* with a little anacrusis (upbeat) on 'a' and a slight change to the second beat.

You can see how the syncopated rhythm is used at the start of both of these rhythmic ideas, but the emphasis is different. In the first example there is a heavy emphasis on the off-beat quaver, but in the vocal melody line the emphasis is not nearly as obvious, even though the rhythm is still syncopated. This subtle difference has a big impact.

Further use of the rhythm from the vocal line can be heard in bars 44–46 of the guitar solo.

(44) Guitar Solo

Area of Study 2: Vocal Music

Melody

Many of Queen's melodies have made it into public consciousness. Songs such as 'We Are the Champions', 'We Will Rock You' and 'Bohemian Rhapsody' have melody lines that are easily memorable, appeal to a wide range of people and are thought of as rock anthems. 'Killer Queen' does not have a vocal line as memorable as these songs, but is still quite catchy. The vocal line is almost entirely **syllabic** throughout the song.

It is not necessary to go through the melody bar by bar, but it is still important to get an overall feel for how the melodic phrases come and go through the piece.

Verse

- The first phrase starts lower in pitch, rising over the four bars.
- The second phrase moves in the same overall direction as the falling bass line with little decorations such as in bar 8 on 'Kennedy' and bar 9 on 'any time'.
- The third phrase is a development of rhythmic motif y, with the melodic line falling through the bar.

Chorus

- The melody is harder to isolate due to the vocal harmonies.
- Bars 20 and 21 use the same idea as the third phrase of the verse, based on rhythmic motif y.

Guitar solo

- This develops the falling melodic phrase from the third phrase of the verse.
- In bar 55 the top part starts the same as the second phrase of the verse, but soon introduces new melodic material.

Texture

The texture in 'Killer Queen' is frequently changing. The song is much more 'orchestrated' than a standard rock song – every sound has its place, and many parts come and go. Only the piano seems to be present for almost all of the song.

- The music is given room to breathe.
- The opening is **homophonic** from when the vocals enter.
- The opening introduces parts gradually: even the piano comes in one hand at a time.
- There are clear contrasts between sections.
- The articulation of the verse is staccato in most of the parts so, even when there are several instruments playing, the overall texture is quite light and relatively sparse.
- Although backing vocals appear in the verse, they come to the fore in the chorus.

- The legato nature of the chorus backing vocals contributes to a thickening of the texture and an increase in dynamics.
- The first chorus is still homophonic.
- From the second phrase of the second verse, there is an increase in polyphony as more interweaving parts are introduced.
- The second half of the guitar solo features a textural trick where the chords are gradually layered by delaying the entry of the second and third guitar parts.
- The use of **panning** (see next section) creates an antiphonal feel in places (for example, in the backing vocals in bars 42–43 and 67–68).
- In the second half of the guitar solo the texture dramatically thins as several parts drop out. This makes the entry of the three-guitar broken chord part all the more effective.

Music technology as a musical element

In any recorded piece of popular music, the use of music technology affects several musical elements, to the extent that it can almost be thought of as an element in its own right. The art of using **effects** in the appropriate place, panning parts to the centre, left and right, balancing all the different sounds and mixing all the ingredients into a cohesive whole can add a considerable amount to the success of a song.

In 'Killer Queen', the following use of music technology can be heard:

- much use of panning, especially of the backing vocals (for example, bars 73–74) and guitar parts (for example, bars 55–61)
- the distinctive swooshing sound of a **flanger** on the whole mix (bars 77–78) and for **word-painting** on the word *laser-beam* (bar 17) in the vocal part
- the dependence on multi-track recording and overdubbing for the basic sound of the band
- use of effects on the guitar – **distortion** throughout the track, creating the 'creamy', sustained tone; **wah-wah** at the start of Verse 3 (bar 62)
- **reverb** on all tracks to some extent, though this is not a major feature of the piece other than to create a sense of space
- clever use of microphone positioning when recording the guitars, to create different timbres.

 Listen

Spot the panning

Listen to the track on headphones, focusing on how the sounds have been placed on the left or the right.

Are there any particular sounds that are always in the centre?

Glossary

Panning: giving sounds different levels in the left and right speakers so that it sounds as if they are coming from a new direction.

Effects: electronic devices designed to enhance or alter the basic sound quality (for example, delay, reverb).

Flanger, flanging: an effect creating a swirling or swooshing sound.

Word-painting: depicting a word in music to imitate its meaning.

Distortion: an effect that increases the volume and sustain on an electric guitar as well as making the timbre more gritty or smooth depending on the settings.

Wah-wah: a filter effect in which the peak of the filter is swept up and down the frequency range in response to the player's foot movement on a rocker pedal.

Reverb: an effect which creates the impression of being in a physical space.

Glossary

Pull-offs: when a note is sounded on the guitar by plucking the string with the fretting hand.

Vibrato: a technique used to cause rapid variations in pitch. The term 'vibrato' is Italian and is the past participle of the verb 'vibrare', which means to vibrate.

Guitar techniques

Brian May focuses on articulating each note in a particular way to help phrase his melodic lines, aided by his use of a sixpence instead of a plectrum. Most of his work is based on single notes layered on top of each other rather than strummed chords. There are some chords in the background in this song, but they are not strummed like an acoustic guitar – they are either played staccato, like an 'oom-pah' piano accompaniment (as in the second half of the chorus), or as more forceful sustained chords that thicken the texture.

There are also the following techniques audible in the guitar solo:

- string bends
- slides
- **pull-offs**
- **vibrato**.

Exam-style question

List three effects that have been used on the guitar part during the guitar solo. **(3 marks)**

Wider listening

In addition to this set work you should also listen to the following:

Beach Boys: 'God Only Knows' from *Pet Sounds*

Released in 1966, the album *Pet Sounds* was produced and arranged by Brian Wilson. After he had stopped performing live shows with the Beach Boys, he chose to concentrate on his composing instead. This album is a testament to his originality and wide-ranging musical tastes. The album was much better received in Britain than in the USA, but has since become a favourite worldwide.

The song 'God Only Knows' is another example of how vocal parts can be layered to dramatic effect and how different sounds can be combined to create an interesting musical texture. Multi-track tape recorders had only recently been invented when *Pet Sounds* was recorded, and Wilson was keen to explore the potential that these devices offered. The song was originally mixed in mono (the same signal coming from both speakers), partly due to the relatively recent popularity of stereo recordings and also because Wilson was almost completely deaf in one ear.

Alicia Keys: 'If I Ain't Got You' from *The Diary of Alicia Keys*

Alicia Keys studied classical piano from a young age and later at a performing arts school. Unlike many performers in her genre, Keys also writes her own music.

Released in 2003, *The Diary of Alicia Keys* is her second studio album. It reached number 1 in the album charts as soon as it was released, demonstrating how popular Keys had become. The song 'If I Ain't Got You' reached number 4 in the charts and won an award for the best R&B video at the MTV Video Music Awards. It is an example of a more straightforward, melody-driven song with a standard, verse–chorus structure.

Alicia Keys: 'Dragon Days' from *The Diary of Alicia Keys*

This track is harmonically relatively simple, but uses music technology to good effect. The use of overdubs and multi-tracking creates a complex, layered texture. The extra sounds and instrumental/vocal parts are not all added at the same time, instead being used to create interest at the right moment. If you listen to the start of the song, you can hear a crackling sound, which is sampled noise from vinyl records. The vocal part is frequently doubled up using overdubs, but only on isolated words and phrases.

Checkpoint

Strengthen

S1 Create a table with two headings: 'heavy rock' and 'songs from musicals'. List the elements of 'Killer Queen' under the appropriate heading.

S2 Write out the overall structure of 'Killer Queen' using fewer than 30 words.

S3 Where is a 'circle of fifths' chord sequence used in 'Killer Queen'?

Challenge

C1 Describe how the use of music technology has enhanced this song.

C2 What are the key elements of 'Killer Queen' that reflect Mercury's love of the theatrical?

Summary of the key musical features

Key points to remember:

Structure
- based on verse–chorus song structure
- unusual phrase lengths
- clever reuse of phrases in different sections.

Tonality and harmony
- key of E♭ major – unusual for rock music
- many modulations
- inspired by musicals rather than blues
- use of harmonic sequence.

Instrumentation and sonority
- limited number of instruments
- use of multi-tracking to layer parts
- carefully crafted backing-vocal parts
- guitar parts sometimes try to emulate other instruments
- no synths!

Rhythm, metre and tempo
- $\frac{12}{8}$ compound time
- swung feel
- use of syncopation
- important rhythmic motif that appears throughout the song
- fast tempo.

Melody
- return of a similar melodic motif through several sections
- syllabic vocal line
- development of vocal melody in guitar solo.

Texture
- careful placement of parts so as not to crowd the texture
- clear contrasts between sections
- use of homophonic, polyphonic and antiphonal textures.

Music technology as a musical element
- music technology plays a fundamental role in the overall sound
- multi-tracking and overdubbing used frequently
- effects such as flanger, wah-wah and distortion used
- panning helps to separate out sounds and creates antiphonal effects.

Guitar techniques
- use of string-bends, slides, vibrato, pull-offs
- no strumming
- careful articulation of each note.

Area of Study 3: Music for Stage and Screen

Stephen Schwartz: 'Defying Gravity' from *Wicked*

Getting started

- How is *Wicked* different from the *The Wizard of Oz*? Which do you prefer and why?
- How many musicals are currently running in Britain?
- Are they all in London?
- Why do more people go to musicals than to operas? Should they?

Learning objectives

In the study of this set work you will learn about:

- the musical in the 20th and 21st centuries
- the life and works of Stephen Schwartz
- the background to *Wicked: The Untold Story of the Witches of Oz*
- patterns and harmony in 'Defying Gravity'
- how to analyse 'Defying Gravity'
- the orchestration of 'Defying Gravity'
- the key musical features.

Musical contexts

The musical in the 20th and 21st centuries

The musical as an art form was designed for the entertainment of mass audiences, and not aimed (as, for example, opera often was) solely for the upper classes who had the money to pay high ticket prices. Musicals have tried not only to entertain the audience with a story, but sometimes also to educate. Some have been based on biblical stories, such as Andrew Lloyd Webber's *Jesus Christ Superstar*. Others are based on historical events, such as Claude-Michel Schönberg's *Les Misérables*, which is based on Victor Hugo's historical novel of the same name. Some of the earliest forms of musical – such as vaudeville – contained popular songs with the words changed for comedic effect. Mozart's own opera music was often parodied by others into farce. Mozart enjoyed these entertainments, where people came along to drink, eat and smoke during performances as well as join in the songs. These evenings were an escape from the harsh realities of life. The same can be said today of course: we go to musicals mainly to be transported to a different time and place, which is pure escapism by any other name.

The musical started in amphitheatres of Ancient Greece, where stories were acted and sung. Since then it has evolved into many different styles of entertainment.

In the 20th century, the rise of the musical began in America. The first of the Broadway musicals was *Show Boat* (1927), written by Jerome Kern. This started the golden age of the musical, whose most spectacular partnership was between Oscar Hammerstein and Richard Rogers. Their works included *Oklahoma!* (1943), *Carousel* (1945), *South Pacific* (1949), *The King and I* (1951) *and The Sound of Music* (1959). Other beautiful musicals from this period include *Annie Get Your Gun* (1946) by Irving Berlin, and *Anything Goes* (1934) and *Kiss Me, Kate* (1948), both by Cole Porter.

The same few decades also saw the rise of cinema as an art form, and many stage musicals, including all those already mentioned, were later made into even more successful films.

For many musicians Leonard Bernstein's *West Side Story* (1957), which was also made into a film, is the best stage musical ever written. It combines Classical, Jazz and Latin American music and is based on Shakespeare's *Romeo and Juliet*. Most musicals, however, are not that adventurous, and some of the most popular composers of the past few decades have thrived precisely by sticking to a limited musical language that they know people like. Another significant composer of musicals over the last fifty years is Stephen Sondheim. He actually worked on *West Side Story* as the lyricist. His own musicals include *Into the Woods, Company* and *Sweeney Todd*.

The composer Andrew Lloyd Webber has had a spectacular career, with *Joseph and the Amazing Technicolor Dreamcoat* (1968), *Jesus Christ Superstar* (1971), *Evita* (1978), *Cats* (1981), *Starlight Express* (1984) and *The Phantom of the Opera* (1986) among many other successes.

Musicals have also taken the form of 'rock operas' or 'jukebox musicals' based on rock or pop music: *Tommy* (1969) (The Who) is an example of the former, while *Mamma Mia!* (1999) (Abba) and *We Will Rock You* (2002) (Queen) are examples of the latter.

The life and works of Stephen Schwartz (1948–)

Stephen Schwartz was born in New York. He attended piano and composition classes at the famous Juilliard School of Music while still at school and then graduated in Drama from Carnegie Mellon University.

Schwartz first came to public attention by writing new material for the musical *Godspell*. This was followed by the English texts in collaboration with Leonard Bernstein for Bernstein's *Mass* (1971) which opened the Kennedy Center for the Performing Arts in Washington, DC. Over the following three years, he wrote the music and lyrics for *Pippin* and *The Magic Show*, both of which ran on Broadway. In addition to many other music theatre productions, Schwartz has worked in film, too, most notably with the composer Alan Menken on Disney's *Pocahontas, The Hunchback of Notre Dame* and *Enchanted*. The musical *Wicked* opened in 2003 and is currently running on Broadway and in the West End.

Stephen Schwartz

Background to *Wicked: The Untold Story of the Witches of Oz*

The musical *Wicked* (2003) is based on the 1939 film *The Wizard of Oz* and the book *Wicked* by Gregory Maguire. It tells the story of two women who are initially arch-enemies:

- **Elphaba** the Wicked Witch of the West
- **Glinda** the Good Witch.

Elphaba is born green and is an outcast from society. She meets Glinda at college. Elphaba is made to feel quite valueless at school and is told that she is only there to look after her sister. Glinda, by contrast, is pink and popular! Elphaba, though, has a talent for magic and the headmistress of the college decides it would be a good idea to send both Elphaba and Glinda to the Emerald City, with a view to assisting the Wonderful Wizard of Oz. However, the Wizard turns out not to be the wonderful person he was thought to be. He is busy segregating the talking animals in Oz from the rest of society. Elphaba, who sees it as her mission to save the inhabitants of Oz from the Wizard, is so enraged that she speaks out against the Wizard and defies his laws. As a result, Elphaba is considered to be 'wicked' for standing up to the Wizard, but she also learns that you can do anything if you set your mind to it; her character is all about strength of mind. By the same token, Glinda is considered 'good' because she lacks the courage to stand up to him.

In the end, Elphaba escapes the Wizard and Oz, but Glinda is changed by the events and becomes a better person… and they all live happily ever after!

The song 'Defying Gravity' ends the first act of the musical and is delivered by both witches. By this point Elphaba has vowed to fight the Wizard of Oz, after discovering he is not the hero she thought he was. The song title 'Defying Gravity' refers to Elphaba's vow not to give in and accept the rules and limitations placed upon her. Just like defying the law of gravity, Elphaba is attempting literally to *rise above* her place in life.

> **Activity** ?
>
> If you were to base the plot to a musical on an existing work – just as Bernstein's *West Side Story* was based on Shakespeare's *Romeo and Juliet* – what would you choose and how would your plot differ from the original?

A scene from *Wicked*

> **Did you know?**
>
> In 2010 the song 'Defying Gravity' was used to wake up the astronauts on the Space Shuttle – appropriately enough, on the day of a spacewalk.

Area of Study 3: Music for Stage and Screen

Glossary

Leitmotif: a recurring musical idea which is associated with a particular theme, character or place.

Motif: a short melodic phrase of just a few notes.

Use of leitmotifs and other recurring patterns in 'Defying Gravity'

(N.B. The intention of this section on **leitmotifs** and **motifs** is to give you a taste of the compositional techniques Schwartz used to construct the song. You are not expected to understand the analysis in detail.)

Schwartz uses a number of leitmotifs throughout his score to *Wicked*.

Schwartz, who has also written music for films, brings this cinematic technique to the score of *Wicked*, and further links its plot to *The Wizard of Oz* by basing its most prominent leitmotif (we're calling this motif X below) on the first seven notes of the song 'Somewhere Over the Rainbow' from *The Wizard of Oz* film (one additional note is shown here in brackets).

Schwartz calls this the **'Unlimited' theme**, after the lyrics that appear with it in 'Defying Gravity'. It first appears in bar 93. Notice that motif X has four pitches – D, E, F♯ and G – spanning an interval of a fourth which, as will be shown, is an important interval in 'Defying Gravity', along with the fifth. Those pitches are also a cipher (musical code) for **DEF**ying **G**ravity!

Did you know?

Schwartz has explained – probably in jest – why he chose only the first seven notes of 'Somewhere over the Rainbow'. Copyright law dictates that, once eight notes of another composer's tune have been used, the person using the notes is 'stealing' another composer's tune. Schwartz therefore uses only seven notes of 'Somewhere Over the Rainbow', but disguises them rhythmically and harmonises them using different chords.

Activity ?

1. Take some manuscript paper. Copy out the melody from 'Somewhere Over the Rainbow'. The melody is printed at the bottom of this page as motif X. See if you can reorder them to make your own hit song for a musical. Use any rhythms you like, as long as they are different from those in the songs.

2. Choose a motif, write it out on manuscript paper and see if you can find one or more examples in the score of the song without reading further in this book.

Schwartz also uses the following accompaniment figure (we'll call it motif B) throughout. Motif B is Elphaba's theme and is derived from the seven pitches of motif X. It appears several times in 'Defying Gravity', starting in B major at bar 20 (the motif X notes are shown with larger note heads in the second part of Figure 1). The bass rises through an interval of a fourth (which, along with the interval of the fifth, plays an important role in this song). The two bracketed notes in the second half of Figure 1 show the pitches of motif X that are not used.

Motif X and motif B appear throughout the show, and therefore in 'Defying Gravity'.

Figure 1: motif B and its reduction to show its relationship to motif X (and therefore to 'Somewhere Over the Rainbow')

Motif X pitches in B major and G major (compare to bars 93–94):

112

Schwartz uses a third motif (motif C), again derived from motif X, to generate much of the melodic material in 'Defying Gravity', in both the lead vocal and the orchestral accompaniment.

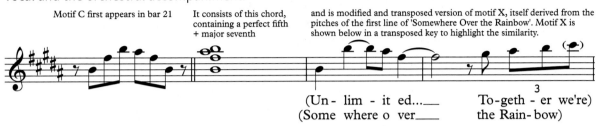

Motif C first appears in bar 21. It consists of this chord, containing a perfect fifth + major seventh, and is modified and transposed version of motif X, itself derived from the pitches of the first line of 'Somewhere Over the Rainbow'. Motif X is shown below in a transposed key to highlight the similarity.

(Un - lim - it ed...___ To-geth - er we're)
(Some where o ver___ the Rain- bow)

Figure 2: motif C and its relationship to motif X

From motif C, Schwartz creates the accompaniment figure (motif D) that leads into the chorus, and the accompaniment figure to the main chorus **hook** (a short, memorable group of notes forming a melody that recurs throughout the music) at bar 51.

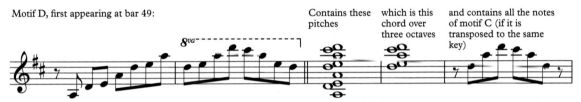

Motif D, first appearing at bar 49:

Contains these pitches which is this chord over three octaves and contains all the notes of motif C (if it is transposed to the same key)

Figure 3: motif D's relation to motif C

The second, third and fourth note of motif C, shown here are reversed (with the A moved up an octave) to form the main accompanying figure to the chorus hook at bar 51:

Figure 4: derivation of chorus accompaniment figure

In choosing a three-note pattern, Schwartz creates **metrical shifting** – the downbeat keeps falling on a different note in different parts of the chorus. Metrical shifting was often used by 20th-century composers such as Stravinsky, and became a technique often used in Minimalism (music built on hypnotically repeated short phrases).

These three notes (C♯, D and A) are used also to create the melody at the start of the verse (bar 34). The rhythm is very similar to motif B, with its quaver–crotchet focus.

> **Glossary**
>
> **Metrical shifting**: the downbeat is shifted to a different part of the bar.

The role of perfect intervals

The intervals of motif C (an ascending perfect fifth, followed by an ascending perfect fourth) are used to derive the melodic material for the main verse. These fourths and fifths help create a strong and assertive melody. The whole verse is derived from perfect fourths and fifths, and each phrase is based on a collection of five pitches which, as Figure 5 shows, are all formed from chords I, IV and V. The only two notes common to each phrase are D and A – also a perfect fifth apart!

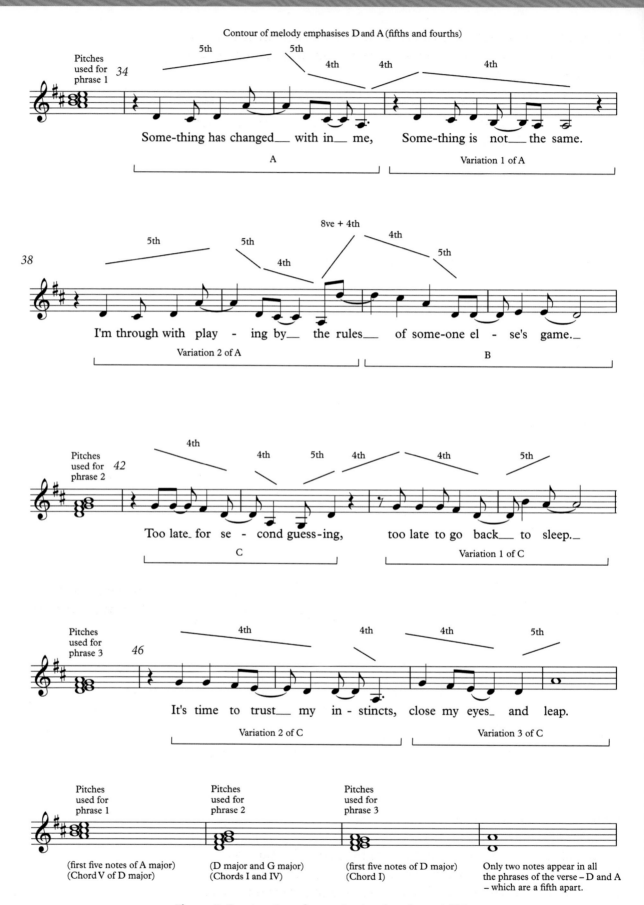

Figure 5: Construction of verse 1 using fourths and fifths

Notice, too, how the verse is constructed from an initial phrase followed by variations of that phrase. Schwartz varies the melody again in verse 2 (bar 63 onwards).

Schwartz also uses perfect fifths at the beginning of the chorus (… *and leap. It's time to try*…) and in a small accompaniment idea in bar 54 based on perfect fourths and fifths:

Figure 6: prominent fifths at the beginning of the chorus

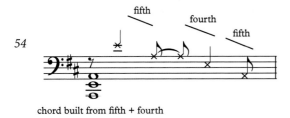

Figure 7: accompaniment figure based on perfect fourths and fifths in bar 54

Schwartz's obsession with the intervals of fourths and fifths was clearly a compositional aid for him and will perhaps also register in the mind of the listener. The interval of the fifth even filters into the chords from bar 68 (last quaver beat) to bar 71, which are a fifth apart (D to G to C) creating a harmonic sequence.

Starting at bar 88, Schwartz uses G and C majors together to create the magical feeling at the beginning of the middle dialogue section. These bars are **bitonal**, since they combine two keys simultaneously. The G chord also has an added major seventh (F♯) – a key feature of motif C (see Figure 2).

> **Glossary**
>
> **Bitonal**: refers to music in two keys at the same time.

Figure 8: Pattern in bars 88–89

Notice, too, that this melody starting at bar 93 is set in G major – a fourth away from the main key of the song (D major). So the interval of a fourth also influences the key relationships, as well as the melody and the harmony.

The iconic scene of 'Defying Gravity'

Close analysis of 'Defying Gravity'

Commentary on bars 1–14 (Introduction)

'Defying Gravity' starts with dramatic *marcato* (very strongly accented) chords reflecting the anger between Glinda and Elphaba in this scene.

The **texture** is **homophonic** (consisting of just melody and harmony) and almost like a **recitative** in opera – a section that quickly moves the action on through fast-paced lines and modulating phrases in order to get to the next number.

The first phrase – *I hope you're happy* – is half-shouted (indicated by crossed notes that denote the approximate pitch). Each phrase in the opening bars is an extended and varied version of this.

The **harmony** in bars 1–6 moves chromatically, first down and then up – D major, C♯ minor, C major, B major, etc. – so that the **tonality** (key) remains uncertain. There are moments where a key is implied, but the music never settles for more than a bar. In bar 4, for example, Schwartz uses the chord of C major, but has F♯s in the melody. This further helps to unsettle any sense of key.

The melody in bar 6 introduces the interval of a fifth on the word *ever* – the same interval that plays such an important role in 'Defying Gravity'. The melody in bar 6 is sequenced then repeated up a semitone in a sequence in bar 7. The fifth is stretched to a minor sixth (C–A♭) on the word *clever* and has an **augmented chord** below, which is used to move the music towards D♭ major at the beginning of bar 8 – a semitone below where we started. This creates a contrasting sense of key when Elphaba responds with *I hope you're happy*.

In the same way that the two witches are at odds, Schwartz gives each witch an initial 'key area' – D major for Glinda and D♭ major for Elphaba – placing them at odds with each other. Notice how the initial phrase sung by each witch has the same words: *I hope you're happy*. This allows Schwartz to further emphasise the use of the same melodic material.

Commentary on bars 15–49

Bars 15–19

The melody for the words *So though I can't imagine how* is also based on the opening phrase, *I hope you're happy*. The introduction ends with a perfect cadence (V7–I) in B major in bars 19–20, in the course of which Schwartz chromatically alters the fifth degree of chord V7 by flattening it from a C♯ to a C♮. This is done to prepare us for the key change to come at the end of bar 21, which is in itself a shift of a diminished fifth from B to F. There is now a different section, marked Andante, which creates a change in mood before the first verse begins, in bar 32.

Bars 20–23

Short dialogue section: motif B appear, followed by motif C – in the full stage show version there is a longer dialogue section here.

Bars 24–29

Schwartz inserts a quotation from an earlier song, 'The Wizard and I', in which Elphaba dreams of how the all-powerful Wizard of Oz will make her his assistant. Since singing that song, Elphaba has met and been disillusioned by the Wizard, who has turned out to be not quite as powerful as his reputation implies. Schwartz therefore quotes the earlier song – this time reflectively – to give greater effect to Elphaba's uncertainty as to whether she wants to pursue the path of being the Wicked Witch of the West. Instead of the pulsing quavers that accompany the original song, Schwartz here uses a slightly syncopated figure.

Bars 29–32

The melody for the words *but I don't want it* is based on the opening *I hope you're happy*. Motifs B and C again appear in bars 32 and 33 respectively.

It is worth noting that the melody for *I can't want it anymore* is very similar to 'Somewhere' from *West Side Story*, a musical that Schwartz admires.

The key changes from F major to D major between bars 31 and 32 to take us into the first verse.

Bars 32–49   Verse 1

The verse opens with motif B played by the brass and motif C on the synthesiser. At bar 34 strings playing **tremolando** accompany the voice and are marked ***colla voce***. This is to continue until bar 49, where Allegro is marked.

We are now in D major. The chords used feature **bare fifths**. This helps create a sparse feeling to the music. These bare fifths here create a sense of possibility, of wide-open spaces – in this case the freedom the character is beginning to imagine for herself. Look at the bass part to see these fifths – for example, in bar 34 (last quaver beat) tied to bar 35.

Glossary

Tremolando/tremolo: rapid playing on the same note to produce a wavering, tremulous sound.

Colla voce: literally, 'with the voice'. This is an instruction to the band and the musical director to follow the vocalist's tempo.

Bare fifth: chords lacking the third and therefore ambiguous in terms of major/minor tonality.

In bars 34–42 the melody uses only five pitches. Schwartz is using the number five to pervade all elements of the song. Look back at figures 2 and 5 to see how the melody here relates to motif C, and is built around the intervals of a fifth and a fourth.

In bars 42–45 the melody uses a new collection of five pitches: G, F♯, D, A, and B. Then in bars 46–49 the melody uses another new collection of five pitches: the first five notes of D major, the home key.

There is a further connection between the collections of five pitches that Schwartz uses for the verse. The only constant notes common to all the collections are D and A – themselves a fifth apart, and the tonic and dominant of the home key. This of course reinforces the sense of this key.

Commentary on bars 49–80

Bars 49–59   Chorus 1

This starts with an interrupted cadence (V–VI) between bars 50 and 51, and the interval of a fifth in the melody (*It's time to…*) accompanied by a figure of ascending fourths (see Figure 3). Schwartz uses an ostinato of three notes (C♯, D and A). These are the second, third and fourth notes of motif X, but reversed (see Figure 4), and with the A put up an octave. In choosing a *three*-note pattern, Schwartz creates metrical shifting – the downbeat keeps falling on a different note over the chorus.

The melody in bars 51–53 (first note) is triadic, whilst the left-hand piano accompaniment contains the same construction of chords as the verse (namely, bare chords without a third). A small accompaniment figure consisting of descending fifths and fourths appears in bar 54 in the drum fill (see Figure 7). Bars 55–57 are a variation on bars 51–53. The accompaniment figure in bar 58 is based around the pitches of motif C (see Figure 3). Motif B appears in bar 59.

Bars 59–63   Link 1

Triplets are introduced to create cross-rhythms against the quaver movement that has been established in the chorus. Schwartz cleverly reflects Glinda's on-stage objection to Elphaba's actions (*Can't I make you understand you're having delusions of grandeur?*) The melody for bars 60–62 is based on the melody in bars 46–49.

Bars 63–79   Verse 2

There is a *perfect* cadence (V–I) in bars 62–63, which portrays Elphaba's increased confidence. Compare this to the *interrupted* cadence (V–VI) in bars 50–51. A perfect cadence always sounds decisive, whereas an interrupted cadence sounds hesitant, even nervous.

The melody for verse 2 is a variation of verse 1. The left-hand accompaniment in bars 63–69 derives from motif B.

The harmony moves through a short '**circle of fifths**' progression in bars 69–70 (D to G to C).

Glossary

Circle of fifths: a series of chords in which the root note of each chord is a fifth lower or a fourth higher than that of the previous one.

Commentary on bars 71–177

The melody (but not the accompaniment) in bars 71–79 is **hexatonic** – meaning it is based on six of the seven pitches in a major scale. Schwartz in the preceding passage has been using chords based on the flattened seventh with which the C♯ would clash. He deliberately does not use the seventh degree of D major (C♯) as this leading note wants to resolve onto the D, so he holds it back for the climatic hook line *defying gravity*.

Bars 80–88   Chorus 2
The chorus again begins with an interrupted cadence, in bars 79–80. The three-note ostinato returns, along with the descending fifths and fourths figure in the left-hand part of the keyboard accompaniment in bar 83.

Bars 88–92   Second dialogue section
The tonality moves up a perfect fourth from D major to G major at bar 88, although we remain in the tonic key of D major. Schwartz uses two keys at once from bar 88 – the left hand of the keyboard part plays a chord of C major, whilst the semiquaver figuration in the right hand of the keyboard is the chord of G major with an added major seventh, the same interval that features prominently in motif C (see Figure 2). Notice that the two keys used (C and G major) are themselves a fifth apart. Although this can be seen in the notation, to the ear the effect is that we remain in D major. Schwartz has used a G major key signature in order to use the chord on the flattened seventh degree, that is, a chord of C major, and thus not having to have to write in lots of C♮! The overriding key we hear is still D major.

Bars 93–103   First bridge
Schwartz introduces the 'Unlimited' theme (see Figure 2) in bars 93–94, featuring the same three-note motif (motif X) that is present in the accompaniment. Bars 95–96 are variations of bars 93–94, with a sequential auxiliary note figure introduced in bar 97. This additional idea in bar 94 has the range of a perfect fourth. The metre changes to $\frac{3}{4}$ in bar 101. Schwartz writes the melody featuring a scalic descent over a perfect fourth to the words *we cannot win*, followed by a scalic ascent up a perfect fourth for *just you and I*. Bar 102 contains a chord of E♭ major with an added major seventh note D.

Bars 103–111   Chorus 3
Elphaba and Glinda now sing together, harmonising in fifths and fourths in bars 106 and 109.

Bars 111–114   Link 2
This is based around motif B, with bar 112 containing a small figure containing a melodic fourth (from the D down to the A and then G down to D) accompanied by a harmonic fifth (G and D together) with added second, known as a sus2 chord.

Bars 115–129　　Revised version of the introduction

The *I hope you're happy* melody takes on a different feel now the witches have reconciled their differences. Schwartz uses the same lyrics at the beginning of the section to create an aural cue for the audience that this section is referring to the beginning of the song, but he changes the lyrics slightly after the initial phrase. The accompaniment now consists of long sustained chords with shifting harmonies. The version here is a shortened version of the introduction. Schwartz uses the interval of a third in the vocal parts to add warmth to the music at bars 125–128.

Bars 129–135　　Vamp section

This section is much longer in the full show version to allow the actress playing Elphaba to run to the back of the stage and clip herself into the harness that will raise her above the rest of the cast in the final chorus. This edition of the score has a reduced six-bar version. The music moves from C major to D major.

Bars 135–151　　Second bridge

A plagal cadence (IV–I) in bars 134–135 leads into the most dramatic section of the song. Schwartz bases the material for bars 135–141 on the chords from verse 1. The melody for *as someone told me lately* is the same melody used for the words *something has changed within me*, but now sung powerfully and assertively.

The melodic idea of a descending fourth returns in bars 143–144, and bars 145–151 are a more powerfully accompanied version of bars 73–78.

Bars 152–162　　Chorus 4

Schwartz alters the melody in bars 156–157 and introduces a top F♯ (that lies towards the top of the 'chest' register of a voice, and so is one of the most powerful notes a musical theatre singer can sing).

Bars 162–168　　Link 3

A six-bar link to slow the momentum in preparation for the coda. Melodic material is based on the descending fourth figure. The harmony includes a B♭ chord in bar 161, immediately before this passage, which is the flattened submediant of D major.

Bars 168–177　　Coda

There is an **interrupted cadence** in bars 167–168. The coda combines a number of ideas. Elphaba continues to sing an augmented version of the melody at the beginning of the chorus (*tell them how I…*), but to the words of *bring me down*. Her melody continues to feature the prominent interval of a perfect fifth. The ensemble sing *look at her, she's wicked* to music from the opening number of the show, 'No One Mourns the Wicked'. Since 'Defying Gravity' ends Act I, there is a sense of symmetry in referring to the beginning at the end of the act. Notice how the ensemble is primarily singing in fifths (between sopranos and altos, and tenors and basses). The orchestra play a *fortissimo* and altered version of motif B (a version first heard in the overture of the show).

Did you know?

The 'chest' register of the voice is roughly at speaking pitch. Some musical theatre singers can take this chest voice very high, in a kind of controlled shouting. This technique is known as 'belting'. Such singers have to take great care not to damage their voices.

The soprano ensemble part for the words *so we've got to bring her* rises in alternating tones and semitones. It is part of an **octatonic scale** (a scale with eight notes, built from alternating tones and semitones). This is set to a series of **polytonal chords**: bar 173 has a chord of C major on top of a chord of F major; and bar 174 contains a chord of B♭ major on top of a chord of E♭ major, as well as a chord of C major over a chord of D♭ major.

Note that in the first two chords, the keys chosen are again a fifth apart. In the final chord they are a semitone apart, and therefore create a strong dissonance. There is a final **vocalisation** figure sung to *ah*, again based on the interval of a fifth, which interrupts the ensemble's lyric of *so we've got to bring her down*. The ensemble complete the word *down* with a six-part triad in the home key of D major. They and the orchestra crescendo before a *sforzando* (incredibly loud and forced) 'door-slam' on a unison D. This final note is also the cue for the lighting blackout.

Glossary

Polytonal chords: chords that are built from two or more keys simultaneously.

Vocalisation: wordless singing using a vowel syllable such as 'ah'.

Exam-style question

Describe how Schwartz sets the words *defying gravity* whenever the phrase occurs the song. Describe how he varies the melody, rhythm and pitch each time. **(3 marks)**

Exam tip

Remember to make **three** different points: one each on melody, rhythm and pitch. Think about the obvious – the shape of the melody, the type of rhythms used and how high or low the pitch is. You will hear these words many times to help you with your answers!

Orchestration of 'Defying Gravity'

Schwartz's music was orchestrated by the veteran arranger William Brohn. Brohn's orchestration achieves weird sonorities to conjure up the world of the witches, combining traditional orchestral sounds with more modern ones (electric guitar, drums, synthesisers).

The orchestration is large by the standards of the usual musical band: flute, oboe, bass clarinet, bassoon, baritone saxophone, two horns, two trumpets, two trombones, percussion, drums, two guitars, harp, two violins, a viola, a cello and a bass. There are also three electronic keyboards, which are programmed with 'patches' (different digital sounds). The players are of course required every night of the show's run, unlike the orchestra players used to record the *Star Wars* music, so this is a considerable expense for the production of the musical.

The keyboard patches include fast attack strings, tremolo strings, contrabass (very, very low) clarinet, celeste and bass trombones. The role of the keyboards is to bulk out the sound made from each instrument family, hence at various points in 'Defying Gravity' string or brass patches are used to give the impression that the orchestra is larger than it is.

One of the electric guitars uses an 'E-bow' (pioneered by Brohn) – a small device held over the guitar that emits electromagnetic radiation to vibrate the strings. The guitarist does not need to pluck the strings, as the sound generated by the E-bow is continuous. Brohn uses this incredibly bizarre

Did you know?

Stravinsky used octatonic scales as well as polytonal chords in his ballet *The Rite of Spring*.

sound to allow the guitar to sweep over the orchestra (for instance, at bar 15 and bars 123–124). The guitars also use distortion, chorus, flange, 'seek-wah', 'wah-wah' and other effects. They also use palm-muting and extreme vibrato at various points in the song.

The trumpets use straight mutes (for example, bar 68); the horns hand-stop their notes (denoted by a + above the note) in bars 36–40. Both techniques alter the instruments' timbre (the 'colour' of the sound). The violins, viola and cello play pizzicato in bars 51–58, but remain bowed (arco) for much of the song. The show is very percussion-heavy, and Brohn uses unusual percussion instruments to create a stranger feel in the music – for example, a bell tree in bar 50, chimes in bars 55–58 and bars 147–150, a shaker in bars 63–75, a suspended cymbal in bar 102, crotales in bars 152–159, a tin maraca and nut rattle in bars 88–90, and a tam-tam in bar 169!

Brohn instructs the timpani to 'pedal-gliss' in the vamp in bar 92 – the timpani have a pedal to change their pitch, so by continually moving the pedal and playing a tremolo, the player can change pitch.

Listen

Some of the features under the section 'Orchestration of Defying Gravity' on pages 121–122 are not notated in the Pearson Anthology. See if you can hear them on the Pearson Anthology CD whilst following the score.

Wider listening

Tim Minchin: 'Naughty' from *Matilda*

Matilda the Musical is based on Roald Dahl's book. It was written by Dennis Kelly, with music and lyrics by Tim Minchin. The instrumentation uses a 13-piece orchestra, including keyboards, reeds, brass, strings and percussion. The musical is about Matilda, a precocious five-year-old girl with the gift of telekinesis – the power to manipulate and move objects with her mind. She loves reading, and one of the stories in her books gives her the idea to get even with her cruel father. She adds some of her mother's hydrogen peroxide to his hair oil, thus leaving her father with bright green hair. This forms the subject of the song 'Naughty'. Listen to this solo song and identify some similarities and differences when compared to 'Defying Gravity' from *Wicked*.

Marc Shaiman: 'Mama, I'm a Big Girl Now' from *Hairspray*

Hairspray is a musical with music by Marc Shaiman and lyrics by Scott Wittman. The story is based on the film *Hairspray* (1988) and is a social commentary on the injustices of American society in the 1960s. In terms of musical style there is a mixture of 1960s-style dance music, and rhythm and blues numbers. The story, set in 1962, is about teenager Tracy Turnblad's dream to dance on a local TV show called *The Corny Collins Show*. Tracy manages to get on the show and becomes an overnight celebrity. This solo song again is worth comparing to the style of the set work, 'Defying Gravity'.

Checkpoint

Strengthen

S1 Explain what a **motif** is and give an example from the song.

S2 Describe the music of the **opening introduction** (bars 1–14), referring to the melody, harmony, tempo and texture.

S3 Describe the structure of the song after this opening introduction, mentioning at least three different sections.

S4 Give a bar number where the mood of the song changes and say in what way the music changes to effect this mood change.

S5 **Give two** musical reasons why you like or dislike this song.

Challenge

C1 Explain how Schwartz uses the perfect intervals of the fourth and fifth in this song as a unifying device.

C2 Listen to 'Mama, I'm a Big Girl Now' from *Hairspray*. Can you identify **three** similarities and **three** differences between this song and 'Defying Gravity'?

C3 If you were to write a musical based on a pre-existing plot from a novel, film or play, what would you choose and why? Would you change the point of view of the characters from the original, as Schwartz did in *Wicked*?

Summary of the key musical features

Key points to remember:

- **Context**. The musical *Wicked* (2003) is based on the 1939 film *The Wizard of Oz*, and the book *Wicked* by Gregory Maguire. The song 'Defying Gravity' is a **dramatic song** sung by both Elphaba and Glinda. Elphaba has vowed to fight the Wizard of Oz, after discovering he is not the hero she thought he was. The song title 'Defying Gravity' refers to Elphaba's vow not to give in and accept the rules and limitations placed on her.

- **Melody**. Schwartz uses a number of leitmotifs throughout his score to *Wicked* (based largely around collections of five pitches and largely focused on the interval of a fifth or its inversion, the fourth below). The most important melody is based on the first seven notes of the song 'Somewhere Over the Rainbow' from *The Wizard of Oz* film. This is called the **Unlimited theme**. Other motifs litter the score.

- **Importance of perfect intervals**. The two intervals of the **perfect fourth** and **perfect fifth** provide the melodic material for the main **verse**. These fourths and fifths help create a strong and assertive melody in the song.

- The **structure of the song** is quite **extended**, comprising the introduction – dialogue section 1 – verse 1 – chorus – link – verse 2 – chorus – dialogue section 2 – first bridge – chorus 3 – link 2 – revised introduction – vamp section – bridge 2 – chorus 4 – coda.

- **Articulation**. Full range used, from **marcato** (very accented) **stabbed chords** in the introduction to long **legato** phrases. Three-note **ostinato** is played **staccato**.

- **Dynamics**. Full range used, from *fortissimo* to *pianissimo*. The song has a large dynamic range, and some more unusual dynamics for example, *sforzando* 'forced' and *fp* 'loud then immediately soft'.

- **Texture**. 'Defying Gravity' starts with **homophonic marcato** chords from the orchestra and **monophonic** lines from each of the witches, Schwartz gradually builds up the **texture** to melody-dominated homophony for *you can still be with the wizard* and for the **bridge**, and then a full **polyphonic** texture for the choruses. A **full range of textures** is used.

- **Harmony/tonality (keys)**. Both major and minor harmonies are used throughout, but with additional **augmented** chords (where the fifth of the chord is raised – for example, bars 7 and 122) and **half-diminished** chords (where the fifth is flattened – for example, bar 19). 'Defying Gravity' begins by deliberately **alienating any sense of tonality** with **continually shifting harmonies**. Schwartz also uses chords based on the flattened degrees of the D major scale. The verse and chorus structures are major, with the coda starting in a minor key. The ensemble and soloist sing a major triad to end the song.

- **Rhythm and metre**. The main rhythmic focus alternates between **slow chordal accompaniments** and **driving quaver rhythms**. Melody is often **syncopated** and **rubato** is used. Heavy **percussion** is used for **rhythmic emphasis**. 'Defying Gravity' starts in $\frac{2}{2}$, before remaining in $\frac{4}{4}$ for most of the time. There is one bar of $\frac{3}{4}$ (bar 101).

- **Instrumentation**. The orchestration combines **traditional classical** instruments with **popular music** instruments (for example, electric guitar, drums, synthesised sounds on keyboard), plus a heavy emphasis on **percussion**. The arranger William Brohn conjures a magical and unfamiliar world by using more **unusual instrumental techniques** (such as palm muting, chorus, delay, flange and E-bow on guitars, and timpani pedal glissandi) and more unusual percussion instruments (such as a bell tree, chimes, a shaker, a finger cymbal, crotales, a tin maraca and a nut rattle).

John Williams: 'Main Title/Rebel Blockade Runner', from *Star Wars Episode IV: A New Hope*

Getting started

- Find a favourite scene from a film of your own choice where there is no spoken dialogue. Watch the scene first with the sound on then with it off. What does the music add to the overall experience?
- Take an excerpt around 30 seconds long from an action scene in one of the *Wallace and Gromit* films and compose some music of your own to fit. This can be done using any instruments and sound effects!

Learning objectives

In the study of this set work you will learn about:

- music for film
- the life and works of John Williams
- the *Star Wars* films
- how to analyse 'Main Title/Rebel Blockade Runner'
- the key musical features.

Musical contexts

Music for film

Before the invention of the soundtrack, films relied on music played live in the cinema itself. The performer was usually a pianist (but an organist or even a small band might be used). The pianist might rely on a 'scene music' book, which recommended pieces of existing music (often by the Norwegian composer Grieg) to play over a particular type of scene.

The first film *with* a soundtrack was *The Jazz Singer* (1927). This contained songs but only a few fragments of speech.

The invention of the soundtrack changed the role of music in film, and in the 1930s the role of the *film composer* began to emerge.

Some producers continued to prefer music composed for other purposes – for example, a Rachmaninov piano concerto was used in *Brief Encounter* (1945). Even much later there were still film directors, such as Stanley Kubrick in the 1960s and 1970s, who used pre-existing music by other composers in their films. Broadway musicals, too, were often successfully turned into film, for example *West Side Story* (1961).

By far the majority of films, though, in the sound era have used music specially commissioned for the soundtrack. The basic pattern, which does not vary all that much, even today, begins with music for the opening titles, rather like an overture to an opera; our set work, the main title music from *Star Wars* (1977), is a very good example. Music was also needed for parts of the film where there was no dialogue – for example in car chases. Composers have often been criticised for following the action in the film a

Area of Study 3: Music for Stage and Screen

Did you know?

- Amazingly, Hitchcock originally resisted the idea of having music for the shower scene in *Psycho*. The composer Bernard Herrmann defied these instructions but won Hitchcock over. However, their relationship did appear to sour from then on. Eventually, composer and director parted company.

- Herrmann's last score – for Martin Scorsese's *Taxi Driver* (1976)– was in a completely different, haunting, jazzy style, and is considered by many to be his finest. He died the day after it was recorded and so was not around to pick up the many awards it won.

Glossary

Diegetic music: this is music contained within the action of the film and included in the story – for example, music played in a bar. If a character in the story can hear the music, it is diegetic. Most film music is non-diegetic.

Background music, underscore, underscoring: non-diegetic music adding to the mood of the scene, reinforcing dramatic developments and aspects of character.

little too closely, rather as in a cartoon, a technique which for that reason has come to be known as 'Mickey Mousing'.

With the Second World War came patriotic movies requiring patriotic music. Such films continued to be popular in the postwar years with films such as *The Dambusters* (1955, music by Eric Coates), *633 Squadron* (1964, Ron Goodwin) and – probably the most famous of these – *The Great Escape* (1963, Elmer Bernstein).

Thrillers also demanded musical skills to conjure up dramatic moments. The famous shower scene from Alfred Hitchcock's *Psycho* (1960) is an unforgettable example.

The James Bond films – from the 1960s on – feature ultra-dramatic film scores. Many are by the composer John Barry, whose music defines the films more than any individual star, hence the saying, 'John Barry *is* James Bond'.

In the *Star Wars* series, Williams, like Barry, uses the full symphony orchestra. He expands the use of melodies to represent characters (both good and bad). These themes are called **leitmotifs** (a term borrowed from opera). Of course, only where large budgets exist can composers write for large orchestras. Blockbusters such as *Titanic* (1997, James Horner), the *Harry Potter* series (2001–11, John Williams and others) and the *Lord of the Rings Trilogy* (2001–03, Howard Shore and others) are all composed for full orchestra.

In recent years, computers and other technology have been used to create film music, often using sampled sounds. High budget films still maintain the tradition of using an orchestra (as for Hans Zimmer's *Pirates* etc.), but that lower budget films now often use sampled sounds. It is simply much cheaper to employ one person to record the whole 'orchestral' score from the computer keyboard than to employ 100 orchestral musicians! Composers such as Hans Zimmer (2003–17, *Pirates of the Caribbean* series) and many others have produced music tracks in this way.

Music composed for films essentially falls into two categories: **diegetic music** and **background music**.

As we shall see in our set work, the role of the title music is to establish atmosphere, time and place. The music is called **underscoring** as it accompanies moving pictures, in this case 'under' the rolling credits in the opening.

Listen

A director may rely on the underscore to provide elements entirely missing from an existing scene – for example, suggesting that a character is lying.

Or the music may warn of an impending danger unseen in the images. Think of a film where the music tells us that a large and unfriendly fish is about – long before we see it.

See if you can find similar examples – for instance, in a TV detective series.

The life and works of John Williams (1932–)

Williams – probably the most famous living composer of film music – was born in New York and relocated to Los Angeles when he was 16. He studied classical composition at the University of California before returning to New York to study piano at the famous Juilliard School of Music. Williams started his career in film studios in Los Angeles, working with Bernard Herrmann, Alfred Newman and Franz Waxman, all of them legendary names by then.

Early success in writing music for television in the 1960s led to his first film credit for *Because They're Young* (1960). His big break came in the early 1970s with Steven Spielberg's *The Sugarland Express* (1974). This led to numerous other collaborations with Spielberg, including the film *Jaws* (1975), which received an Oscar. Further Oscars were nominated for *Star Wars* and *Close Encounters of the Third Kind* (1977). Since then success has followed success, with other well-known work including *E.T. – the Extra-Terrestrial* (1982), *Schindler's List* (1993), the first three *Harry Potter* films, *Jurassic Park* (1993), the *Star Wars Trilogy* (1977–83), the *Indiana Jones Trilogy* (1981–9), *Home Alone* (1990) and *Empire of the Sun* (1987). In total, Williams has been awarded five Oscars, seven British Academy Awards, twenty-two Grammys and four Golden Globes. In addition to his film music, he has composed two symphonies as well as concertos for violin, cello, flute, clarinet, bassoon, trumpet and tuba.

John Williams

Did you know?

Spielberg and Williams have a mutually respectful working relationship. Usually composers write their music for the *finished* film. However, in the case of *ET*, Williams persuaded Spielberg to re-edit the section where the boys start to fly on their bikes, so that the action could fit his music – to wonderful effect.

The *Star Wars* films

Star Wars is a series of adventure films created by George Lucas and set a long time ago *in a galaxy far, far away*. It portrays battles between good and evil forces.

Star Wars Episode IV: A New Hope (1977), originally titled just **Star Wars**, was the first film in the series. The film starred Mark Hamill, Harrison Ford, Carrie Fisher, Peter Cushing and Alec Guinness.

The story is about the mission of Princess Leia, the leader of the Rebel Alliance, to destroy the Galactic Empire's space station, known as the Death Star. Meanwhile, Luke Skywalker has in his possession a pair of droids that own stolen plans for the construction of the Death Star. The Rebel Alliance are searching for the missing droids and Luke agrees to go with the Jedi Knight Obi-Wan Kenobi on a mission to return the plans to help the Rebel Alliance and thus save the galaxy from the destructive power of the evil Galactic Empire. We will now focus on the music itself.

Glossary

Cue: a section of music in a film. Here it refers to the whole track.

Fanfare: a celebratory piece for brass instruments (and sometimes percussion) often marking the opening of an important event or ceremony. The music is short and loud and often features arpeggios and broken chords. In the Main Title here, it serves a similar purpose, namely, to introduce the main melody of the *Star Wars* theme. An inspiring example of a fanfare for brass and percussion is Aaron Copland's *Fanfare for the Common Man*.

Close analysis of 'Main Title/Rebel Blockade Runner'

The main title music to the *Star Wars* films is probably one of the most famous **cues** in film music history. From its 1977 debut in *Episode IV: A New Hope*, it has remained the iconic theme to the *Star Wars* films. The main theme tune is also the melody associated with the character Luke Skywalker.

The Rebel Blockade Runner or CR90 Corvette is the iconic ship with twin turbolaser turrets and eleven turbine engines that features in the film.

Sound to picture

The scene opens in silence until the words *Star Wars* flash onto the screen. This is the cue for the dramatic *forte* opening fanfare and main theme music. Whilst this music is being played, the script on the screen rolls forward, telling the background story. At the conclusion of the main theme at bar 30, the music becomes much more mysterious and static. The words on the screen have passed by into space. The texture is light and we hear a solo piccolo and string accompaniment. As the camera then focuses on the Death Star, there is a change of mood again as the string writing rises in pitch and dynamic level until at bar 51 there is a passage in *forte* octaves and strong brass chords. The picture changes to the Rebel Blockade Runner being chased by an Imperial Star Destroyer. The adventure begins…

Commentary on bars 1–11 (Introduction and Section A)

Bars 1–3 Introductory *fanfare*

The music starts with a blast from the full orchestra on a B♭ major chord marked *ff*. B♭ major is a comfortable key for horns and brass (whose natural pitches are usually F, B♭ and C) and the first three bars feature them prominently. Immediately we are given a powerful impression of something grand and important. The writing is heroic and this, of course, suits the mood of the film.

The music of the first three bars features overlapping lines starting with the trumpets and trombones, then the horns, then the tubas joining at bar 3. Rhythmic features include triplet semiquavers and quavers. This triplet rhythm permeates all the music and is used as part of the main theme, too. The interval of the fourth is important, as is the seventh. Look at the motif in bar 2, beats 2 and 4, as well as in bar 3, beat 2, in the trumpet part. This three-note motif is used as part of the main theme tune that follows the introduction. Notice how these three bars feature a predominance of fourths, suggesting power and strength.

Darth Vader conducting an orchestra in homage of John Williams

The whole of the three bars of the fanfare are essentially built on the B♭ chord with added fourths and sevenths. If you listen to the first three bars, you can sense that the fourth note (E♭) is part of a 4–3 suspension that finally resolves to D (the third of the B♭ chord) at bar 4, beat 1.

The harmony of the brass parts that follow the opening chord comprises broken chords. Looking at the harmony produced vertically reveals a chord built on fourths, or what is known as a **quartal harmony**. The chord generated in bar 2 comprises the notes F–B♭–E♭–A♭.

Quartal harmony: chords built on superimposed fourths

In bar 3 the B♭ harmony with added fourths and sevenths continues until Williams writes octave dominant triplet Fs on beat 4. This is the triplet upbeat to the main *Star Wars* theme. The first chord of bar 4 is a tonic B♭ chord, completing a perfect cadence from bar 3, beat 4.

This pattern of harmony underlines the entire main theme that follows:

- bar 1: B♭ major chord
- bar 2: F quartal
- bar 3: beats 1 and 2 quartal; beat 3 chord 17 d; beat 4 octave f dominant note.

The whole piece is highly unified in both its musical structure and its expressive qualities. We hear the same melodic motifs, the same harmonies, and the same rhythms played again and again but in slightly different guises.

The main theme is organised into a **ternary structure (ABA)**.

Bars 4–11   Main *Star Wars* theme – Section A

The grand *Star Wars* theme is played by the full orchestra. The melody opens with a strong upward fifth interval from the tonic to the dominant (B♭ to F) in bar 4. The triplet feature of the introduction is used in every bar in bars 5–11. Notice the intervals of the fourth and seventh in both the melody and harmony.

Melody

Interval of the fourth

Bar 4 (beat 3) to bar 5 (last quaver triplet note of beat one) in descending pitches F to C. Then from the high B♭ minim (bar 5 beat 2) down a fourth to the crotchet F (bar 5 beat 4). Then from this F down a fourth in step to C in bar 6 (last quaver triplet note of beat 1).

Interval of the seventh

Bars 5 and 6, both from last note of the triplets – C up to B♭.

The same pattern can be found when this repeats in bars 8–11.

The accompaniment from bar 4 is chordal, again using the triplet figuration. The off-beat rhythms in bars 5 and 6 add to the excitement of the music. The chords from bar 4 follow the same pattern as that of the introduction. The superimposed fourths (**quartal chord**) can be seen in bars 5 and 6.

The long held B♭ in bars 4–6 played by **tremolo strings** is a **tonic pedal**. As it is at the top of the musical texture it is called an **inverted pedal**.

Bar 7 roots us to the dominant chord of F on beats 2–4, as a string flourish takes us to a repeat of the opening part of the theme at bars 8–11. The accompaniment is now varied. The strings play a tremolo B♭ in bars 9–11, whilst the accompanying chords are a little more regular and triadic (simple three-note chords), but still feature the triplets in bars 8, 9 and 11.

A dominant chord is reached at bar 11 to link to the central part of the *Star Wars* melody. This starts on the last beat of bar 11 and finishes at bar 19.

It is interesting to note that the intervals of the fourth and seventh feature prominently in both this *Star Wars* music as well as in 'Defying Gravity'.

Commentary on bars 11–41

Bars 11–20   Central section of main *Star Wars* theme

This middle section sounds more restrained after the *fortissimo* opening section and is marked **mf**. The accompaniment to the melody in octave strings comprises simple chords, although many have *added notes*. For example, the two chords in bar 12 are Eb major chords, with the notes Eb–G–Bb plus the **added sixth** C. This added sixth chord is a common chord in jazz music. Another example of this type of chord can be seen at beat 4 of bar 13: F–A–C–D.

Glossary

Added sixth chord: a common chord in Jazz and Popular Music, a triad with the sixth added above the tonic.

The repeated F in the bass in bars 11–14 not only keeps the march beat going but also functions as a **dominant pedal**.

The melody also uses the intervals of the fourth and seventh that we analysed in the introductory fanfare bars. For example, the second half of bar 12 uses the falling fourth interval in scalic form from Eb to Bb. This same pattern occurs from the end of bar 13 and into bar 14 when the melody is repeated. Also notice the fourth at bar 15 (F down to C) and, as before, the use of the fourth and seventh in bar 16 last beat (C to B♮ is a major seventh, Eb to Ab is a perfect fourth and B♮ to melody note Eb is a diminished fourth) to bar 17 first beat (bass C to F then the F to Bb is a perfect fourth and this B to Eb is a perfect fourth which forms quartal harmony).

The crescendo in bar 17 to **ff** at bar 18 leads to a full orchestra three-bar linking section before the theme returns at bar 21. Bar 18 is a strong contrary-motion dotted-rhythm figure landing on a strong dominant seventh chord at bar 19. The horns and lower brass pound out the chord in triplets, taken over by the trumpet and strings in bar 20. The slowing down in bar 20 (**rit.**) takes us straight into the opening section of the *Star Wars* theme again.

Bars 21–29   Reprise of main *Star Wars* theme – Section A1

The theme is played by the full orchestra. The accompanying chords feature the triplet figuration and off-beat rhythms. See bar 23 as a good example of both of these features. The bass reiterates strong tonic and dominant notes, Bb and F. The section ends slightly differently this time, at bars 28 and 29. The trumpet triplet figure at bar 28 now rises in pitch to a dominant F major chord on beat 2. The beat 1 triplet chords provide chromatic interest. Look at how the B♭ is chromatic (meaning it is not in the key) but is followed by a B♮ in the next chord. And the horns quote part of the melody below the sustained dominant F major chord. This melodic phrase stands out above the full orchestra as other parts have rests. This also helps the harp **glissando** (fast scale) to be heard in bar 29 too. This is the end of the title theme tune and the 'Rebel Blockade Runner' section now starts with a key change to three flats.

Bars 30–35   Link

Bars 30–35 have similar ingredients to the opening fanfare. The strong repeating Fs in the bass continue as the brass play triplet broken-chord figurations. Again, notice the build-up in fourths in bar 30 over the bass F to add B♭ then E♭ then A♭ in the brass triplets. As before, this creates **quartal harmony**. This is used in chords, too, for example on the last beat of bar 30.

The strings take over the triplet idea, this time extending to sextuplet groupings playing a swiftly ascending figure in (**compound**) thirds. The trombones, tuba and timpani join in with a crescendo on a chord made up mostly of fourths at the end of bar 32.

The following three bars (33–35) take us through some chromatic chords:

> **Glossary**
>
> **Compound interval**: one extending over more than an octave. A compound third could be a tenth, or a seventeenth and so on up.

Bar 33 is a D♭ chord, D♭–F–A♭ plus the major seventh (C) and sharpened ninth (E♭), giving the chord D♭maj7♯9.

Bar 34 is an unrelated chord of A minor.

Bar 35 is an augmented chord of A♭–C–E♮.

The chords help to unsettle us as the music moves from bright heroic major keys to dark and uncertain, even sinister, tonality. Above these chords, the violins and harp play triplet and demisemiquaver broken chords as the dynamic level gets softer and softer to reach *piano* in bar 36.

Bars 36–38   'Rebel Blockade Runner' theme

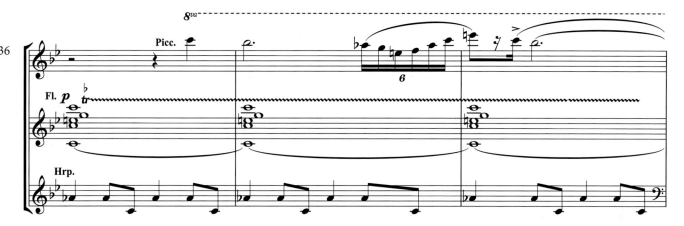

These are three very quiet bars in what is generally a very loud piece. Note values have lengthened to make these three bars feel almost static and 'spacy'. The space feel is achieved by the very high pitch of the piccolo. All other parts are in the treble clef, with simple accompaniment from the harp and sustained and tied C major woodwind chords. In the flute part the high C trills add to the eeriness of the music at this point. Notice that the sextuplet grouping is still present in the piccolo melody. During this section of music the rate of chord changes (called the harmonic rhythm) slows down. The tonality of this section is based on a six-note scale called hexatonic. This tonality also features in the 'Defying Gravity' song.

Bars 39–41   Link

Another three-bar link suddenly propels the music forward. This literally interrupts the quiet reflective bars with a sudden jolt to *forte* in bar 39 by the strings and brass chords. The sextuplet groupings take flight as the patterns ascend in pitch. The bass part repeats each two beats as an **ostinato**. The brass build up an unrelated C major chord (in second inversion), creating a sense of drama and expectation. The dynamics crescendo throughout bar 41 to herald the final section of music.

Glossary

Ostinato: a persistent phrase or motif repeated over several bars or more.

Commentary on bars 42–56

Bars 42–50   March

Following the dramatic build up in texture in the previous three bars, the bare octave Cs of bar 42 temporarily take the heat out of the music. However, marked *ff*, the timpani and basses pound out a military-sounding rhythm to the accompaniment of tutti (full orchestra) chords. The bass of the entire last section is centred on a long repeated pedal C (replaced twice with the dominant G).

The chords are quite chromatic. For instance, in bar 43 there is a B♭ chord followed by a G major chord followed by a D♭ major chord. The common denominator is that they are *all major chords*, adding strength to this final section.

The metre changes to $\frac{3}{4}$ at bar 44 and the triplet chords dominate. From this point to the end, rhythm and harmony rather than melody conjure up a warlike feel. From bar 43 up to the end of bar 50 the music comprises just one chord, added to in rising pitches.

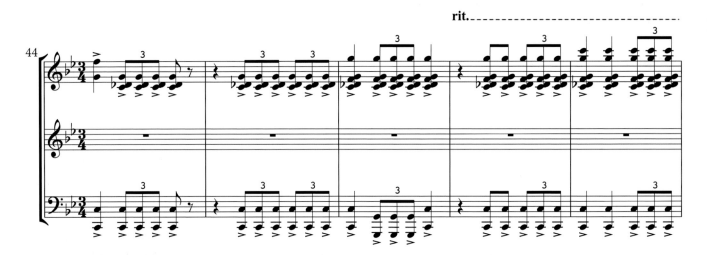

Glossary

Rit./ritardando: slowing down.

Neapolitan chord: a chord built on the flattened supertonic note.

The notes are C–D♭–F–G. Within this chord are *two sets* of fourths, C–F (perfect fourth) and D♭–G (augmented fourth)!

The music grinds to a dramatic stop and pause on the last beat of bar 50 with a three-bar **ritardando** (slowing up).

Bars 51–60   Codetta

These last few bars return to a very fast tempo. Each bar contains a rhythm of two crotchets and a group of triplet quavers. These form a driving ostinato over which are punctuated chords. The D♭ chords in bars 53–56 are built on the **flattened supertonic note** in C major. D is the supertonic, so the flattened supertonic is D♭. The chord based on this note is called the **Neapolitan chord**. Its effect is to temporarily take the music out of key. More chromatic F♭ major chords follow at bars 56–58, before the last triplet Cs are sounded in the bass. This is a dramatic and highly charged final section. It does not develop: instead, the music suddenly reduces to *pp* and ends on a long sustained pedal C. This will lead into the next **cue**.

Wider listening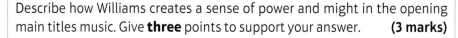

The driving march rhythms of the last 16 bars of the set work sound similar to the dramatic rhythm used in Gustav Holst's 'Mars' from *The Planets Suite* (1914–16). Mars was the Roman god of war and the music, like the *Star Wars* piece, evokes strong, warlike images.

Listen to this movement for similarities to and differences from the *Star Wars* music.

Exam-style question

Describe how Williams creates a sense of power and might in the opening main titles music. Give **three** points to support your answer.　　**(3 marks)**

Exam tip

The key thing to remember is that you need to make **three** points. Think chronologically in the music as you list your points. What happens at the start? (Opening brass and percussion fanfare set scene. This is very loud and sets an heroic and ceremonial mood.) What happens next? (Main theme is played – again *forte* (loud) dynamics, strong melody based on triads that repeats for emphasis. Use of triplets in the rhythm – military sounding etc.)

Wider listening

Deborah Lurie: 'The Pier', 'Walk on the Beach', and 'Dear John Letter' from *Dear John*

The 2010 film *Dear John* is an American romantic war film starring Amanda Seyfield and Channing Tatum. It is an adaptation of Nicholas Sparks's 2006 novel of the same name. The musical score was composed by Deborah Lurie. She is an American composer and arranger who has had success with a number of other films including *Justin Bieber: Never Say Never*.

The film is about a soldier called John Tyree who is home on leave. The love story centres on him and Savannah Curtis, a college student he meets. The film spans seven years of their relationship. With John often away on dangerous combat missions, they stay in touch through letters that unfortunately lead to a fateful ending…

The music to each of the three suggested listening pieces – 'The Pier', 'Walk on the Beach' and 'Dear John Letter' – has similar features. Each is played at a sedate or Andante tempo. Each one is also in a major key (the key of G), with a simple homophonic accompaniment and a diatonic melody organised into regular eight-bar phrases. Listen for the folky sound of the fiddle using open D and G strings and the pitch-bending on some of the notes in the first two pieces. There are some blue notes, too, giving the music its Cajun, Deep South American folk feeling. The influence of Scots and Irish folk tradition is another apparent influence on the music. The pieces are all short (between 1 and 2 minutes) and conjure up a relaxing and romantic mood, suitable to the film. They are in total contrast to the *Star Wars* music.

Howard Shore: 'The Prophecy', 'Concerning Hobbits', 'The Bridge of Khazad Dum' and 'The Breaking of the Fellowship' from *The Lord of the Rings: The Fellowship of the Ring.*

The Lord of the Rings: The Fellowship of the Ring: Original Motion Picture Soundtrack was released on 20 November 2001. It was composed, orchestrated and conducted by Howard Shore and performed by the London Philharmonic Orchestra. The music is composed very much in the way opera is written, with over 90 leitmotifs (short themes) across all three films relating directly to the characters and subject matter of the plot. Listen to this selection of pieces from the first film in the trilogy and compare them to each other in terms of mood, orchestration, melody, rhythm, tonality, etc. How different are these pieces from the *Star Wars* set work?

Checkpoint

Strengthen

S1 Describe what you understand by quartal harmony.

S2 How does background music (underscoring) enhance the moving pictures on screen? Give **two** contrasting examples from the score to illustrate your points.

S3 Name **three** ways in which Williams creates a grand opening to this main title music.

Challenge

C1 Compare this music with the title music to *Raiders of the Lost Ark*, also by John Williams. What are the similarities in the title music of these two films?

C2 Now compare the *Star Wars* music with the title music to *Schindler's List*. This time explore the many *differences* between the pieces. Why are there so many?

Summary of the key musical features

Key points to remember:

- Film music as in this set work is background music, referred to as **underscoring**. It adds to the **mood** of the scene, reinforcing **dramatic developments** and aspects of **character**. The music is called underscoring as it accompanies (plays 'under') moving pictures, in this case the rolling credits in the opening story of *Star Wars*. The complete section of music – that is, the 'Main Title/Rebel Blockade Runner' themes – is called a **cue**.

- The piece starts with an introductory three-bar **fanfare** followed by the **main *Star Wars* theme**. A fanfare is a celebratory piece often marking the opening of an important event or ceremony. The music of the fanfare is scored for **brass** instruments and often **percussion** and is **short** and played **loudly**.

- The **main theme** is in a three-part **ternary** structure. There then follows a **link** section taking us to the 'Rebel Blockade Runner' theme. Another short link takes us into the **'March'** and the piece concludes with a short **codetta** to round off the cue.

- Williams uses some common devices in his harmony. **Fourths and sevenths** are important intervals throughout the piece. In addition, **quartal harmony** can be seen in many bars. This is harmony produced by chords built on intervals of **superimposed fourths**. The chord in bar 2 is a good example, made up of the notes F–Bb–Eb–Ab. Williams also uses **added sixth chords**. This is a major or minor **triad** with a sixth added. The two chords in bar 12 are Eb major chords, with the notes Eb–G–Bb plus the added sixth C. This added sixth chord is common in jazz. Finally, there are **Neapolitan chords** in bars 53–56, built on the **flattened supertonic note** in C major. D is the supertonic, which makes Db the flattened supertonic.

- Williams uses **leitmotifs** (a recurring musical idea which is associated with a particular theme, character or place). The main melody is associated with Luke Skywalker. It is a **strong**, **bold**, even **heroic** theme, and is of course suited to the character it represents. It is played at the outset by the **full symphony orchestra**. The melody is in the key of **Bb major**. It is **diatonic** and the opening **perfect fifth** from tonic Bb to dominant F is **strong**. Notice, too, the intervals of the **fourth** and **seventh** in both the melody and harmony. Elements from the fanfare add to the power of the melody – for example, the **triplets**.

- The 'Rebel Blockade Runner' theme provides a strong **contrast** to the main theme. It is much **quieter**, **lighter in texture** and **very slow** in tempo. It uses **longer note values** to achieve a **static** feeling. Note the **high piccolo** writing and light accompaniment from the harp. All other parts are in the treble clef with sustained and tied C major woodwind chords. The **high C trills** in the flute part add to the **eeriness** of the music.

- The 'March' sees a return to a robust and *fortissimo* mood, with the timpani and basses pounding out a military-sounding rhythm to the accompaniment of **tutti** (full orchestra) **chords**. The bass features a long **pedal** of C, replaced twice with the dominant G. Other features include **driving ostinato**, **changing metre**, **triplets**, **chromatic chords**, and chords built on **fourths** again.

- The **codetta** is a short end section featuring a very fast tempo and the driving ostinato of two crochets and a group of triplet quavers. This is a dramatic and highly charged final section, though one which does not develop further. The music suddenly reduces to *pp* and ends on a long sustained pedal C. This will lead into the next cue in the film sequence.

Afro Celt Sound System: 'Release' from
the album *Volume 2: Release*

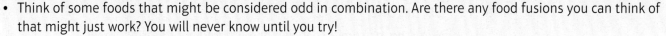

Getting started

- Think of some foods that might be considered odd in combination. Are there any food fusions you can think of that might just work? You will never know until you try!
- What musical combinations might be considered odd? Are there any two styles that could never work together under any circumstances?

Learning objectives

In the study of this set work you will learn about:

- the Afro Celt Sound System and the background to 'Release'
- how to analyse 'Release'
- music technology as a musical element
- the key musical features.

Musical contexts

The formation of the Afro Celt Sound System

The Afro Celt Sound System is more of a collaborative musical collective than a band. It began in 1995 as an experiment by Simon Emmerson to see what would happen if he brought together expert musicians from different cultures and let them improvise over some **techno** drum **grooves**. Stunned by the results, the four founder members and key contributors to the collective (Emmerson, James McNally, Iarla Ó Lionáird and producer Martin Russell) took it to Peter Gabriel's Real World Studios where a recording week is held to allow people from all over the world to come together and inspire each other, form links and record some new and original music. The **fusion** of Irish and African cultures was what originally inspired Emmerson. In that one week when they recorded most of the first album, the musicians didn't all share the same spoken language, communicating largely through their music, but the results proved that the concept worked. The resulting album, *Volume 1: Sound Magic*, was released in 1996 after they finished off the recording. The music critic Tim Sheridan described the album as 'a sort of hip-hop jig and reel, like the Chieftains meet the Chemical Brothers'. The group then toured with various personnel for the next two years, building up their audience and their live show to critical acclaim.

Background to 'Release'

In 1997, as they were preparing to record their second album, one of their keyboard players, Jo Bruce (the son of Jack Bruce from the band Cream), died suddenly. This tragedy almost stopped the project from happening, but when they were in the recording studio, Sinéad O'Connor happened to be in the same studio complex. She met with the group and contributed some lyrics in keeping with its collective nature. The lyrics took a different view of the tragedy and inspired the group to continue with what they were doing. O'Connor was invited to sing her lyrics, so she is the female vocalist you can hear on this set work.

Glossary

Techno: a style of electronic music.

Groove: in the context of the text this is a drum loop. It can also mean 'rhythmic feel'.

Fusion: the blending of two or more musical styles, usually from different cultures.

Close analysis of 'Release'

Structure

Note: the instruments shown here in **bold** are described later.

Time	Section	Phrase structure and general points
0:00	Introduction	A synth **pad drone** with filter sweeps establishes the key. A talking drum solo joins in. There is no **metre**. A shaker starts to introduce the rhythm, but the pulse isn't really clear until…
0:48		12 bars – a **bodhrán** rhythm helps us to feel the pulse. Male, African, spoken vocals are heard in the texture.
1:17		8 bars in which a simple **kora** riff can be heard twice over the loops.
1:38	Verse 1	8 bars: Sinéad O'Connor sings the first line of the verse (this whole verse is in English). Each line is split into two-bar phrases.
1:55		8 bars: second line of the verse. The instrumentation gradually builds up.
2:15		8 bars, with an ascending chromatic line from G to B♭ (two bars per note).
2:34	Break	8 bars of bodhrán, bass guitar, percussion and breath **sample**.
2:55	Verse 2	8 bars: Iarla Ó Lionáird sings this verse in Gaelic (not notated in the Pearson Anthology). He splits the phrases a little more irregularly than O'Connor.
3:12		8 bars: second line of the verse.
3:31		8 bars with the ascending chromatic line. Ó Lionáird's phrasing generally anticipates the beat and soars over the other parts. The bass drops out.
3:51	Solos 1 and 2	8 bars: **uilleann pipes** solo (doubled by the **tin whistle** in the second four bars).
4:10		8 bars: low whistle solo over the ascending chromatic line. The bass drops out and the bodhrán part is much simpler and sparser.
4:29	Break	2 bars of repeated vocal sample with the accordion rhythm as the main driving force while most of the other parts drop out.
4:34	Solo 3	8 bars: **hurdy-gurdy** solo with vocal sample (the other parts join in again).
4:55	Verse 3	8 bars: this is the same as the second line of the first verse (with O'Connor singing), but the hurdy-gurdy solo continues in the background.
5:12		8 bars: the same as the third line of the first verse with the uilleann pipes solo added.
5:31		8 bars: the same as the third line of the second verse (the ascending chromatic line) with a slightly different rhythm in the last four bars.
5:51	**Build/Outro**	4 bars: bass guitar, bodhrán and drum **loop**.
6:00		8 bars: interweaving loops of plucked and electronic instruments – more are added in the second four bars.
6:19		8 bars: another hurdy-gurdy solo accompanied by wordless vocals, joined in the second four bars by the uilleann pipes.
6:38		8 bars: a subtle version of the ascending chromatic line which is buried under the ostinatos played by the other instruments.
6:59		8 bars then loop to fade: the third line of verse 1 (with the ascending chromatic line) followed by the interweaving loops of plucked and electronic instruments to fade.

'Release' gives the feeling of being improvised and, indeed, many of the melodic lines are improvised, but the structure is carefully constructed to allow some relatively simple ideas to be extended over 7 minutes of music. Unlike some of the other set works, where tonality is a major factor in the structure, this song relies on how the texture evolves over time. The sense of direction is maintained by the use of build-ups through the different sections. The ascending chromatic line at the end of most sections also gives a feeling of increasing tension.

The structure is not the normal verse–chorus structure of a pop song, and the term 'verse' is used here mainly for convenience. It is an evolving structure that uses the sung sections as an anchor for the instrumental sections. The last section listed in the table is the build/outro section. This can all be considered as an outro or it can be viewed as another instrumental build-up followed by a short **coda** (the final eight bars). However, it seems appropriate to view the whole passage as a balancing section to the long introduction; both are of a similar length and both are mainly instrumental with some wordless vocals and vocal samples.

This sort of music can be described accurately in several ways. It is not like the music of the Baroque, Classical and Romantic eras, which – after centuries of study – has a generally agreed set of terms to describe its structure. In tackling this set piece in an exam, you will be given credit for any well-justified structural analysis; or in a short-answer question several equally valid options will be given in the mark scheme.

Tonality and harmony

From the very beginning of the track, the scene is set by a synth drone on the note C. This note persists almost throughout the track, so it is safe to say that the song is in the key of C, though it is not clear whether this is major or minor until the wordless vocals come in. Gradually, as more and more parts join in, the following notes can be heard:

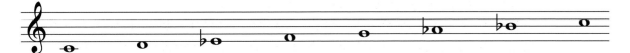

This is the Aeolian **mode** (transposed to begin on the note C), so the piece can be said to be **modal**. It would be acceptable to say that the song is in the key of C minor (and in fact the key signature in any notated score will reflect this), but it would be more accurate to say that it is in C Aeolian. Normally, in the key of C minor you would expect some B♮s to allow for the use of the G major triad (the dominant triad), but if B♭s are present then the dominant triad will be G minor, giving a modal sound. Most music that is strongly influenced by the folk music tradition of the British Isles will have a modal flavour.

> **Glossary**
>
> **Pad**: a synthesiser sound designed to be used in chords as opposed to lead lines.
>
> **Drone**: a continuously held or repeated note, usually low in pitch.
>
> **Metre**: the number of beats in a bar and how they are subdivided.
>
> **Sample**: a pre-recorded segment of sound, often manipulated in some way.
>
> **Loop**: a short repeated passage, often involving electronic drums.
>
> **Build**: in the context of the text this refers to the gradual introduction of more instruments.
>
> **Coda**: a section sometimes added at the end of a piece or movement.

> **Activity** ❓
>
> Try playing scales on a keyboard using just the white notes and starting each scale on a different note. These will all be in different **modes**.

Despite the fact that the C drone continues through almost the entire piece (it stops briefly when the synth, accordion, fiddle and hurdy-gurdy all stop playing), the tonality is not the same throughout. During the uilleann pipes solo, the Dorian mode is used. This differs from the Aeolian mode in that the sixth is not flattened:

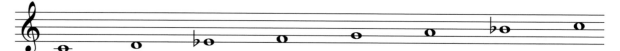

This mode has a slightly different sound – it still sounds modal, but as the sixth is not flattened, it has a particular flavour. This is because the triad built on the subdominant (the fourth degree of the scale) will be a major chord – in this case, F major.

Listen to the uilleann pipes solo (3:51 to 4:10)

There is a quiet synth part in the accompaniment that plays the following:

The presence of the A♮ gives a C Dorian tonality.

The second bar of the hurdy-gurdy solo (approximately 4:36) is another example that you might find a little easier to hear. It is repeated several times.

Can you find any other examples of the use of the Dorian mode in the piece?

Chords

Although this track is clearly influenced by Western popular music in its use of technology, instrumentation and drum loops, etc., it does not contain chord sequences in the same way. When you analyse 'Killer Queen', there are clear chord sequences that help to determine how the piece is structured. In 'Release', the harmony is mostly determined by which melodies happen to be playing at the time.

Why is this?

- The synth parts often contain chords, but these are sometimes open fifths (containing the notes C and G only) and are generally part of the background texture, so are rather quiet in the overall mix.
- The accordion has a rhythmic **riff** that drives through much of the piece consisting of a repeated C minor chord.

- The hurdy-gurdy has a rhythmic part that drones on the note C.
- The bass guitar plays a repeating riff, frequently repeating the tonic note of C.
- The only time the harmony really changes is during the ascending chromatic passage at the end of most sections, but even here, the C drone is reinforced by several parts.
- Several instruments play **ostinatos** – even the solos are repeated.

If the chords were to change in a way that would be recognisable as a chord sequence, at least some of the chords would clash horribly with all the other music going on. Hence, although other chords are hinted at, everything is based on the C drone.

The harmony is said to be **static**.

> ## Glossary
>
> **Ostinato**: a persistent phrase or motif repeated over several bars or more.
>
> **Static harmony**: when the harmony remains on a single chord for a prolonged period of time.

Instrumentation and sonority

Listen to the solos (3:51 to 4:53)

Describe the sound of the three main solo instruments during this passage:

1 the uilleann pipes – 3:51 to 4:10
2 the low whistle (a large tin whistle) – 4:10 to 4:29
3 the hurdy-gurdy – 4:34 to 4:53

Try to be as detailed as possible when you describe the sound:

- Is it soft or harsh?
- Does it sound as if it is blown, plucked, bowed or struck?
- How do the notes start and end?
- Are there any note bends or other techniques used?
- Are there many changes in dynamics?
- Are there any odd features of the sound, or mechanical noises?

- The **uilleann pipes** are played by pumping bellows which are placed under the arm (rather than blowing into them as with Scottish bagpipes). Their name translates as 'elbow pipes', referring to the way they are played. They are the national bagpipe of Ireland and have a much sweeter, quieter sound than other bagpipes. The 'chanter' is the part of the bagpipe that looks a bit like a recorder, with holes that the player covers and uncovers to create the different pitches. On the uilleann pipes, the chanter can cover a range of two octaves with chromatic notes. There are also three 'regulators' on a full set of pipes which are like the drones on a set of bagpipes; these can be turned on or off and the pitch can be changed, allowing simple chords to be played.

Uilleann pipes

A hurdy-gurdy

A kora

A bodhrán

- The **hurdy-gurdy** is sometimes called the 'wheel-fiddle' because it looks a little bit like a violin and the player sounds the notes by using a crank to turn a wheel which rubs against the strings (instead of a bow). Hurdy-gurdies often have drone strings so that they can create a bagpipe-like effect. A little keyboard attached to what would normally be the fingerboard of a violin lets the performer change the pitch of the melody notes by pressing wedges of wood called 'tangents' against the strings. They are common in various European folk music traditions.

- The **kora** is a West-African string instrument that looks like a cross between a harp and a lute. It normally has 21 strings, which are plucked in a similar way to a harp, though the playing style is generally more like a guitar than a harp. Kora performers often come from storytelling families known as 'griot' families. This is the case with the Afro Celt's kora player, N'Faly Kouyaté, whose voice is heard in the introduction.

- The **bodhrán** is a frame drum from Ireland that is played with a double-headed stick known as the 'bone' or 'tipper'. The pitch can be altered by applying pressure to the skin with the hand that holds the drum.

One of the key features of this set work is the way the instrumental sounds combine in a way that probably had not been heard before. Instruments that were normally restricted to use within their own cultures were being integrated with each other and with electronic sounds and looped drum parts. Through the 20th century, songwriters and composers had been searching around the world for different sounds that they could use in their works. The concept of bringing a kora or a set of uilleann pipes into some music other than their standard African or Irish context was not new, but when the first Afro Celts album was released, this particular combination of instruments used in this way was a fresh idea that had a profound impact on all who heard it. People were amazed that the different musical cultures could gel in such a seamless way and that the performers could improvise together when music was their only common language.

Exam-style question

Make a list under the headings 'Africa', 'Ireland', 'European folk' and 'Western popular music' and place the instruments in this recording in the appropriate columns. **(8 marks)**

Exam tip

You need to be able to recognise the instruments used in this piece and to divide them into the parts of the world they come from.

Other than the instruments from Africa and Ireland, there are also synthesisers, the bass guitar and pre-recorded loops used to create the full-sounding texture. The use of synthesisers and loops will be discussed in the music technology section.

Rhythm, metre and tempo

The introduction of 'Release' starts with no regular pulse – it is free and has no metre. The sense of metre begins when the shaker loop enters approximately 26 seconds into the track. The talking drum solo is used more for effect than for creating a pulse as it does not provide a steady beat. Since the talking drum is much more in the forefront of the mix than the shaker loop, the regular pulse is not obvious until the bodhrán enters after 48 seconds. From here, the tempo remains the same throughout the song (100 beats per minute).

The bodhrán rhythm is the rhythmic backbone of the track against which the other rhythms work. It is syncopated and is elaborated on slightly during the piece, but the basic one-bar rhythmic ostinato remains the same throughout:

The real rhythmic drive is provided by the player accenting some of the notes (although this is not marked in the music). If all the notes were played at the same volume, the rhythm would be really dull.

Other rhythmic ostinatos interweave with this rhythm, creating a **polyrhythmic** texture (one with several simultaneous rhythms). One of the most obvious can be heard in the accordion part (listen from 4:10 to 4:34):

A talking drum

The rhythmic interest is created by the combination of the accented notes in both parts (and in the other driving, rhythmic parts). Since the accents are on different parts of the beat, there is a sense of movement between the different parts of the texture, rippling under the main melodic parts. Notice how both of these rhythms are based on splitting the beat into four semiquavers and accenting different semiquavers within the beat. Most of the elaborations in the bodhrán part involve playing more of the semiquavers within the beat – that is, the part becomes a little busier. In keeping with the Irish folk tradition, additional rhythmic interest is added by adding semiquaver triplets, particularly at the end of the bar. Since the rest of the rhythmic drive is straight semiquavers, the triplets are particularly noticeable.

Melody

The melodic content of 'Release' is provided by the two main vocalists and the solo instruments. O'Connor's vocal lines are more repetitive than Ó Lionáird's and fit into regular two-bar phrases.

In general, O'Connor's melodic phrases are based on the initial motif:

The penultimate note is sometimes a B♭, sometimes a C and sometimes somewhere in between! This motif forms the basis of much of the melodic material in the vocal parts. Ó Lionáird's vocal starts with the same motif, which he develops when he sings the higher part over the ascending chromatic line (at 3:31 to 3:40). The range of Ó Lionáird's vocal melody is wider than O'Connor's, spanning the interval of a tenth.

The instrumental solos are based on folk melodies and mostly move in semiquavers. The uilleann pipe solo oscillates around a C, often repeating notes, creating a rather rhythmic feel within the melody itself. This is part of the playing style of the uilleann pipes, showing that the melodies played by certain instruments are often determined by the physical characteristics of that instrument. A melody is said to be idiomatic if it sounds as if it belongs on the instrument playing it.

The low whistle solo is much more flowing than the uilleann pipes solo – there are far fewer repeated notes and the melody has more rhythmic variety. Both solos avoid the use of the sixth degree of the scale (the A♭ or A♮, depending on whether it is the Aeolian or Dorian mode).

The hurdy-gurdy solo contains A♮s in the second bar of the loop, so at this point it is in C Dorian, though in using A♭s later on it shifts to C Aeolian. Shifting tonality like this within a single melody line is common in folk music.

Texture

'Release' has a layered texture that makes use of music technology to blend the parts together and to fade them into and out of the mix. In general the texture evolves through the different sections with any abrupt changes carefully placed for maximum effect.

In the introduction:

1 We first hear a synth pad drone with a filter sweep effect.
2 More synth parts are subtly added, thickening the texture almost imperceptibly because our ears are drawn to the addition of the talking drum.
3 Then a shaker rhythm is added and an African vocal in the 'griot' storytelling style enters.
4 As the talking drum stops, the bodhrán enters along with some other percussion loops.
5 Then the female voice with a wordless melody replaces the mostly spoken male African voice.

In verse 1:

As each eight-bar phrase begins, more parts are added. Note that the bass guitar has not yet entered. Obviously, it is not good just to keep adding parts indefinitely, so in bars 7 and 8 of the last eight-bar phrase, several parts drop out. This makes the entry of the bass guitar more dramatic, because it is taking over from several other instruments instead of fighting them for space (and our attention) in the **mix**. Similar textural effects occur in the other verses.

Textural effects

One of the more striking textural effects in the set work occurs during the rising chromatic line at the end of the verses and the second solo: the bass guitar drops out (along with some other instruments). Why is this so striking? The bass guitar provides most of the sound in the lowest part of the register. Psychologically, it feels like the rest of the track builds on this foundation. We don't notice this in the introduction because the bass has not yet made its entrance but, after we have heard it in context, it is rather jarring when this is removed. We expect that the bass will return at some point. This, when combined with the rising chromatic line, creates a real sense of anticipation.

This effect is perhaps at its most striking before the solos enter. In the last two bars of verse 2, many parts drop out (in addition to the bass which stopped several bars earlier). This is almost a held breath or a pause before the entrance of the uilleann pipes solo and the return of the bass guitar along with several of the other parts.

Music technology as a musical element

It would be very difficult to recreate the textural effects described above without the use of music technology. Layering parts is a very natural process when using multi-track recording techniques because of the way multi-track recorders are set up. Microphones and sound sources are routed to individual tracks, which are generally recorded separately. Other parts are added on different takes, building up the potential layers in the piece. Often some of what is recorded is not used because the producer decides that it does not suit the piece at that point – this is achieved by the simple method of muting or fading out the part.

Mixing is the art of balancing all the recorded parts, panning them to different points in the **stereo field** (where they are positioned from left to right), and applying certain effects such as reverb and delay to make the parts sound as if they are in a real space rather than a small studio. An example of mixing in action can be heard at the end of the hurdy-gurdy solo – when the hurdy-gurdy is the solo part, it is at the front of the mix (meaning it is louder), but when the vocals enter it is turned down a little so that it does not detract from the vocals, which are now the main part. Mixing techniques like this are used many times through the piece, mostly in very subtle ways which you will not notice unless you listen out for them specifically.

> ### Glossary
>
> **Mix**: the relative volume of the different parts in a recording and their place in the stereo field.

> ### Exam tip
>
> The process of gradual (and not so gradual) changes in texture is repeated with variations several times throughout the track, so there is no need to go through each section in detail. In your exam you will hear an extract from the piece and may be asked to describe the texture. It is important to be able to *listen* to how instruments are added to and taken away from the texture rather than just *learning* information by rote. Practise this by starting the track from a random position and describing the textural changes in detail over the space of 30 to 40 seconds. This will require you to be able to identify each of the instruments aurally.

Spot the panning

Listen to verse 3 through headphones. On a piece of paper, draw a diagram of where the different parts are in the stereo field.

Another aspect of music technology that plays a significant role in this set work is the use of synthesisers and loops.

Synthesisers

Abbreviated to 'synths', these are devices that can be programmed to create different sorts of timbres. In this piece they are mostly used to create sustaining pad sounds for chords and drones. In the introduction, the timbre is altered during the note to create the filter sweep effect – different parts of the frequency range are emphasised as the control is moved. Synths can also be used to create timbres that are similar to acoustic instruments but are much easier to adjust. Some synths can also take sounds from acoustic instruments (samples) and edit these either subtly so that they sound like the original source, or not so subtly so that they are unrecognisable as the original sound.

Loops

There are many loops used in 'Release'. Many of these will have been pre-recorded for the musicians to improvise over. The electronic plucked sounds, most of the percussion sounds and most of the synth parts will have been pre-recorded as loops. The producer (Martin Russell) can then position these as he sees fit. The live, improvised parts will have been recorded and some of these will have been used as loops after the initial recording session.

Wider listening

In addition to this set work you should also listen to the following:

Capercaillie: 'Beautiful Wasteland' from _Beautiful Wasteland_

Released in 1997, _Beautiful Wasteland_ is Capercaillie's seventh studio album. Like most of their other albums, it contains a mixture of songs sung in Gaelic, songs sung in English and instrumentals. It received the 'Album of the Year' accolade from the music magazines _Mojo_ and _Folk Roots_ and was generally a critical success. In a similar way to the Afro Celt Sound System, Capercaillie marry elements of Celtic music and Western popular music without diluting the essence of their roots, hence bringing the music to a wider audience than would generally listen to it. Unlike the Afro Celts, Capercaillie are not a musical collective, with the lineup remaining largely stable (with a few members coming and going) since their formation in 1984.

The title song, 'Beautiful Wasteland', is a pop song with Celtic tinges (such as the use of uilleann pipes), while 'Hebridean Hale-Bopp' is a modern take on three folk songs featuring vocalist Karen Matheson's virtuosity, and 'Kepplehall/25Kts' shows off the band's instrumental credentials. The song 'Thiocfadh Leat Fanacht' has most similarities with the Afro Celts in that the band has invited the female duo Sibeba from Equatorial Guinea to contribute vocals.

Demet Akalın: 'Pırlanta' from *Pırlanta*

Demet Akalın is a Turkish singer, model and actress who started her singing career in 1996 at the age of 25. The album *Pırlanta* was released in 2015, and this song is the title track. It combines elements of Turkish music with modern popular music production. The use of multi-layered, 'choppy' synthesiser sounds, a four-to-the-floor bass drum, heavy compression and filters show that this track is intended to be played in clubs and danced to. It also includes the tonality of Turkish music and some synthesised sounds as well as sounds sampled from Turkish folk instruments.

Demet Akalın: 'Ders Olsun' from *Pırlanta*

This track is perhaps more of a fusion than 'Pırlanta'. There is some very complex production in the track, again with synthesisers and drum loops that would be at home in a club, but the samples of Turkish folk instruments are brought more to the fore, certainly during the **breakdown** where the synth parts drop out to give them more space in the mix.

Glossary

Breakdown: when many of the parts drop out of the musical texture for a short period of time.

Checkpoint

Strengthen

What aspects of 'Release' make it a fusion?

When you are asked an open-ended question like this, split it into the different musical elements. Some musical elements are more relevant than others, depending on what the question is asking for, so in this case focus on the following elements:

1 instrumentation and sonority (timbre)

2 rhythm

3 melody

4 texture

Make at least two points under each element heading, using appropriate musical vocabulary.

Challenge

C1 What are the elements that make African and Irish music work so well together as a fusion?

C2 Why do many popular music productions include instruments sourced from different musical cultures around the world? What challenges would you face in trying to use these instruments in your own compositions?

Area of Study 4: Fusions

Summary of the key musical features

Key points to remember:

Structure

- Intro – Verse 1 – Break – Verse 2 – Solos (including break) – Verse 3 – Build/Outro
- mostly split into eight-bar phrases
- determined mostly by texture rather than tonality.

Tonality and harmony

- modal
- C Aeolian and C Dorian
- static harmony.

Instrumentation and sonority

- synths, bass guitar, percussion and synth loops
- kora and talking drum
- uilleann pipes, bodhrán, tin whistle, low whistle
- fiddle, accordion, hurdy-gurdy
- vocals: male African (mostly spoken), female (in English), male (in Gaelic).

Rhythm, metre and tempo

- $\frac{4}{4}$ time
- mostly straight semiquavers
- use of syncopation and occasional triplets
- polyrhythms
- has no metre at the beginning
- steady tempo after bodhrán entry (100 bpm).

Melody

- vocal melody mostly based on opening motif
- solo parts play melodies based on folk tunes
- idiomatic (suited to the instrument).

Texture

- multi-tracked and layered
- gradual builds
- sudden drop-outs to prepare for new sections.

Music technology as a musical element

- multi-tracking allows for many textural effects
- parts faded in and out and panned in stereo field
- synths and pre-recorded loops used extensively
- reverb used on all parts to create a sense of space.

Esperanza Spalding:
'Samba Em Prelúdio' from
the album *Esperanza*

Learning objectives

In the study of this set work you will learn about:

- Esperanza Spalding and the background to 'Samba Em Prelúdio'
- Bossa Nova
- how to analyse 'Samba Em Prelúdio'
- the basics of jazz harmony
- the key musical features.

Esperanza Spalding

Glossary

Acoustic guitar: does not require amplification, unlike an electric one.

Musical contexts

Esperanza Spalding

Esperanza Spalding was born in Portland, Oregon, USA on 18 October 1984. She went to the local high school and during her time there experimented with the violin, oboe, clarinet and cello. At 16 she left high school, claiming that she found it 'easy and boring'. By then, however, a teacher at the school had taught her a **riff** (short repeated phrase) on the bass which earned her a first **gig** (paid musical job), so she did owe her school something! Having discovered the bass, Spalding developed a love for the instrument that surpassed her enthusiasm for the other instruments, so this is what she concentrated on, along with her singing.

After leaving school, Spalding became the singer of an **indie band** (a band *independent* of a label) called Noise for Pretend for whom she wrote songs (both music and lyrics), but at the same time she also performed regularly with musicians in a local Blues club. These musicians took her under their collective wing and helped her to develop as a performer.

She later attended Berklee College of Music in Boston, where she studied double bass. After graduating at the age of 20, Spalding was asked to stay on as an instructor, becoming one of the youngest instructors the college had ever had. She then formed a jazz trio with Francisco Mela (drums) and Aruan Ortiz (piano), with whom she recorded the album *Junjo* in 2006. This was mostly instrumental, but showcased her abilities on the bass. She went on to release *Esperanza* in 2008 (from which this set work is taken), *Chamber Music Society* in 2010, and the more Pop-oriented *Radio Music Society* in 2012. In her live shows, Spalding sings and plays double bass, electric bass guitar and **acoustic** bass guitar, the instrument she plays in this set work. She sings in English, Spanish and Portuguese, and has a particular love for the music of Brazil, where Portuguese is spoken.

Spalding won a Grammy Award in 2011 for Best New Artist, the first time a jazz musician had done so. She has since gone on to win several more Grammy Awards in other categories.

The background to 'Samba Em Prelúdio'

This set work is a **cover** of a song written by Roberto Baden Powell de Aquino and Vinícius de Moraes. It was originally intended as a love song performed as a duet between a man and a woman. A Samba is a Brazilian musical style with a signature rhythm (which we will look at in the section on rhythm). The *em* in the title does not refer to the key of the piece, but is Portuguese for 'in'. This piece is not really Samba, but is in a style called Bossa Nova that is closely related to Samba.

Bossa Nova

Literally translated as 'new trend', Bossa Nova is a fusion of Brazilian Samba and American jazz. Antônio Carlos Jobim and João Gilberto were credited with developing the new style in the late 1950s, although figures such as de Moraes were also involved. Then, in 1964, the American saxophonist Stan Getz collaborated with Gilberto on *The Girl from Ipanema*, and Bossa Nova gained widespread popularity beyond the borders of Brazil. The style is essentially a much more laidback version of Samba, with a slowed-down version of the Samba rhythm (see the rhythm section for more details). Bossa Nova was often performed by a soloist accompanying themselves on nylon-string guitar, although the piano, organ, double bass and drums were also frequently used. The self-accompanied examples also featured a return to a Brazilian folk song style of vocal delivery, which was much more nasal and subdued than was the case with Samba. In this set work, the guitar playing is clearly influenced by Flamenco (traditional Spanish) guitar styles, as was the case with some other examples of Bossa Nova using similar instrumentation.

Close analysis of 'Samba Em Prelúdio'

Structure

In jazz, the structure is often determined by the chord sequence, otherwise known as 'the changes'. One statement of the chord sequence is called a 'chorus'. One of the most common structures in jazz is also one of the simplest – a 'head arrangement'. A head arrangement consists of the following elements:

- the main melody (or 'head') is played over the changes
- the soloists take turns to improvise over the changes
- the music finishes with a repeat of the head.

Other music often includes more complex patterns such as verse–chorus format, binary form, ternary form and sonata form, which you will also find in this book.

This set piece, being in fusion style, sits between the two (the simple head arrangement and one of the more complex structural forms) in terms of structure.

The following analysis is only one way to look at how the song has been put together.

Lyrics

English translation by Rodrigo Maltez-Novaes

First stanza

Eu sem você não tenho porquê
Porque sem você não sei nem chorar
Sou chama sem luz, jardim sem luar
Luar sem amor, amor sem se dar

Without you I'm aimless
Because without you, I can't even cry
I'm a flame with no glow, a garden with no moonlight
Moonlight with no love, love with no giving

Second stanza

Eu sem você sou só desamor
Um barco sem mar, um campo sem flor
Tristeza que vai, tristeza que vem
Sem você, meu amor, eu não sou ninguém

Without you I'm only unlove
A boat with no sea, a field with no flower
Sadness that ebbs, sadness that floods
Without you my love, I'm no one

Third stanza

Ai, que saudade
Que vontade de ver renascer nossa vida
Volta querido
Teus abraços precisam dos meus
Os meus braços precisam dos teus

Oh, what longing
A desire to see our life reborn
Come back, darling
Your embraces need mine
My arms need yours

Fourth stanza

Estou tão sozinha
Tenho os olhos cansados de olhar para o além
Vem ver a vida
Sem você, meu amor eu não sou ninguém

I'm so lonely
My eyes have tired of gazing beyond
Come, behold life
Without you, my love, I'm no one

Bar number	Section	Description
1–3	Intro	Bass solo in free tempo
4–21	Verse 1	Bars 4–11: First stanza Bars 12–19: Second stanza Note that these sections are only 8 bars long rather than the 16 bars in the rest of the song – this is because of the slower tempo at this point.
19–22	Break	Bars 19– 21 overlap with the last note of Verse 1. The bass sets the Bossa Nova groove for four bars before the guitar joins in.
23–54	Verse 2	Bars 23–38: Third stanza Bars 39–54: Fourth stanza The chord sequence is played through once for each stanza.
55–87	Instrumental section (not transcribed in the Pearson Anthology)	The guitar **solos** over two sets of the 16-bar chord sequence from Verse 2 with the bass guitar continuing to accompany.
88		The guitar plays an altered B minor chord for one bar before the voice returns.
88–104	Verse 3	Although the guitar drops out, the tempo is maintained – this is not free tempo like the intro. Bars 88–104: Third stanza repeat In bar 104 the marking D.S. al Coda means Dal Segno al Coda (From the Sign to the Coda). This in turn means: 1. Jump back to the Sign (Segno). This is the symbol at the beginning of bar 39. 2. Continue from here to the Coda mark. This is at the end of bar 51. 3. Jump to the Coda. This starts at bar 105.
105–end	Coda	This consists of two repetitions of the last line of the lyrics over **turnaround** chords followed by a guitar flourish.

Exam-style question

1 Both the first and second stanzas start with the phrase, 'Without you…'. The third stanza begins differently, with 'Oh, what longing…'. State two ways in which this change is reflected in the Bossa Nova section starting at bar 19. **(2 marks)**

2 In what other ways does the music match the mood of the lyrics of this song? **(2 marks)**

Glossary

Solo: an extended, improvised melodic line played by a single instrument (guitar, sax, piano, etc.) over a given chord sequence, usually as an interlude in the middle of a song.

Turnaround: a set of (usually four) faster-moving chords to get the music back to a repeated section.

Area of Study 4: Fusions

Glossary

Hi-hat: a pair of cymbals mounted on a special stand so that they can be sounded by pressing a pedal that clamps them together as well as by striking.

Ride: a type of cymbal sometimes used to offer a counter-rhythm to the main beat.

Kick drum: also known as 'bass drum' – the biggest drum in a drum kit, set sideways-on to the audience and drummer. It is played by pressing a pedal which moves a beater to strike the drum skin.

Clave: the rhythm closely associated with the Latin percussion instrument known as 'claves' (short squat sticks that are struck together).

Side sticks: hitting the edge of the snare drum with the sticks held sideways.

Snare: a drum with a series of loosely strung metal wires in contact with the lower skin which create a distinct 'buzzing' or 'rattling' noise when the drum is struck.

Activity ?

Try adding in the imaginary drum part as described here to see if it fits. You might need to split the part between several people to start with as the syncopation can be tricky. Try adding a straight rock beat and see if this fits as naturally as the Bossa Nova beat. If it doesn't, this is because the existing parts do not imply a straight rock beat just as they don't imply a waltz or country groove.

Tonality and harmony

- This piece is in the key of B minor.
- The chords are very rarely simple triads – the main complexity of this set work lies in the use of harmony. A section has been included in this chapter to investigate the basics of jazz harmony as they relate to this piece. You should endeavour to understand as much of it as you can.
- Dissonance is common in this piece owing to the complex nature of the jazz chords, but the dissonance is nonetheless controlled, and resolved according to the conventions of jazz harmony.

Instrumentation and sonority

In this set work, the instrumentation is rather stripped back. This is similar to the more mellow Bossa Nova tracks of the early 1960s.

- female vocal
- acoustic bass guitar
- nylon-string acoustic guitar.

Listen

After you have listened to this song on the CD, listen to 'Music for a While' and 'Killer Queen'. Try to decide which song most resembles this one, (1) in terms of rhythm, then (2) in terms of harmony, then (3) in terms of texture.

Rhythm, metre and tempo

Antônio Carlos Jobim often quoted Debussy's saying, 'Music is the silence between the notes'.

Rhythm

With a stripped-down instrumentation, the arranger leaves it to the listener to 'feel' notes and parts that are not included (which humans subconsciously do). As mentioned previously, the rhythm in this set work is based on the Bossa Nova rhythm, but this is implied rather than clearly stated in any one part. It is easy to imagine a drum kit playing straight quavers on the **hi-hat** or the **ride** cymbal with a repeated dotted crotchet–quaver figure in the **kick drum** and a **clave** rhythm played as **side sticks** on the **snare**:

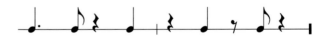

Bossa Nova groove

The dotted crotchet–quaver rhythm that might be expected on the kick drum can be heard frequently in the bass part from bar 19 onwards.

A typical Salsa groove would be:

156

If you double the note lengths, you can perhaps see some similarity between the two grooves and how the syncopated Salsa rhythm has developed into the Bossa Nova groove.

The notated music in the Pearson Anthology is a transcription of the music recorded by Esperanza Spalding's band. The rhythms that they played would have felt natural – they would all be responding to the same request to create a Bossa Nova groove. When the rhythms are transcribed they look much more complicated than they would feel for the performing musician. In fact, it is likely that the musicians would have had only a chord chart to read from rather than any staff notation, so they would have been improvising not just the groove but also the chord voicings and any additional fills and solos.

Metre and tempo
- The track starts in free tempo, but it does have a metre – the pulse is pulled around freely, but the music can be readily written in a straightforward time signature.
- By bar 4 the music is clearly in $\frac{4}{4}$ metre, although the tempo is still somewhat '**tempo rubato**'.
- By bar 19, the pulse becomes steady and the instruments lock into the Bossa Nova groove.

Melody
- The melody is **syllabic** throughout the song. This may be because the singer is also playing her bass guitar and so has to concentrate on the bass lines rather than on improvising **melismatic** vocal lines.
- At the beginning of the track Spalding sings ascending **broken chords**. The bass and voice are working together to create a sense of harmony even though they are (mostly) performing single notes.
- From verse 2 onwards, the melody contains mostly stepwise movement.
- The melody often consists of the highest notes of the sevenths or of even more **extended chords** (described in a later section). For example, in bar 35 the chord is G♯dim7 and Spalding sings the highest note of the chord, F. In bar 37 the chord is G13 and she sings an E, which is the thirteenth of the chord.
- Occasionally she will sing a note which is a deliberate dissonance with the harmony, such as in bar 44, where the B7 chord clashes with the C in the melody (which is a flattened ninth).

Texture
- The piece begins with a bass guitar solo. It is, however, **monophonic** only at the start of the first bar and end of the third bar, as the open strings are left to ring in the rest of the passage.
- The voice enters in bar 4. The bass alternates between a chordal accompaniment and **counterpoint** with the melody line.
- When the Bossa Nova rhythm is introduced, the guitar and bass are accompanying the melody line but also include **contrapuntal** melodic lines of their own, as would be expected in the style.

Glossary

Tempo rubato: literally means 'robbed time'. This is a technique where the performer can pull back (or speed up) the tempo for expressive effect.

Syllabic: when one note is sung per syllable.

Melismatic: refers to vocal melody with several or even many notes per syllable.

Broken chord: when the notes of a chord are played one at a time rather than being sounded simultaneously.

Monophonic: refers to a musical texture comprising a single line which can be sung or played by several people.

Counterpoint: literally means 'tune against tune'. It is the simultaneous combination of two or more melodies with independent rhythms.

Contrapuntal: when two melodies are played 'against' each other and interweave – almost the same as 'polyphonic'; written in counterpoint.

Glossary

Overdubbed: recording an instrumental or vocal part over previously recorded music.

- The texture briefly increases to three parts during the instrumental starting at bar 55 (not transcribed in the Pearson Anthology). It is likely that one guitar part was **overdubbed** during recording and that live shows would have a work-around by the guitarist simplifying the solo a little and adding some chords filling in the gaps.
- The texture drops to the two-part texture of vocal and bass at the start of verse 3. This is even sparser than in verse 1 as the bass is playing fewer notes and no chords.
- The set work ends with a flourish from the guitar as the last vocal note dies away.
- When the texture drops to just the vocal and bass (for example, in verse 3), a sense of intimacy is created with the listener as if we are being invited into the singer's innermost emotions.

The basics of jazz harmony

Refer to the 'Understanding Music' chapter and read the section titled 'Chords and inversions' before continuing with this section.

Jazz harmony can look quite complicated on the page, but a logical system can be applied to understand any jazz chord you encounter.

Western Classical harmony is based on triads:

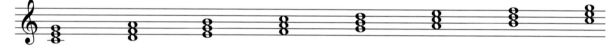

Jazz harmony is based on sevenths:

Jazz chords are named after the root note and whether the seventh (not the chord) is minor or major. Here *major* seventh is abbreviated to *maj*, *minor* seventh to *m* and ♭5 means that the fifth of the chord has been flattened.

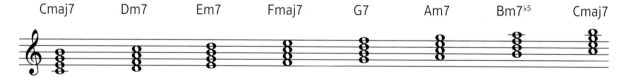

The numbers of the chords are the same (chords I to VII), but this time the name has been given in a different format, as would be more common in jazz music (such as Cmaj7). Each chord has an additional note, continuing the visual pattern of all spaces or all lines and each chord is a type of seventh. Notice how the pattern is 'play one – miss one – play one – miss one – play one – miss one – play one'. This describes what happens when you stack thirds on top of each other, and the same process continues for extending the chords further.

There are four different kinds of jazz shorthand shown in the table below.

Chord	Triad	Seventh interval
Major seventh (C and F or chords I and IV)	Major	Major
Minor seventh (D, E and A or chords II, III and VI)	Minor	Minor
Dominant seventh (G or chord V)	Major	Minor
Half-diminished seventh (B or chord VII)	Diminished	Minor

Extended chords

The seventh chords all have one note (the seventh) in addition to the basic triad, but you can keep on adding notes in the 'play one – miss one' pattern until you get back to the starting note. The chord that is most commonly extended is the dominant seventh – that is, the chord based on the fifth degree of the scale, in this case G7:

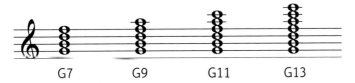

G7   G9   G11   G13

The number beside the chord name comes from how many notes you would have to count from the root (which is 1) until you get to the top note of the chord. So G9 includes an A on top, which is the interval of a ninth from the G root. G13 has an E on top, which is a thirteenth above the root.

Extended chords are normally based on these numbers: they follow the 'play one – miss one' pattern of stacking thirds on top of one another.

It is not necessary to play all the notes of the chord, as long as the top note is present along with the root, third and seventh (surprisingly, the fifth is not necessary in extended chords). In fact, it would be unusual to play all the possible notes – for example, G13 includes all the notes of the scale, so it would sound odd if you used them all. Nor does it matter what order the notes are in, so the voicing can be altered to suit the circumstances. The following are examples of extended chords:

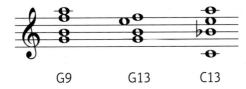

G9   G13   C13

Altered chords

Bm7^{b5} is an example of an altered chord: one in which one of the notes has been altered by sharpening or flattening it. In Bm7^{b5} the fifth has been flattened.

Flattened with respect to what? In a normal Bm7 chord, the notes would be B, D, F♯ and A. In Bm7^{b5} the notes are B, D, F and A, so the F has been flattened with respect to the main chord symbol, Bm7. Many altered chords are also extended chords, but the same principle applies – figure out what the notes would be in the main chord symbol (without the alteration) and then apply the change, which is always to move a note up or down a semitone.

Notated chord	Explanation
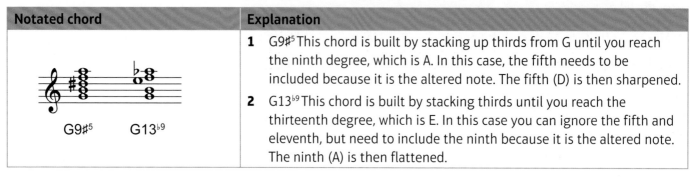 G9#5 G13♭9	**1** G9#5 This chord is built by stacking up thirds from G until you reach the ninth degree, which is A. In this case, the fifth needs to be included because it is the altered note. The fifth (D) is then sharpened. **2** G13♭9 This chord is built by stacking thirds until you reach the thirteenth degree, which is E. In this case you can ignore the fifth and eleventh, but need to include the ninth because it is the altered note. The ninth (A) is then flattened.

The same principles discussed above can be applied to minor keys. If we use the key of B minor as our example then some of the chords from the set work may start to make sense:

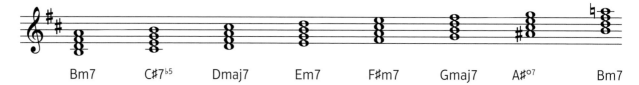

Bm7   C#7♭5   Dmaj7   Em7   F#m7   Gmaj7   A#°7   Bm7

Glossary

Enharmonic equivalent: two identically sounding pitches with different names – for example, E♭ and D#.

Spelling: deciding between enharmonic equivalents.

At chord VII, A#°7 is shorthand for 'A sharp diminished seventh' which consists of an A# diminished triad with a diminished seventh on top. B♭ is the **enharmonic equivalent** of A# and is much easier to read, but doesn't make sense in the key of B minor, so you need to keep the **spelling** as it is.

Substitution

In jazz music it is usual for musicians to develop the chord sequence on different repeats by substituting one chord for another that can have the same effect, but sound a little more colourful (chromatic). The new chord is often an altered chord.

So let's take this process in the opposite direction and simplify the chord sequence from 'Samba Em Prelúdio' a little and then consider some of the more complicated extensions and alterations.

Harmony in 'Samba Em Prelúdio'

The simplified chord sequence:

Bar	1	2	3	4	5	6	7	8
Chord	Bm7	Bm7	C#m7♭5	F#7	B7/F#	B7	Em	Em

Bar	9	10	11	12	13	14	15	16
Chord	C#m7♭9	F#7	A#dim7/B	Bm7/A	G#dim7	G#dim7	G13	F#7

- The bar numbers refer to the position of the chord relative to where the sequence begins, so Bm7 is the first chord of the sequence *every* time it occurs.

- The chords shown here are simplified in that some of the extensions have been removed (see table below) and the alterations changed, but they could still be used without any nasty clashes.
- The chord symbols followed by a forward slash and another note indicate that you need to play the note after the slash as the lowest note in the chord (the bass note) – so Bm7/A is a B minor seventh chord with an A in the bass.

Many of these chords can be found directly from the harmonisation of the minor scale with triads and sevenths. Those that cannot be found in the B minor harmonisation are either passing chords or indicate a momentary change of key. G13 is a passing chord between G#dim7 and F#7, while the B7 and Em indicate a brief modulation to E minor.

So let's pick a couple of examples from the score and see if we can work out what the notes should be:

Chord	Explanation
C#m11$^{\flat 5}$ (bar 41)	This is based on chord II (C#m7$^{\flat 5}$), but includes the eleventh degree counting from C#, which is F#. Notes: C#, E, G, B and F#
F#7#^{5} (bar 26)	This is based on chord V (F#7), but the fifth has been altered by sharpening it, so the C# is sharpened to C⹀, which is the enharmonic equivalent of D. This is an augmented triad with a minor seventh. Notes: F#, A#, C⹀ and E

Wider listening

In addition to this set work you should also listen to the following:

Buena Vista Social Club: *Buena Vista Social Club*

Buena Vista Social Club is an unusual album in that it was recorded in 1996 and released in 1997 but was the result of a project that aimed to capture the sounds of Cuban music's 'golden era'. As such, although it was recorded in the 1990s, it captures the music of the 1940s and 1950s, performed by musicians of the period in a 1950s Havana studio. The main vocalist on the album, Ibrahim Ferrer, was a Cuban star in the 1950s, but had long since stopped making music. He was brought in off the streets to record the album along with many of Cuba's other famous musicians from that era. The recording took about six days in total.

The album itself tells the story of Cuban music stretching back to 'La Bayamesa', which was written in 1869. It includes songs about Cuba's history and mixes musical styles from the city and the country. There are also some instrumentals with a strong jazz influence, highlighting the fusion element of the album. The 89-year-old singer and guitarist Compay Segundo was central in choosing which songs should be included on the album. Other musicians included the American guitarist Ry Cooder and the Cuban trumpeter Manuel 'Guajiro' Mirabal. The album became a worldwide sensation and relaunched the careers of many of the musicians who contributed.

Area of Study 4: Fusions

Dizzy Gillespie y Machito: *Afro-Cuban Jazz Moods*

The jazz trumpeter Dizzy Gillespie was well known for his flamboyant trumpet-playing technique and was central in the development of the Bebop jazz style. The singer Machito brought the rhythms of Cuban music into Big Band jazz arrangements. His exact place and date of birth remained shrouded in mystery, but he certainly had Cuban roots. The album *Afro-Cuban Jazz Moods* is short by modern standards at just over half an hour in duration, but has since been hailed as a very important album in the development of Afro-Cuban jazz. It was recorded in 1975 in New York and features just four tracks. Machito does not actually sing on any of the tracks, instead contributing some percussion and marimba as well as his arranging skills and band leadership.

The Cuban influence can be heard in the percussion parts and the rhythms that underpin the entire album. There are parts of the album in which the rhythm section would be just as at home in any Latin band as they are in this Big Band setup. The jazz influence can be heard in Gillespie's Bebop trumpet solos and in the Big Band arrangements. There is also a synthesiser that makes some unusual and ear-catching appearances during the long first track. Synths were to become more and more of a feature in jazz fusion as it developed.

Checkpoint

Strengthen

S1 In what ways can this set work be described as a piece of fusion?

S2 How do the players learn songs without traditional staff notation?

Challenge

C1 Using the techniques described above, work out all the chords for verse 2. Write out the names of the chords and the notes they contain. Leave out optional notes as the guitar is unlikely to voice them.

C2 Work out an alternative voicing for some of the chords.

Summary of the key musical features

Key points to remember:

Structure

- Intro – Verse 1 – Break – Verse 2 – Guitar solo – Verse 3 – Coda
- mostly split into 16-bar sections.

Tonality and harmony

- B minor
- jazz harmony
- includes extended, altered and substitution chords.

Instrumentation and sonority

- female vocal
- acoustic bass guitar
- nylon-string acoustic guitar (with second guitar overdubbed for solo).

Rhythm, metre and tempo

- starts in free tempo
- in $\frac{4}{4}$ metre
- based on Bossa Nova rhythm
- very syncopated.

Melody

- vocal melody opens by voicing broken chords
- syllabic throughout
- mostly stepwise movement
- melody notes are often the highest extension of extended chords – for example, the ninth of a ninth chord.

Texture

- monophonic at the very start
- counterpoint between parts
- very sparse in places, creating an intimate feel.

4: Preparing for your Exam

What to expect in the exam

Component 3 (Appraising) will be assessed by a listening examination which is worth 40% of your GCSE qualification in music. The paper lasts for 1 hour and 45 minutes and consists of 80 marks. The extracts of music will be played to you on a CD in the examination room. You will sit the examination in the final term of your two-year GCSE course.

The paper has nine questions and you must answer all questions. The questions are split into two sections:

Section A: Questions 1 to 8 and

Section B: Question 9.

In Section A the types of question include:

1 multiple choice
2 short open questions varying from 1 to 4 marks
3 a dictation question (Question 7)
4 a skeleton score question (Question 8).

Section B has one extended writing question featuring a comparison between an extract from one of the set works and one extract of unfamiliar music.

What is the purpose of this exam?

The paper is designed to test your listening and appraising skills through the study of a wide variety of musical styles as represented by the set works. These pieces are grouped into four areas of study, each containing two set works. The purpose is to test your knowledge of the set works through analysis. It also requires you to reflect on the music as well as making critical evaluations about unfamiliar music (in other words, music that you have not studied as part of your course). These critical judgements require careful listening and aural perception skills.

Preparing for this exam

The most important thing is to familiarise yourself with each set work thoroughly before trying to learn all the stylistic features in the music. The chapters covering these pieces identify the historical, social and cultural contexts of the music and also highlight aspects of continuity and change over time from one musical period to another. In addition, it is important as part of your preparation to understand the stylistic features of the music, which includes appreciating how the musical elements are used. This knowledge and understanding of each piece of music includes:

- The structure (or form) of the music.
- The stylistic features of the music, such as the Romantic traits in the Beethoven piano sonata or the Baroque features in Purcell's song or Bach's Brandenburg Concerto. In the latter case, too, you need to draw out common threads in the Baroque pieces.

- How the music relates to the context for which it was written as in, for example, the song 'Defying Gravity' from the musical *Wicked*. For instance, how does this song relate to the drama of the musical at this point in the show?
- The ability to express and justify opinions and preferences. This is quite demanding and features strongly in the extended writing in Question 9. The key word here is ***evaluate***, which means to compare and contrast the familiar with the unfamiliar, to draw out common elements, expressing opinions about each work and giving your preference based on the evidence.

The musical elements

Key to success in this part of the GCSE course is to understand how the following musical elements are used in each of the eight pieces. Every single examination question will target one or more of these features, so spend time learning these elements carefully. It would be a good idea to create revision cards using the musical elements and making points on these for all of your eight set works. These elements feature in all the analyses of the pieces in Section 3. They are defined as follows:

- **Organisation of pitch.** This is about melody and harmony – how the melodies in the set works are constructed and which types of chords are used as supporting harmony. It also covers the use of cadences as well as melodic devices such as sequences.
- **Tonality.** This is essentially the keys or modes used in the music. Common tonalities that you will study are major or minor, or modal. This element also embraces modulations to different keys such as to the dominant or the relative minor or major.
- **Structure.** This is essentially the formal plan of the music and how the musical material is organised. Structures that are covered include ternary form, sonata form and verse–chorus form.
- **Sonority.** This element is about the sounds created by the instruments and/ or voices. In examination questions you might be asked to identify individual instruments and/or a combination of instruments in an extract of music. Different types of articulation, such as legato and staccato playing, are also part of the overall sonority.
- **Texture.** The texture of music relates to the number of parts playing and the way in which they relate to one another. The range of textures covered in the pieces includes, solo, unison, chordal, in octaves, monophonic, homophonic, polyphonic/contrapuntal and fugal.
- **Tempo, metre and rhythm.** This includes the pulse of the music, time signatures and rhythmic devices such as dotted, syncopated and reverse dotted rhythms.
- **Dynamics.** Basic ranges in dynamics from very soft to very loud including crescendos and decrescendos.

How the musical elements are tested in the examination questions

The musical elements listed above will be tested in all questions on your examination paper.

You will need to be able to show your knowledge of the following in each set work extract played to you. These are possible question types that you should be aware of:

1   Identify instruments and groups of instruments and how combinations of instruments are used.

2   Name playing techniques such as pizzicato, use of mutes, col legno, etc.

3   Spot melodic and harmonic devices such as sequences, pedals, ostinato, etc.

4   Identify rhythmic features such as swung rhythms, etc.

5   Name specific tonalities: major, minor, modal, pentatonic, atonal, hexatonic, octatonic, etc.

6   Recognise textures in music and textural contrasts – for example, monophony, homophony, polyphony, heterophony.

7   Name chord patterns and individual chords.

Understanding the questions

This examination paper will use some important command words in the questions themselves. You will need to become familiar with these over the two-year course. As a general rule the commands will appear in progression in order of complexity through the paper, so that the more basic 'name' question could be in early questions and the most difficult 'evaluate' might appear in Question 9. They range in difficulty as follows:

- **State, give, name, identify, list.** These questions rely on your recall of facts and require you to give one or more points.
- **Complete.** Questions such as Question 7, the dictation of melody and rhythm question, or filling in blanks in a score.
- **Describe.** For example, describing the texture of the music. The points you are asked to describe may or may not be linked.
- **Explain.** Providing points that are linked to a justification.
- **Compare.** Making observations of similarities and differences.
- **Analyse.** This will include examining and dissecting the musical elements in detail, working out how certain effects/sounds are achieved through the combination of musical elements.
- **Evaluate.** Making critical judgements about familiar and unfamiliar music, drawing conclusions and then appraising.

Sample answers with comments

In this section we will look at some sample questions to show how the features mentioned above are tested.

For each question we will identify what it is that is being tested and then show an annotated student response. The number of marks awarded for a completely correct response is shown in brackets after the question.

Preparing for your Exam

1-mark question using the command word 'identify'

Beethoven: Sonata in C minor (Pathétique), first movement

Question. Identify the musical genre of this piece of music. (1 mark)

This type of question tests your knowledge of the period and style of this piano work. Basically the question is asking what type of piece this is.

Student answer

Piano sonata.

Verdict

This is a correct response. In fact, the key word for the mark is the word *sonata* as this is the genre or type of piece.

2-mark question using the command word 'name'

John Williams: *Star Wars IV: A New Hope*

Question. Name two types of brass instruments that play in the opening two bars of the extract. (2 marks)

This type of question assesses your ability to identify and name instruments.

Student answer

Trumpets; trombones.

Verdict

This is a correct answer and would score 2 marks. It is also possible to give **French horns** as one of the answers. **Tuba** is incorrect because it doesn't play until bar 3.

2-mark question using the command word 'describe'

Queen: 'Killer Queen'

Question. One of the characteristic features of Queen songs is the use of overdubbing. Describe what this process involves. (2 marks)

The purpose of this question is to test your understanding of the process of recording tracks using overdubbing and how this affects the production of the song.

Student answer

Overdubbing is about recording the tracks.

Verdict

This is an average answer, not a full answer. Overdubbing is about the recording, but this answer is too vague and does not say how the process works. The answer should mention the building of guitar and vocal parts by recording one layer on top of another. In the chorus, there is a four-part choir that has been built up by recording Mercury singing each part individually, one at a time.

3-mark question using the command word 'explain'

J.S. Bach: Brandenburg Concerto No. 5 in D major (3rd movement)

Question. Explain the purpose of the concertino group in a concerto grosso. (3 marks)

This type of question assesses your ability to think carefully about the role of this group of instruments.

Student answer

They are the solo instrument(s) that are pitted against the orchestra.

Verdict

As this is a three-mark question more information is required. A better answer would expand with more information such as, for example, the concertino group in this concerto comprises one flute and one violin.

It is good to name the instruments but now also to think about what they play, such as these two instruments play solos as well as playing with the ripieno group.

A stronger answer might also include some of the following additional points:

The concertino instruments contrast with the main body of strings, sometimes adding to the ripieno in a full (tutti) texture or playing solo passages with a light accompaniment from the ripieno. They also provide opportunities for dialogue with the ripieno.

4-mark question using the command word 'compare'

Henry Purcell: 'Music for a While'

Question. Compare the music of the words 'music for a while shall all your cares beguile' with the following line 'shall all, all, all, shall all, all, all, shall all your cares beguile'. (4 marks)

This question requires you to use your aural perception skills to hear both similarities and differences in the music of these two sets of words.

Exam tip

Always state the obvious in your response: for example, the same tempo, key, time signature, dynamics. Refer to the musical elements defined in this textbook as a guide for your answers.

Student answer

Similarities: Both have constant quaver bass notes forming the ground bass. This is played in both the lute and harpsichord. They are both in same key and have the same time signature. Likewise, the tempo and dynamics are also the same. Both works are written for the same instruments and voice.

Verdict

This answer would probably only gain half the marks. It does mention 6 similarities, but remember that a typical 4-mark question such as this would give 2 marks for similarities and two marks for differences.

A further three points of similarity could be included to achieve more marks:

Both phrases end on tonic A. Both are syllabic settings of the words and both have the same top note: F.

The following points of difference relating to the range of the melody could have been included:

The first phrase has a smaller vocal range (or conversely the second phrase has a wider range). The second phrase also has wider leaps or jumps in the melody.

Other points of difference are:

The second phrase is more fragmented. There are more rests in the second phrase, between 'shall' and 'all'. There are long notes in the first phrase on the word 'music'.

3-mark question using the command word 'analyse'

Queen: 'Killer Queen'

Question. Analyse the common features that are found in the majority of Queen songs. (3 marks)

This type of question assesses your ability to think carefully about what the features in the songs are and then to analyse what is common to all of the songs and not just the set work.

Student answer

They all have guitar solos and complex vocal and guitar parts. Queen songs have unusual structures, such as in the most famous song 'Bohemian Rhapsody', where there are arias, recitatives and chorus bits all inspired by opera. The songs feature a wide range of keys and use music technology to add effects (such as overdubbing) to the music. All of this is performed in a theatrical and dramatic way on stage!

Verdict

Many points are mentioned in this full answer. It was impressive that the student mentioned another work ('Bohemian Rhapsody') to show awareness and knowledge of music other than the set work. The answer covers points about both vocal and guitar parts, as well as the structure, technology and manner of performance.

12-mark question using the command word 'evaluate'

Question. Evaluate how effectively the excerpts from Star Wars IV: A New Hope by John Williams (0.00–2.00) and On the Waterfront by Leonard Bernstein (0.00–2.00) set the mood of these two films. (12 marks)

In this section of the examination, you will be asked to compare in detail an extract from one of your set works with an unfamiliar piece. The pieces will be related – for example, piano pieces, songs from musicals, etc.

The example question above asks you to compare two examples of film music, *Star Wars* (familiar to you) and *On the Waterfront* (unfamiliar to you).

Exam tip

You can only achieve half marks in this question if you write only about one piece, so make sure that both pieces are covered in your answers!

In this question you will be assessed on **two** assessment objectives (AOs). You need to demonstrate and apply musical knowledge (AO3) and also use appraising skills to make evaluative and critical judgements on the two pieces (AO4).

The easiest way to approach the question is to make accurate points about both extracts and give examples from the score extracts taken from the source booklet. Then you need to make comparisons between the works, saying which you think is more effective at setting the mood and why.

The mark scheme will assess the following in the top mark band (level 4):

- There are developed points about both extracts, with examples, demonstrating stylistic awareness of both pieces. (AO3)

- Accurate musical vocabulary is used throughout. (AO3)

- Appraisal presents a cohesive critical argument of both pieces. (AO4)

- The student demonstrates an ability to compare, contrast and draw conclusions. (AO4)

Exam tip

The question focuses on the stylistic features in the music and will draw on your knowledge from the study of the set works. You will be required to evaluate when answering this question – that is, to discuss strengths and weaknesses and form critical judgements.

Twelve mark questions of this type will require you to focus on the following:

- how the musical elements are used by the composer

- how the instruments or groups of instruments are used

- how the two pieces compare to meet a purpose, audience or other factor

- expressing and justifying opinions on the pieces.

In summary, you need to make points about both extracts, using examples from the score provided. Compare the two extracts (that is, highlight the similarities and differences) and then go on to say which you think is more effective and why.

Student answer

The Star Wars piece and On the Waterfront both set different moods in the opening music of the film. Star Wars sets a heroic and celebratory feeling, giving an impressive mood by being bold and brassy, whereas the On the Waterfront piece is far darker and more sinister.

This point is true but no musical detail has been given yet. The student has contrasted the moods of the two pieces and now goes on to back this up with how this is achieved in the music.

In the Star Wars piece, the fanfare opening for brass and percussion immediately sets an upbeat mood. It is in a major key (Bb) and is in a $\frac{4}{4}$ march-like metre.

All good, clear points showing how this mood is created in the music.

The dynamics from the very start (and for most of the music) are very loud.

These are correct observations but the dynamics mentioned are not linked to the mood of the music.

Williams uses the strings only for effects rather than melody.

Correct. It is a pity that the student did not make the comparison with the use of strings in the Bernstein piece, although this is done later in the essay. When making comparisons, it is wise to make points about each piece in the same paragraph.

The strong mood is reinforced by homophonic texture, so that the melody stands out clearly. The harmony is diatonic and is made to sound more modern by the use of quartal harmony.

All good points showing how harmony is used to create a powerful mood.

Williams repeats his main tune a lot, giving emphasis to the strong mood he wants to express throughout.

Good point about how a strong mood is created in the music.

The Bernstein piece starts with a solo horn, which sounds quite solemn and gives the feeling of isolation quite different from the boldness of the opening of Star Wars.

All good, clear points including a comparison with the opening of Star Wars.

The dynamics of the On the Waterfront piece are much quieter.

This implies that Williams is louder. It's always wise to state the obvious, so it would be a better answer if this point was included.

The saxophone solo is very bluesy, too. Like the Williams piece, the strings are used just for special effects.

Good point. It would have been better if made earlier in the answer.

Preparing for your Exam

The second section of the Bernstein piece is much faster and the rhythms suggest a chase going on. Good. Uses the musical elements of tempo and rhythm to match the mood created.

There is a lot of percussion in both pieces, but used on its own only in the Bernstein. The 'tempo barbaro' section marks a distinct change in mood from the opening section. By using fast syncopated rhythms, Bernstein gives the music an exciting feeling.

All good, clear points showing how the mood changes.

The piece I prefer is the Bernstein, as the music is far more varied in terms of orchestral colour and in the range of moods in the two sections. The Star Wars is a bit repetitive, to be honest, and is really just a main theme tune for most of the time.

The evaluation is a bit short but does give musical reasons for preferring the Bernstein over the Williams.

Verdict

There are good points made on both pieces with clear comparisons of similarities and differences. This fulfils the requirement in the top mark band 4 of *developed points about both extracts, with examples showing stylistic awareness and using musical vocabulary (AO3)*. However, the overall answer could be improved further with more detail in the last paragraph showing your evaluation of the pieces and using critical judgements, to say which piece you prefer and why. Do not be afraid to use the first person singular (**I think that, I believe that…**) as this shows **your opinions** and judgements. By doing this, you are evaluating the music – that is, giving it a value in your own eyes and not just reporting facts from textbooks. The essay above therefore only partially fulfils the requirement to *present a cohesive critical argument that compares, contrasts and draws conclusions (AO4)*.

Overall, this is a good answer covering the AO3 points, but needs more in the last paragraph on the AO4 requirements to achieve an 'excellent' rating overall.

A better conclusion would be: ***I prefer the music in* On the Waterfront *as the eerie opening horn melody, I feel, is scary and sets a foreboding feeling to the music. I feel that it conjures up nicely the idea of the lone individual on his own against the world. This is contrasted by the exciting fast section, which sounds like a chase scene. I feel that this adds to the drama and tension of the mood. This, I feel, is effective orchestration. I also think that the music is far more varied in terms of the use of the instruments than Star Wars, which is just one long fanfare and repetitive march theme played for most of the time by the full orchestra. The music is far less subtle than the Bernstein, in my opinion.***

Glossary

Acoustic guitar: does not require amplification, unlike an electric one.

Added notes: notes that are added to a basic triad, such as a seventh or a ninth.

Added sixth chord: a common chord in Jazz and Popular Music, a triad with the sixth added above the tonic.

Affection: the prevailing mood in a Baroque movement.

Alberti bass: a figuration commonly used in the Classical period, made up of broken chords used as an accompaniment. Named after a now forgotten composer called Domenico Alberti.

Altered notes: notes in a chord that have been sharpened or flattened by a semitone, such as a flattened fifth.

Answer: in a fugue, the subject repeated in response to its initial appearance, usually a fourth or fifth lower or higher than the preceding subject. If it is an exact transposition of the subject it is a real answer; if not it is a tonal answer.

Anthemic, anthem: a song with a strong, memorable melody which has rousing or uplifting characteristics.

Antiphonal: music performed alternately by two groups which are often physically separated.

Appoggiatura: an ornament often referred to as a 'leaning in' note. The appoggiatura leans on the main note, commonly taking half its value and starting a semitone or tone higher. For example, if the main note is a crotchet and the smaller grace note a quaver, then the player plays two equal quavers.

Arpeggiated: the chord is spread, normally from the bottom note to the top.

Articulation: the manner in which a note or sequence of notes is played, for example, staccato, legato, accented, etc.

Atonal: music that does not have a key of any sort.

Attack: how the note sounds when it comes in – a slow attack will sound like the note is fading in and a fast attack will sound quite percussive.

Augmented chord: a triad built on two major thirds, here A♭–C and C–E.

Augmented: doubling (or more) of the original notes' durations.

Background music, underscore, underscoring: non-diegetic music adding to the mood of the scene, reinforcing dramatic developments and aspects of character.

Bar lines: vertical lines ruled down through the stave, indicating bars.

Bare fifth: chords lacking the third and therefore ambiguous in terms of major/minor tonality.

Bars: the manageable chunks into which music is divided.

Basso continuo: continuous bass parts are provided for harpsichord and stringed instruments such as bass viol and lute. The players add chords and melody.

Binary form: a structure of two sections, A and B. Each section is repeated. In the A section the music modulates from the tonic to the dominant key. In section B, the music starts in the dominant and explores other keys before returning to the tonic at the end of the section.

Bitonal: refers to music in two keys at the same time.

Block triads: major or minor triads in root position, built up in thirds.

Breakdown: when many of the parts drop out of the musical texture for a short period of time.

Bridge passage: a linking passage often used to change the key of the music (to modulate) in preparation for the second subject.

Broken chord: when the notes of a chord are played one at a time rather than being sounded simultaneously.

Build: in the context of the text this refers to the gradual introduction of more instruments.

Cadential: this refers to a progression of chords forming a cadence. For example, Ic–V7–I is known as a cadential $^6_4$. The $^6_4$ refers to the first chord being in second inversion – that is, a fourth and sixth above the bass (for example, G–C–E).

Canon: parts copy each other in exact intervals, often at the fifth or octave, but at different beats of the bar. The song 'London's Burning' is a good example.

Cantata: the word derives from the Italian *cantare* and means 'sung'. A cantata is an extended piece in several movements, comprising chorus, recitative, chorale and aria with an orchestral accompaniment.

Capo: a clamp fastened across all the strings on the neck of a stringed instrument to raise their pitch.

Chopin, Frédéric (1810–49): Polish composer of piano music in the Romantic style.

Glossary

Chord voicing: how the notes in a chord have been spaced out, and the order in which they occur.

Chromatic: 1 (harmony) from the Greek for 'colour'. The term is used to describe notes that are not diatonic (part of the key of the music). 2 (melody) ascending or descending in semitones.

Circle of fifths: a series of chords in which the root note of each chord is a fifth lower or a fourth higher than that of the previous one.

Classical era: the musical period extending from c.1750 to c.1820.

Clave: the rhythm closely associated with the Latin percussion instrument known as 'claves' (short squat sticks that are struck together).

Coda: a section sometimes added at the end of a piece or movement.

Codetta: a short coda concluding a single section within a movement.

Colla voce: literally, 'with the voice'. This is an instruction to the band and the musical director to follow the vocalist's tempo.

Compound interval: one extending over more than an octave. A compound third could be a tenth or a seventeenth and so on up.

Compound metre: a metre in which the beat is dotted and subdivides into groups of three.

Compound time signature: when the bar feels like it needs to be split into groups of three (having a group of three 'mini' beats in a 'big' beat). For example, $\frac{6}{8}$.

Concertino: the smaller group of soloists in a concerto grosso.

Concerto grosso (plural *concerti grossi*): a concerto for more than one soloist. The phrase literally means a large concerto. It is usually written in three movements in the order fast–slow–fast.

Conjunct: movement by step.

Consonant: intervals or chords that sound pleasant; the triads and intervals of a third and sixth are examples of this.

Contrapuntal: when two melodies are played 'against' each other and interweave – almost the same as 'polyphonic'; written in counterpoint.

Counterpoint: literally means 'tune against tune'. It is the simultaneous combination of two or more melodies with independent rhythms.

Countersubject: the melody played after the subject or answer has been sounded. The melody is literally counter (against) the subject.

Cover: a new version of an existing song.

Crescendo: getting gradually louder.

Cross rhythms: rhythms that cross the usual pattern of accented and unaccented beats, creating irregular accents and syncopated effects.

Cue: a section of music in a film. Here it refers to the whole track.

Da capo aria: ABA or ternary form. Often the repeated A section would be ornamented by the singer. Da capo means 'again from the beginning'.

Dance suite: in Baroque music the suite comprised a series of dance movements. By the time of Purcell, suites were composed of four main movements called the allemande, courante, sarabande and gigue. These movements are based on dance forms from different countries. Optional extra movements include the air, bourrée, gavotte, minuet and prelude.

Decay: how the note dies away after being sounded.

Dialoguing: instruments literally 'in dialogue', playing one after the other, swapping ideas.

Diatonic: notes that belong to the key of the piece (literally 'of the key').

Diegetic music: this is music contained within the action of the film and is included in the story – for example, music played in a bar. If a character in the story can hear the music, it is diegetic. Most film music is non-diegetic.

Diminished seventh: a four-note chord made up solely of minor-third intervals.

Diminuendo: getting gradually quieter.

Disjunct: movement by leap.

Dissonant intervals: the intervals that are dissonant (clashing) are the minor and major second, the minor and major seventh and the tritone (augmented fourth or diminished fifth).

Distortion: an effect that increases the volume and sustain on an electric guitar as well as making the timbre more gritty or smooth depending on the settings.

Dominant preparation: a passage focused on the dominant chord to create expectation for a return to the tonic.

Dominant seventh: chord V with added minor seventh.

Dominant: the fifth note of the scale or key – the strongest note after the tonic.

Drone: a continuously held or repeated note, usually low in pitch.

Drum loops: a pre-recorded drum pattern repeated on a loop, over which other music can be laid.

Dynamics: marks in the score indicating to the performer how loud or soft their part should be played.

Effects: electronic devices designed to enhance or alter the basic sound quality (for example, delay, reverb).

Enharmonic: two identically sounding pitches with different names – for example, E♭ and D♯.

Extended chord: a chord with at least one added note, such as the ninth.

Fanfare: a celebratory piece for brass instruments (and sometimes percussion) often marking the opening of an important event or ceremony. The music is short and loud and often features arpeggios and broken chords. An inspiring example of a fanfare for brass and percussion is Aaron Copland's *Fanfare for the Common Man*.

Figured bass: a form of musical shorthand that the keyboard player reads from the score to play the intended harmony. $\frac{5}{3}$ (often not indicated so players would automatically assume root position if there was no figuring indicates a root position chord; $\frac{3}{6}$ (or just 6) is a first inversion; and $\frac{6}{4}$ is a second inversion ($\frac{6}{4}$ is always written and not abbreviated). In each case the two numbers are obtained by counting upwards from the bass. For example, if the notes are C-F-A, then C to the top note A is a sixth and from C to the F is a fourth. Other combinations of numbers indicate more complex harmony. Accidentals such as a sharp of flat placed in front of the figure affect that note, and an accidental on its own only applies to the third of the chord.

First subject: the first theme or melody.

Flanger, flanging: an effect creating a swirling or swooshing sound.

Fortissimo: very loud.

Forte: loud.

Fugal exposition: the initial statements of the subject and answer.

Fugue: a musical form comprising an exposition, middle section and final section. The music is contrapuntal.

Fusion: the blending of two or more musical styles, usually from different cultures.

Gavotte: a medium-paced French dance in $\frac{4}{4}$ time beginning on the third beat of the bar. It was popular in the 18th century.

Glam: a genre of rock known for over-the-top, glamorous dress sense including platform shoes, glitter and flamboyant hairstyles.

Gospel music: a musical style with roots in the black oral tradition in which vocal harmonies play a prominent role.

Groove: in the context of the text this is a drum loop. It can also mean 'rhythmic feel'.

Harmonic rhythm: the rate at which the chords change.

Harmonic sequence: when a chord sequence is immediately repeated at a higher or lower pitch.

Heterophonic: two or more instruments playing the same melody at the same time, with each embellishing it in a slightly different way.

Hi-hat: a pair of cymbals mounted on a special stand so that they can be sounded by pressing a pedal that clamps them together as well as by striking.

Homophonic: a texture comprising a melody part and an accompaniment.

Imperfect cadence: a cadence ending on chord V and sounding incomplete. Usually preceded by chord I, II or IV.

Independent parts: the instruments or voices are each doing different things. Note that a part that is simply harmonising another (e.g. in thirds) throughout the piece is not considered independent.

Interrupted cadence: most commonly comprises chord V followed by chord VI. So-called because it interrupts an expected perfect cadence V–I.

Interval: the distance between two notes.

Inversions: major or minor triads with either the third (first inversion) or the fifth (second inversion) in the bass.

Jukebox musical: when the score for a musical is made up of existing songs, usually all by the same artist or with a strong thematic link.

Glossary

Key signature: a series of sharp or flat signs placed next to the clef sign on every stave, which tells us the key of the music in the following bars.

Kick drum: also known as 'bass drum' – the biggest drum in a drum kit, set sideways-on to the audience and drummer. It is played by pressing a pedal which moves a beater to strike the drum skin.

Lament: a song with a sorrowful mood. Often slow and in a minor key.

Ledger lines: mini lines used to extend the pitch upwards above the stave or downwards below it.

Legato: played in a smooth fashion (the opposite of staccato).

Leitmotif: a recurring musical idea which is associated with a particular theme, character or place.

Level descriptors: the parts of a mark scheme that describe what you need to do to achieve that level.

Loop: a short repeated passage, often involving electronic drums.

Lyrical: songlike, flowing.

Melismatic: refers to vocal melody with several or even many notes per syllable.

Metre: refers to the number of beats in a bar and how they are subdivided.

Metrical shifting: the downbeat is shifted to a different part of the bar.

Mezzo: the Italian name for half but in the context of dynamics, this means 'moderately'. For example, mezzo forte is moderately loud.

Middle 8: connects two sections of a pop or rock song but is not necessarily eight bars long.

Middle C: the note used as a reference point for all instruments and clefs.

Mix: the relative volume of the different parts in a recording and their place in the stereo field.

Monophonic: refers to a musical texture comprising a single line which can be sung or played by several people.

Mordent: there are two types of mordent: 'upper' and 'lower'. The upper mordent is made up of the main note, the note above the note and the main note again, all played as quickly as possible. The lower mordent again goes from the main note to the note below and back to the main note again.

Motif: a short melodic phrase of just a few notes.

Multi-track: a recording of a performance (or performances) on separate tracks in which each track can be edited individually to change levels, add effects, etc.

Murky bass: the fast octave repetitions in the bass.

Neapolitan chord: a chord built on the flattened supertonic note.

Obbligato: an essential melody part that must be played.

Octave: a series of eight notes occupying the interval between (and including) two notes for example, between one C and the nearest C above or below it.

Onomatopoeic: the music setting sounds like the word, for example, *drop*.

Ornament: notes that decorate a melody. These are shown by small notes (grace notes) immediately before the main note or symbols above it. Examples include the mordent, the trill and the turn.

Ostinato: a persistent phrase or motif repeated over several bars or more.

Ottava alta: a symbol (a little dotted line with 8va at the beginning) indicating that notes should be played an octave higher than written.

Ottava bassa: a symbol (a little dotted line with 8vb at the beginning) indicating that notes should be played an octave lower than written.

Outro: a concluding section, sometimes like a coda in Classical music.

Overdubbing: recording an instrumental or vocal part over previously recorded music.

Pad: a synthesiser sound designed to be used in chords as opposed to lead lines.

Panning: giving sounds different levels in the left and right speakers so that it sounds as if they are coming from a new direction.

Passagework: a constantly moving passage, often in patterns of quick notes such as semiquavers. It often includes sequences.

Passing modulations: modulations where the new key only lasts for a few bars (or less) before modulating to another key.

Patronage: a system whereby composers earned money from a wealthy individual for writing music. The person who commissioned (asked for) the music was known as a patron.

Pedal: a sustained or repeated note in the bass. It may clash with harmonic changes above it. Pedals are usually on the tonic or dominant notes, so would be called either a tonic or a dominant pedal.

Pentatonic: a five-note scale or a melody that uses only five different notes.

Perfect cadence: a cadence comprising two chords. A perfect cadence is chord V followed by chord I.

Piano: quiet.

Pianissimo: very quiet.

Polyphonic: literally, 'many sounds'; more than one melody sounding at the same time or entering at slightly different times so that melodic lines overlap.

Polytonal: chords that are built from two or more keys simultaneously.

Pull-offs: when a note is sounded on the guitar by plucking the string with the fretting hand.

Range: how many octaves an instrument can play. For example, a guitar can play notes over three and a half to four octaves.

Register: refers to how high or low in pitch a piece of music or a musical part sounds.

Relative minor: the minor key based on the sixth note of the major scale.

Reverb: an effect which creates the impression of being in a physical space.

Ride: a type of cymbal sometimes used to offer a counter-rhythm to the main beat.

Riff: a short passage of music that is repeated.

Ripieno: the larger group in a concerto grosso.

Rit./ritardando: slowing down.

Romantic era: the musical period extending from c.1810 to c.1900.

Romanticism: an artistic and intellectual movement that began in Europe in the early 1800s and lasted for approximately 100 years. Romanticism is characterised by an emphasis on the individual's expression of emotions and their freedom of imagination, as well as a love of the natural world. Another common theme was the idea of the individual's rebellion against established social rules and conventions, which led to the rise of the virtuoso heroic soloist in Romantic concertos.

Sample: a pre-recorded segment of sound, often manipulated in some way.

Scalic: music that is based on scales ascending and/or descending in pitch.

Second subject: the second theme or melody.

Semitones: the 12 equally spaced intervals into which an octave is divided.

Sequence: the repetition of a musical phrase at a higher or lower pitch than the original.

Sforzando: an accent showing that a note or chord should be played with greater force than other notes surrounding it. Often shown in the score as *sf* or *sfz*.

Side sticks: hitting the edge of the snare drum with the sticks held sideways.

Simple time signature: when the beat naturally divides into two equal halves.

Simultaneously sounding: there has to be a significant proportion of the music in which there is more than one part being performed at the same time. You cannot just sing one verse and have someone else sing the next verse, because the parts aren't sounding at the same time.

Snare roll: a rapid succession of hits on the snare drum.

Snare: a drum with a series of loosely strung metal wires in contact with the lower skin which create a distinct 'buzzing' or 'rattling' noise when the drum is struck.

Solo concerto: a concerto for a single instrument accompanied by an orchestra.

Solo: an extended, improvised melodic line played by a single instrument (guitar, sax, piano, etc.) over a given chord sequence, usually as an interlude in the middle of a song.

Sonata form: a large-scale form invented in the Classical era comprising three sections: *exposition*, *development* and *recapitulation*. Not restricted to sonatas.

Spelling: deciding between enharmonic equivalents.

Staccato: played in a detached fashion.

Static harmony: when the harmony remains on a single chord for a prolonged period of time.

Stereo field: how the sounds have been positioned in the left and right speakers.

Glossary

Stile italiano: Purcell was influenced by the Italian style, which was characterised by the concertato style, the trio sonata, double-dotted notes, dramatic recitatives, and *da capo* arias.

Stretto: entries of the subject occur closer together than before, heightening the tension of the music.

Subject: the short main theme of the fugue.

Suspension: prolonging a note to create a dissonance with the next chord.

Swung rhythm: often used in Jazz, the first of a pair of quavers is given a slightly longer duration and the second a slightly shorter duration, creating a 'skipping' feel.

Swung: music that has a triplet feel, even when notated with straight quavers.

Syllabic word-setting: one note per syllable of a word.

Syllabic: when one note is sung per syllable.

Syncopated: when a weak bar or a note in between bets is purposely accented.

Syncopation: emphasising beats of the bar that are normally unaccented.

Synthesiser: an electronic musical instrument that creates sounds by manipulating combinations of waveforms or by modifying existing sounds.

Techno: a style of electronic music.

Tempo rubato: literally means 'robbed time'. This is a technique where the performer can pull back (or speed up) the tempo for expressive effect.

Ternary (or **ABA**) **form**: a simple musical form in three sections with an ABA structure.

Texture: the character of a piece of music created by the interaction of its various parts.

Tierce de Picardie: refers to a sharpened third in the tonic chord in music in a minor key.

Ties: small arcs drawn from one note head to the next, indicating that you should add up the tied note values and hold the note on instead of sounding it a second time.

Timbre: the particular tone colour of an instrument or voice.

Time signature: included at the start of a piece of music, it shows what note values are used to count the pulse and how many beats there are in a bar.

Tone: an interval of two semitones.

Transition: a section used to take the music from one key to another by modulation. Sometimes also called a bridge section.

Tremolando/tremolo: rapid playing on the same note to produce a wavering, tremulous sound.

Triads: three-note chords.

Trio sonata: a piece for Baroque ensemble comprising two violins, cello and harpsichord (or organ).

Triplets: a horizontal square bracket that lets the performer know that the three notes should be played in the time it normally takes to play two.

Turnaround: a set of (usually four) faster-moving chords to get the music back to a repeated section.

Tutti: all parts playing at the same time.

Undoubled: the part you are performing is not being performed in another instrument or voice at the same time. It is fine if someone is harmonising, but they can't be playing the same notes as you.

Unison: more than one part playing the same melody at the same pitch.

Vamp: a short repeated accompanying phrase.

Variant: a phrase whose shape resembles the original.

Vaudeville: a form of comic musical theatre from the 1880s.

Vibrato: a technique used to cause rapid variations in pitch. The term 'vibrato' is Italian and is the past participle of the verb 'vibrare', which means to vibrate.

Vocalisation: wordless singing using a vowel syllable such as 'ah'.

Wah-wah: a filter effect in which the peak of the filter is swept up and down the frequency range in response to the player's foot movement on a rocker pedal.

Word painting: depicting a word in music to imitate its meaning.

Index

Note: Page numbers in **bold font** refer to defined terms.

Index

Index

Acknowledgements

We would like to thank Alexander Aitken for the musical analysis of Defying Gravity and for carrying out a technical review of the material. We would also like to thank Rodrigo Maltez-Novaes for the English translation of Samba Em Prelúdio.

The publisher would like to thank the following for their kind permission to reproduce their photographs:

(Key: b-bottom; c-centre; l-left; r-right; t-top)

Alamy Images: AF Archive 53, Chronicle 83, Everett Collection Historical 127, INTERFOTO 66, John McKenna 95, Julio Etchart 96, Lebrecht Music and Arts Photo Library 20, 80, 81, Paul Springett D 144b, Philip Scalia 144c, PRISMA ARCHIVO 8; **Fotolia.com:** a40757se 1, Georgios Kollidas 67, Prudkov 27; **Getty Images:** C Brandon 138, Chris Walter / WireImage 102, Clobo 128, Education Images 145, 151, Frank Micelotta 116, Gijsbert Hanekroot 94, Hiroyuki Ito 55, John Fedele 25, Kristian Dowling 109, Michael St. Maur Sheil / Corbis / VCG 143, Mike Pont 110, Rick Kern 152; **Mary Evans Picture Library:** 52, 71; **NASA:** NASA / JPL-Caltech / SAO 124; **Rex Shutterstock:** Alasdair Muir 111; **Shutterstock.com:** LIUSHENGFILM 29, Platslee 4, rosesmith 144t

All other images © Pearson Education

Picture Research by: Alison Prior

Copyright acknowledgements